FROM AGE TO AGE

FROM
AGE
TO
AGE

How Christians Have Celebrated
the Eucharist

Edward Foley

Illustrated by Robin Faulkner

LTP

LITURGY
TRAINING
PUBLICATIONS

FROM AGE TO AGE © 1991 Archdiocese of Chicago: Liturgy Training Publications, 1800 North Hermitage Avenue, Chicago IL 60622-1101; 1-800-933-1800; orders@ltp.org; fax: 1-800-933-7094. All rights reserved.

Visit our website at www.ltp.org.

Editor: Victoria M. Tufano
Editorial Assistance: Peter Mazar, Theresa Pincich, Lorraine Schmidt
Designer: Ana Aguilar-Islas
Typesetter: Mark Hollopeter
Cover photographs: Details from the sixth-century mosaics in the apse of the church of St. Vitale in Ravenna, Italy. The front depicts Empress Theodora and her court; the back shows Emperor Justinian and his court. Courtesy of The Bettmann Archive.

Printed in the United States of America.

04 03 02 01 00   10 9 8 7 6 5

Library of Congress Cataloging-in-Publication Data
Foley, Edward.
    From age to age: how Christians celebrated the Eucharist/Edward Foley; illustrated by Robin Faulkner.
    Includes bibliographical references and index.
    ISBN 0-929650-41-7 (pbk.)
    1. Lord's Supper—Celebration—History. I. Title
BV825.5.F64 1991   91-30446
264'.02036'09—dc20   CIP

Contents

Introduction

The history of liturgy has always fascinated me. I find it alternately informative, amusing, shocking, sad and inspiring. Most of all, I have experienced a sense of liberation through studying and teaching liturgical history. This sense of liberation grows as I survey the innumerable forms of common worship in the past and ponder a similar richness of possibilities for the future.

Knowing our worship history does not mean that we have to repeat it. A common criticism of liturgical historians is that they sometimes give the impression that the church should return to the glories of the fourth, the twelfth or some other century. Such thinking has no place in a church committed to living in the modern world. Yet knowing how the church prayed in the fourth or the twelfth century is valuable for assessing and understanding contemporary worship.

Even more valuable is knowing how the prayer of the church developed from the fourth century to the twelfth. Such knowledge challenges our sometimes limited image of tradition, which is the name we often give to what we remember with fondness. Studying the development of our worship through the ages also enables us to admit the tremendous pluriformity that has marked Christian liturgy from the very beginning. There was no primitive Christian rite promulgated early in the first century that eventually became more diverse with the passing of time. Rather, a rich variety of worship forms and styles has existed from the start. Such an awareness is of immeasurable value as we forge prayer for the diverse communities of the twenty-first-century church.

It is possible to tell the history of Christian worship in many different ways. One could, for example, discuss the emergence of a single rite, trace the development of particular types of prayer texts, or concentrate on the great figures or geographic centers of liturgy. Each of these approaches has its own value and requires further exploration today. I have chosen, however, to introduce the history of Christian worship in a different way. In this period after the Second Vatican

Council, when we are especially concerned about the participation of the whole worshiping community, it seems particularly useful to consider how worship affected ordinary people. Apart from the writings of great theologians, the instructions of venerable church orders, or the customaries of famed monasteries, what did the ordinary people experience at worship?

Introducing the history of worship from the perspective of the people's experience suggests that we study those tangible aspects of the liturgy that have always been important to the experience of worship. Therefore, instead of beginning with theological treatises or liturgical commentaries, this book will focus on some of the primary symbols of the worship itself. Although there are many such symbols that could be studied, we will limit our considerations to the architecture, music, books and vessels that have served Christian worship throughout its history. While ordinary Christians did not always have access to explanations about worship or understand the explanations that were provided, they did have their own experiences. They entered the buildings, heard (and sometimes sang) the music, saw the books and often tasted the bread. For people of every age, this concrete experience of worship—seen, heard, touched and tasted—shaped their faith. Although ordinary Christians from the past left few words about their experiences, some of the music, vessels, books and buildings that affected them endure. It is from these remnants of primary sources that we will attempt to enter the experience of Christian worship in the past. Because eucharist has traditionally been at the heart of Christian worship, these symbols are considered primarily as they were used at the eucharist, particularly as it developed in the West.

This approach allows us to consider seriously the liturgy as a source of belief and theology. The Christian churches today acknowledge the ancient teaching that worship is the source and embodiment of our common belief. At the same time, worship has the power to shape and change our belief. More than any official proclamation or systematic treatise, the liturgy announces who we are and who we are to become in Christ. Liturgy, therefore, is the bedrock upon which we build our theologies of God, church and salvation. Discovering how these beliefs were embodied and perpetuated by liturgies of the past can help us to look critically at contemporary worship and discover how liturgy is expressing and shaping our faith today.

This book is divided into seven chapters, charting the experience of Christian worship from the first century to our own time. Each chapter begins with a brief introduction noting some of the cultural and historical factors that influenced the development of Christian worship. The introduction is followed by individual considerations of the architecture, music, books and vessels of each age. To elucidate the central text, numerous illustrations are included. The inclusion of so many illustrations is also an acknowledgment that liturgy is not simply a text. Thus, any work about the history of worship must be more than just words. These illustrations are intended to help the reader envision the worship experience of the past. Excerpts from various primary and secondary sources also are provided throughout the book. These have been chosen to exemplify or to further explain ideas examined in the main body of the text. At the end of each chapter, a fictional scenario is included that attempts to enflesh the narrative in an imaginative but historically accurate account of Christian worship. A glossary of terms is provided at the end of the volume. The bibliography employed in the writing of this work is provided as a guide to further reading, while the index will be helpful when looking for a particular subject in the text.

Although this book focuses on worship in the Roman Catholic tradition, the experience of the Protestant Reformation—especially as it emerged in the Lutheran and Episcopal churches, and less so in the Methodist and Presbyterian traditions—is an important part of the last two chapters. The volume has an intentional bias, particularly in the last chapter, toward liturgical developments in the United States.

Reconstructing worship from another era is a perilous endeavor. Attempting to introduce almost 2,000 years of eucharistic liturgy and its architecture, music, vessels and books all in the same volume borders on the foolhardy. In a work of this size, it is not possible to explore thoroughly even one of the symbols of Christian worship examined here. Rather than attempting a comprehensive review of these symbols and the eucharist, I have tried to offer a reasonable synthesis of a vast quantity of material in a manner accessible to the ordinary reader or beginning student of liturgy. Practically, this has meant that the principle of exclusion rather than inclusion has directed the writing of this work. Many important monuments in stone, vellum, silver and song consequently have been omitted. Those that are included were chosen as representatives of a particular age, style, trend or theology significant for Christians' experience of eucharist. Many who read this volume will have favorite examples of the liturgical arts that have not been included in this work. I hope that the material that has been chosen provides an adequate framework for those readers in relating their examples and insights to the history of worship.

There have been many people who have helped in the development of this volume. William Storey and Gordon Lathrop read the entire manuscript and Marchita Mauck reviewed the sections on architecture and vessels. I am most grateful to have benefited from the critical appraisal of such esteemed colleagues and friends. Over the years three graduate assistants helped with the research for this volume. The work of Michael Jennerich, Michael Cruise and Michael Surufka is warmly remembered. James White offered direction for researching eucharistic vessels in Protestant Churches. Kenneth O'Malley, the librarian at Catholic Theological Union, worked long and patiently to assemble the index. Vince Agnew supplied archival material from the John P. Daleiden Company. Gerrie Boberg, also from the library at Catholic Theological Union, was most helpful in securing obscure materials through often difficult interlibrary loans for this project. I am sincerely grateful for the generous contributions of these professionals. I am especially grateful to Robin Faulkner for her splendid illustrations and artistic suggestions that have contributed immeasurably to this volume. Special thanks are also due to Vicky Tufano for her work in editing this volume. Finally, I wish to thank Gabe Huck of Liturgy Training Publications for encouraging me to undertake this project. His patience, professionalism and friendship are a lasting gift.

In my academic career I have had the opportunity to write two theses in liturgical history. The first was directed by Ralph A. Keifer, the second by Niels Krogh Rasmussen. Both of these scholars died tragically in the summer of 1987. It is to their memories that this volume is lovingly dedicated.

Edward Foley, Capuchin

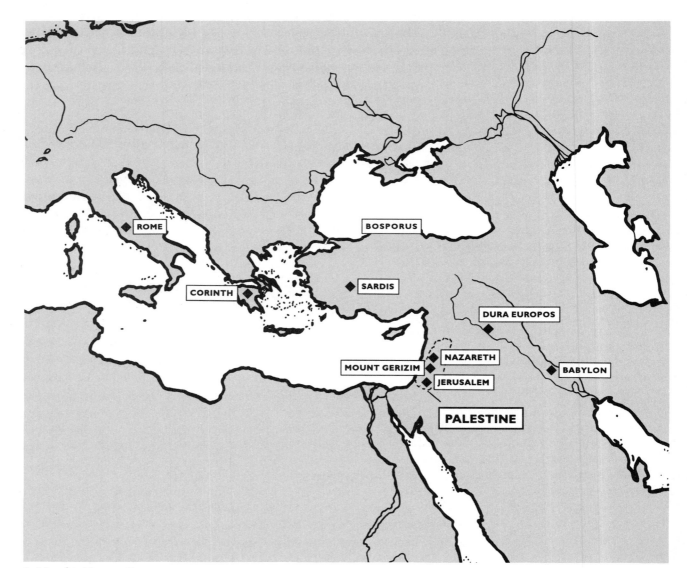

1. Map for Chapter One.

Emerging Christianity: The First Century

Quotation 1. *I give you a new commandment, that you love one another.* John 13:34

Quotation 2. *Alexander spread Hellenism in a vast colonizing wave throughout the Near East and created, if not politically, at least economically and culturally, a single world stretching from Gibraltar to the Punjab.* Robert Grant

Pope Pius XI (d. 1939) once commented that every Christian must become a spiritual Semite. Though it is possible to disagree with the way he formulated this idea, it is not possible to dismiss the insight of these words. Christianity originated in a Jewish milieu and even today continues to be shaped by these Jewish beginnings. Christians believe that Jesus—as both human and divine—was unique in the history of salvation, establishing a new covenant [quotation 1] and revealing himself as God's fullest self-communication to humankind. Jesus was a Jew, and his Jewishness unquestionably shaped his mission and ministry. Thus Jesus' unique message is linked to a specific time, place and culture, though it is not confined by these. Jesus' message and the Christianity that emerged from those who accepted that message can be understood only in the context of the Jewish culture in which they originated.

It is not enough, however, to state that Christianity emerged in a Jewish setting. First-century Palestine was deeply influenced by Hellenistic culture. Almost four centuries before the birth of Christ, Alexander the Great (d. 323 BCE) conquered the whole of the eastern Mediterranean region, including Palestine [illustration 1]. Alexander also transformed the Near East and, ultimately, Western civilization by imposing his own culture and language on the peoples he subdued [quotation 2]. Although Alexander's empire was divided among his generals after his death, the influence of his Hellenizing campaign continued for centuries. This was true even in Palestine, where the Jews did not reestablish their political independence until almost 150 years after the death of Alexander. The Jews attempted to assert their cultural independence from Hellenism as well, but this effort was short lived and ultimately unsuccessful. Rome conquered the Jewish monarchy in 63 BCE and continued the process of Hellenization. Thus it was in a Jewish milieu under the political and cultural influence of the Greco-Roman world—in what sometimes is called "Hellenistic Judaism"—that Christianity emerged.

The sect that came to be called Christianity was, at its root, a small reform movement within rural Palestinian Judaism, where the Hellenistic influence was weak and Aramaic was the common language. After the death of Jesus, this rural movement gravitated toward the Jewish communities in the larger towns and cities, where Hellenism was more influential and Greek was the common language. People such as Paul carried Jesus' message outside the Jewish community to Gentiles, especially those living in the great cities of the Greco-Roman world. Although born in rural Judaism, this religious movement increasingly wedded itself to an urban, Hellenistic culture and was accepted by a growing number of Gentiles. It was in this context that the followers of Jesus of Nazareth were first called Christians [quotation 3].

Quotation 3. *It was in Antioch that the disciples were first called "Christians."* Acts 11:26

ARCHITECTURE

Jews at the time of Jesus did not confine their worship to a single location or type of building. A pious Jew was expected to pray not only in some specially designated room or structure, but in every place and at every time [quotation 4]. No matter what the location, the believer was expected to bless God continuously throughout the day. Breaking bread, seeing lightning, purchasing a vessel and watching the sun set all were occasions for blessing God. Though prayer was not confined to any specific location in Judaism, certain types of prayer or ritual came to be identified with specific sites. The most important of these were the temple, the synagogue and the home.

Quotation 4. *A man is obliged to recite one hundred benedictions each day. Babylonian Talmud, Menahot 43b*

Temple

Following the instruction of his father King David (d. about 962 BCE), Solomon (d. about 922 BCE) built the first temple in Jerusalem [quotation 5]. This small but sumptuous structure quickly became the national religious center of Israel, overshadowing every other sanctuary in the country. Destroyed by the invading Babylonians in 587 BCE, the temple was rebuilt after the period of captivity in about 515 BCE. By the first century BCE, this structure, ravaged by time and wars, was in considerable disrepair. Herod the Great (d. 4 BCE) demolished this second temple and began building a magnificent replacement about the year 20 BCE. Construction was completed by 64 CE.

Quotation 5. *Then [David] called for his son Solomon and charged him to build a house for the LORD, the God of Israel. David said to Solomon: "My son, I had planned to build a house to the name of the LORD, my God. But the word of the LORD came to me, saying 'You have shed much blood and have waged great wars; you shall not build a house to my name, because you have shed so much blood in my sight on the earth.'"* I Chronicles 22:6–8

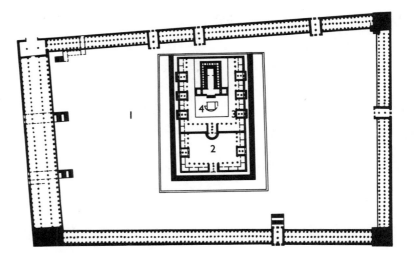

1. Court of the Gentiles
2. Court of the Women
3. Court of Israel
4. Court of the Priests

2. Plan of Herod's temple. (After Vincent-Steve as cited in Perrin-Duling, p. XX.)

The new temple, like the two before it, sat high on a hill overlooking the Kidron valley. This temple was about the same size as Solomon's building. It seemed more magnificent because it was set off by a series of walls and courtyards: [illustration 2] the outermost Court of the Gentiles, open to all; the Court of the Women, open to all Jews; the Court of Israel, open only to Jewish men; and the innermost Court of the Priests, open only to the priests. The altar for the daily sacrifices stood within the Court of Israel.

Although sacrifices had once been offered throughout Israel, the temple in Jerusalem came to be the only place of sacrifice for the Jews, except for the Samaritans, who offered sacrifices in their temple on Mount Gerizim. The destruction of the temple during the Jewish revolt against the Romans in 70 CE marked the end of ritual sacrifice among the Jews.

Jesus is remembered as having traveled to the temple in his childhood at Passover (Luke 2:41–50). The gospels also record that he frequented the temple during his public ministry. In the temple, he prayed, taught, cured the sick and challenged contemporary religious practice [quotation 6]. After his resurrection, the disciples also continued to worship and evangelize in the temple precincts. As the early Jewish-Christians began to distinguish themselves from other Jews, the temple became a place of tension for them. But they never completely rejected the temple or its worship [quotation 7].

Quotation 6. *Then Jesus entered the temple and drove out all who were selling and buying in the temple. . . . The blind and the lame came to him in the temple, and he cured them.* Matthew 21:12, 14

Quotation 7. *One day Peter and John were going up to the temple at the hour of prayer, at three o'clock in the afternoon.* Acts 3:1

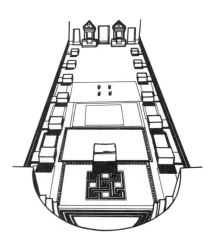

3. Synagogue at Sardis, originally built as a Roman basilica (first century CE). In the foreground is the apse with three rows of benches for the elders of the community. Beyond the apse is the marble table, probably used for the reading of Torah. Toward the back of the hall are the bases of four pillars, which may have supported the reader's desk. At the far end are three entrances with shrines between them, which may have been used for storing the Torah scrolls. (Text and illustration after Widoger, pp. 32–33.)

Quotation 8. *Then Jesus, filled with the power of the Spirit, returned to Galilee, and a report about him spread through all the surrounding country. He began to teach in their synagogues, and was praised by everyone. When he came to Nazareth, where he had been brought up, he went to the synagogue on the sabbath day, as was his custom. He stood up to read.* Luke 4:14–16

Quotation 9. *For several days [Saul] was with the disciples in Damascus, and immediately he began to proclaim Jesus in the synagogues, saying, "He is the Son of God."* Acts 9:19–20

Synagogue

The synagogue may have developed while the Jews were exiled from their homeland during the sixth century BCE. Whatever its origins, by the first century BCE, a synagogue existed in almost every place that Jews lived. In the synagogue, the local community gathered for the study of the Law and for prayer on the Sabbath, on some weekdays and during festivals.

The popularity of this institution resulted in a wide variety of styles and shapes for the buildings. Some, like the great synagogue of Jerusalem, were splendid edifices. Others were similar to the modest dwellings of the rural folk they served. Often they were rectangular buildings [illustration 3], built on the highest point in the town, facing Jerusalem. Inside, commonly, was a raised wooden platform for the readers and prayer leaders. The scrolls of the Law and the Prophets were kept in a special cupboard or niche decorated according to the size and means of the congregation. Seats were available, at least for the more notable guests and members. In some instances, benches for the people lined the walls. This relatively open, unrestricted space architecturally lived up to the name "synagogue," which means "a gathering place."

Jesus would have attended synagogue services while growing up in Nazareth. From early in his public ministry, he is remembered as having visited the synagogues to pray. There he cast out demons, taught, and began his preaching ministry. In his hometown synagogue, he is remembered as having read a prophecy from Isaiah and declaring himself to be the fulfillment of those words [quotation 8]. Following his example, the disciples continued to preach in the synagogues. Many times, the Acts of the Apostles tells of Paul, Silas, Barnabas and others preaching in the synagogues. Just as Jesus is remembered as first having preached his message in the synagogue, so is Paul remembered [quotation 9].

If the synagogues were the places where Jesus and his disciples preached, they also were the places where many Jews came to believe in this new way. These Jewish disciples did not reject Judaism initially and so did not reject the practice of study and prayer in the synagogue. Consequently, for most of the first century, the Jewish followers of Jesus continued to frequent the synagogue. Eventually, however, they came to be identified more as a separate sect than as a reforming agent within Judaism. About the year 80 CE, a malediction against the followers of Jesus was inserted into one of the central prayers of the daily Jewish service [quotation 10]. This suggests that the departure of the disciples from the Jewish synagogues occurred about this time. The Jewish followers of Jesus, however, did not abandon the way of prayer

4. Reconstruction of a multistory apartment block. (After Gardner, p. 186.)

of the synagogue. In places such as Jerusalem where there was a large Jewish-Christian population, these followers probably had their own synagogues at least into the second century.

Home

If the temple was a place of sacrifice and the synagogue a place for study and gathering, then the home was a place for blessing and prayer. Although certain prayers such as the *Shema* or "Hear, O Israel" came to be central elements in the synagogue service, they first were prayers to be offered in the home [quotation 11]. The home was especially important for emerging Christianity as the center for that familial and social institution, the meal. For the Jews, every meal was a sacred act. In a singular way, the meal recalled God's faithfulness and became a living sign of the covenant that God had sealed with a meal. Festival meals had their own repertoire of prayers and ritual actions. Some of them, such as the Passover meal, developed into elaborate and treasured traditions.

Jesus certainly learned to pray as he ate with his family at home in Nazareth. At that table, he heard the accounts of God's wondrous deeds that confirmed and continued the covenant with Israel, and there he must have learned the traditional prayers of blessing before and after festival meals. Many believe that these prayers were the predecessors of the Christian eucharistic prayers [quotation 12]. This pattern of table learning for the child became a pattern of table ministry for the adult. Time and again, Jesus is remembered as having entered the home of an outcast or a dignitary and sharing a meal [quotation 13]. In these homes and in an upper room, Jesus continued the ministry that was manifest in the temple and the synagogue, where he prayed, taught, and cured the sick.

Quotation 11. *Hear, O Israel! The LORD is our God, the LORD alone. You shall love the LORD your God with all your heart, and with all your soul, and with all your might. Keep these words that I am commanding you today in your heart. Recite them to your children and talk about them when you are at home and when you are away, when you lie down and when you rise. Write them on the doorposts of your house and on your gates.* Deuteronomy 6:4–7, 9

Quotation 12. *And Isaac, too, sent by the hand of Jacob to Abraham a best thank-offering that he might eat and drink. And he ate and drank, and blessed the Most High God, who hath created heaven and earth, and given them to the children of men that they might eat and drink and bless their creator.* The blessing after a meal from the *Book of Jubilees* (c. 100 BCE)

Quotation 13. *Then Levi gave a great banquet for [Jesus] in his house; and there was a large crowd of tax collectors and others sitting at the table with them.* Luke 5:29

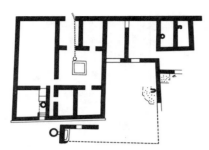

5. Roman villa excavated at Corinth, dating from the time of Paul. (After Murphy-O'Connor, p. 157.)

Quotation 14. *For, to begin with, when you come together as a church, I hear that there are divisions among you; and to some extent I believe it. When you come together it is not really to eat the Lord's supper. For when the time comes to eat, each of you goes ahead with your supper, and one goes hungry and another becomes drunk. What! Do you not have homes to eat and drink in? Or do you show contempt for the church of God and humiliate those who have nothing?* I Corinthians 11:18, 20–22

After Jesus' resurrection, the disciples continued to gather in believers' homes or apartment houses [illustration 4], as well as in borrowed rooms of public buildings. Here the word was proclaimed, teaching was imparted and healing was offered. In these places, the members of this first community gathered for the breaking of the bread. Jesus had celebrated his last ritual meal with his disciples in a borrowed room, and he appeared to them there after the resurrection. These borrowed rooms continued to serve the fledgling community through the first century.

The spacious homes or villas of wealthy believers became central gathering places as the community expanded into the urban centers of the first century. These homes, built in the tradition of Roman domestic architecture, often were large four-sided structures, built around a square courtyard or atrium that was open to the sky. Radiating off this courtyard were the dining room and private apartments for the family [illustration 5]. Such a home was probably the setting for Paul's famous tirade, which was recorded in his First Letter to the Corinthians [quotation 14].

As Jerome Murphy-O'Connor has suggested, a gathering for worship would have been confined to the two most public areas of the home, the dining room and the atrium. A recently excavated Roman house from Corinth, dating from the time of Paul, had a dining room that measured about 18 feet by 24 feet, though the floor space was diminished by the couches that lined the walls. This space would have been too small for the 40 or 50 members of the Corinthian Christian community. Consequently, the friends of the host or important guests would have been invited to recline in the dining room for the meal that was interwoven with the eucharist. Those who were less well known to the host, or some of the poorer community members who arrived late because they had to work longer, were relegated to the open-air atrium. This space was not only more uncomfortable—especially if the weather was inclement—it also was farther from the food and drink. Apparently, some guests never received dinner. No wonder that Paul suggested that people should eat at their own homes before gathering for eucharist. Even after the eucharist and the meal were separated, an early development in Christian worship, private homes continued to be employed for worship.

Summary

The emerging Christian community had no architecture of its own, but rather continued to use the places of Jewish cult: the temple until its destruction in 70 CE, synagogues and homes. As this religious movement gravitated toward large Hellenistic cities and evangelized large numbers of Gentiles, the villas of wealthy believers became important gathering places. Distinctive Christian rituals developed primarily in these homes.

Despite the growing preference for domestic settings, however, Christianity retained the Jewish perspective that God could not be confined to a single place. Prayer could and should be offered anywhere. Consequently, little tendency existed in the beginning to develop a distinctive design or arrangement for worship. Even the language of these first believers stressed that the people were more important than the space. The assembly, not the building, is the true temple [quotation 15]. Similarly, the Greek word *ekklesia*, which often is translated as "church," did not refer to the structure but to the believers. The only true Christian architecture of the first century was one of living stones and not of brick or mortar. This ideal accompanied the development of Christianity from its rural Jewish origins into the urban Gentile mission.

MUSIC

Ralph Martin once wrote that "the Christian Church was born in song." While this certainly is true, the difficulty with speaking about music in this period is that it was not a separate worship element, as it often is today. Many ancient peoples did not make a clear distinction between singing and speaking. The audible nature of all reading, for example, presumed rhythmic and melodic features that today would be more quickly classified as music rather than as speech. Public speaking, too, presumed a kind of chanting in cadence that fell someplace between modern categories of speech and song. Though many religions did have specially trained musicians, the ritual music of the ancient world was not confined to their performance. In Judaism and emerging Christianity especially, to the extent that there was audible worship, that worship was lyrical [quotation 16]. Furthermore, liturgical leadership was not separate from musical leadership; every leader of public prayer in Israel would have rendered that prayer in a musical manner. Musical leadership and ritual lyricism developed different forms according to the sites in which they took place.

Temple

The splendor of the architecture of Herod's temple certainly found a parallel in the temple's music. The temple had a large staff of professional musicians drawn from the tribe of Levi. According to the Bible, the musician-king, David, appointed some of the Levites as temple

---

Quotation 15. *Like living stones, let yourself be built into a spiritual house, to be a holy priesthood, to offer spiritual sacrifices acceptable to God through Jesus Christ.* 1 Peter 2:5

Quotation 16. *Hebrew and Greek have no separate word for music. The frontier between singing and speaking was far less precise. As soon as speech turned to poetry, or when public or ceremonial speaking was involved, rhythmic and melodic features were incorporated which today would be classified as musical, or at least premusical.* Joseph Gelineau, p. 444

6. Shofar.

7. Shofar calls. (Werner, *The Sacred Bridge,* Volume II, p. 12.)

Quotation 17. *David and the leaders of the army also set apart for the service the sons of Asaph, and of Heman, and of Jeduthun, as who should prophesy with lyres, harps, and cymbals.* I Chronicles 25:1

Quotation 18.
Praise him with trumpet sound;
  praise him with lute and harp!
Praise him with tambourine and dance;
  praise him with strings and pipe!
Praise him with clanging cymbals;
  praise him with loud clashing cymbals!
    Psalm 150:3–5

musicians [quotation 17]. Although this account was written centuries after the events it recounts, it reflects a tradition about David's musical interests and the Levites' early involvement in temple music.

At the time of Jesus, professional, rigorously trained instrumentalists and singers served in the temple. Instrumental music was an integral part of worship in Herod's temple. Of the various instruments mentioned in the Bible, some, such as the trumpet and *shofar* [illustrations 6 and 7], primarily were used to signal ritual moments such as the entrance of the priests. Other wind and string instruments accompanied the singing of the choir. Eric Werner believes that these instruments would have reproduced the vocal line of the singers with only slight ornamentation.

On certain occasions, a mixture of all the instruments with percussion joined with the voices of the augmented choir to offer a fitting song to the Lord [quotation 18]. The choir, which numbered at least 12 adult male singers, could be augmented by an unlimited number of adult males and by male Levite children. The orchestra, which required at least 12 instruments, also could be augmented with other instruments according to need. On certain days, the combined forces of voices and instruments may have numbered more than 50!

The psalms were one important part of the temple repertoire, and certain psalms came to be prescribed for specific events or festivals. Psalm 15, an examination of conscience for worshipers, probably was employed as a preparation for worship. Psalms 113 to 118 came to be sung at the three great pilgrim festivals of Passover, Pentecost and Tabernacles. Besides the psalms, Levites also sang a variety of canticles and other poetic texts from the Bible, and possibly even nonbiblical texts.

Though professional singers and instrumentalists were the primary musical force in temple worship, the people were not excluded from ritual song. Carroll Stuhlmueller's analysis of Psalm 44, for example, suggests how individual singers, a choir and the larger assembly could have joined together in this hymn [illustration 8]. Psalm 136 was

Hymnic Introduction: vv. 1–8

vv. 1–2: Call to praise, sung by everyone
We have heard with our ears, O God,
 our ancestors have told us,
what deeds you performed in their days,
 in the days of old:
you with your own hand drove out the nations
 but them you planted;
you afflicted the peoples,
 but them you set free;

v. 3: Motivation by large choir
for not by their own sword did they win the land
 nor did their own arm give them victory;
but your right hand, and your arm,
 and the light of your countenance,
 for you delighted in them.

v. 7: Confidence
For you have saved us from our foes,
 and have put to confusion those who hate us.

vv. 4, 6: individual cantor or special choir
You are my King and my God;
 you command victories for Jacob.
For not in my bow do I trust,
 nor can my sword save me.

v. 8: refrain by everyone
In God we have boasted continually,
 and we will give thanks to your name forever.

Community Lament: vv. 9–16

v. 15: individual cantor or choir
All day long my disgrace is before me,
 and shame has covered my face

vv. 17–22: reflection in which different choirs speak:

to God (vv. 17–19)
All this has come upon us,
 yet we have not forgotten you,
 or been false to your covenant.
Our heart has not turned back,
 nor have our steps departed from your way,
yet you have broken us in the haunt of jackals,
 and covered us with deep darkness.

about God (vv. 20–21)
If we had forgotten the name of our God
 or spread our hands out to a strange god,
would not God discover this?
 For he knows the secrets of the heart.

to God (vv. 22)
Because of you we are being killed all day long,
 and accounted as sheep for the slaughter.

Prayer of Petition: vv. 23–26

Rouse yourself! Why do you sleep, O Lord?
 Awake, do not cast us off forever!
Why do you hide your face?
 Why do you forget our
  affliction and oppression?
For we sink down to the dust;
 our bodies cling to the ground.
Rise up, come to our help.
 Redeem us for the sake of your
  steadfast love.

8. Structural analysis of psalm 44

composed with a continuous refrain that probably was echoed by the assembly, while Psalms 146 to 150 may have been punctuated by a continuous "Alleluia" by the people. Though the assembly might have joined in singing a refrain or even a whole psalm known by heart, the professional musicians dominated temple music. Musical participation on the part of the people was limited, and they often were silent onlookers during the temple sacrifices.

Synagogue

The great differences between the rituals of the temple and those of the synagogue produced divergent forms of music in these two institutions. Only one temple existed for the whole nation, while synagogues were present wherever there were Jews. The temple cult essentially was sacrificial, while the synagogue was a place of study and prayer. Only adult Jewish males were allowed into the inner court of the temple, while the main assembly in the synagogue was comprised of women, men and children. The temple was staffed by a large body of professional ministers, while the synagogue and its worship were led by townsfolk, with no need or place for priests. After the destruction of the temple, this was to change. The need for stability in the synagogue—which now was the institution that largely defined Judaism—as well as the influx of professional ministers from the temple contributed to the development of more formal ministries in the synagogue. Until this time, however, the synagogue clearly had been a lay organization.

In the synagogue, the modern distinction between music and public speech became especially blurred. The choirs and orchestras in the temple clearly indicate the presence of music as a distinct element. The synagogue, however, never was a place of instrumental music nor of choirs, but a place of prayer and proclamation. The performance of this word-centered worship continuously migrated back and forth between what today would be called speech and song.

Despite the pluriformity of practice and the lack of written records, at least two standard elements can be discerned in the daily services of the synagogue during the first century. The oldest of these was the recitation of the *Shema* [quotation 11]. Centuries after the destruction of the temple, various blessings that traditionally surrounded the *Shema* were standardized and became mandatory. A second element was the Eighteen Benedictions, also called the *Amidah* or "standing prayer" because it was prayed while standing [quotation 19]. The reading of scripture was also an integral part of some synagogue services. The Sabbath morning service included a reading from the

Quotation 19. *You are praised, O Lord our God and God of our fathers, God of Abraham, God of Isaac, and God of Jacob, the great, mighty and awe-inspiring God, God Supreme, Creator of heaven and earth, our Shield and Shield of our fathers, our trust in every generation. You are praised, O Lord, Shield of Abraham.* The first of the Eighteen Benedictions, current Ashkenazi version of Babylonian provenance, translated by Jakob J. Petuchowski

9. Some of the notational signs of ancient Jewish music, with their rendition according to Syrian practice. (Davidson and Apel, I:8.)

Torah and another from the Prophets. It also is probable that the Torah was read in the synagogue on the market days, Monday and Thursday.

These various elements were rendered with a certain degree of musicality. Because every Jew knew the *Shema* by heart, it could have been chanted in unison by the whole assembly during the service. In some places, a prayer leader appears to have recited the first line with the congregation responding with the second line, and so on through the entire prayer. Either style would require relatively simple musical settings for these congregational chants.

In contrast, the *Amidah* probably was not chanted by the whole assembly. This was due, in part, to the unfixed nature of these blessings in the first century. Though a general outline of the prayer was in place by the time of Jesus, the *Amidah* required improvisation and expansion. This could be accomplished only by a single voice, though the assembly might have added some phrases of blessing or affirmation at the end of the prayer. Little evidence exists for the congregational singing of psalms in the synagogue. Because the Book of Psalms was considered one of the prophetic books, it was regularly chanted like the rest of these readings.

The musical building blocks for the *Shema* and the *Amidah* probably were derived from the repertoire of chants that had developed for the cantillation of scripture. Cantillation was a way of chanting that consisted of employing a series of set melodic formulas [quotation 20]. The scrolls from which one chanted were marked with signs or accents that indicated the appropriate formula [illustration 9]. Though many variations in this practice existed, cantillation generally respected the structure and sense of the text being proclaimed. Because this musical declamation was intended to serve the word and enable its proclamation, it could not be too florid or distracting in its artistry [illustration 10].

Quotation 20. *He who reads the Pentateuch without tune shows disregard for it. Babylonian Talmud,* Megilla 32a

Home

The various services of the synagogues and the temple left a musical impression on the early followers of Jesus. This shaped them in a cultural context where public speech naturally migrated toward music.

Wa-jiq-ra moše   lehol ziqne jisra-el waj-jomer a-lehem, mi-še-hu   uq-hu lahem šon   lemiš-pe-hotehem wešaha-tu

hap-pe-sah. Ulqah-tem   a;-gudat e-zob   ut-baltem   baddam ašer bassaf wehig-ga-tem el hammašqof we-el še-te

hame-zu-zot min haddam a-šer bassaf we-at-tem   lo te-še-u   iš mippe-tah beto ad boqer.

10. Intonation pattern used in reading from the Pentateuch, according to Syrian practice. (Davidson and Apel I:8.)

Quotation 21. *To the only wise God, through Jesus Christ, to whom be the glory forever! Amen.* Romans 16:27

Quotation 22.
Amen. Galatians 6:18
Hallelujah! Revelation 19:1
Hosanna! Mark 11:9
Maranatha. I Corinthians 16:22

Quotation 23. *[Jesus Christ] is the image of the invisible God, the firstborn of all creation; for in him all things in heaven and on earth were created, things visible and invisible, whether thrones or dominions or rulers or powers—all things have been created through him and for him. He himself is before all things, and in him all things hold together. He is the head of the body, the church; he is the beginning, the firstborn from the dead, so that he might come to have first place in everything. For in him all the fullness of God was pleased to dwell, and through him God was pleased to reconcile to himself all things, whether on earth or in heaven, by making peace through the blood of his cross.* Colossians 1:15–20

In the home rituals of the first followers of Jesus, this lyrical environment shaped emerging Christian worship. Some of the blessings chanted before and after meals, the psalms and other songs of the Christian home were indistinguishable from those of other Jewish households. As the community began to reshape its prayer in the memory and example of Jesus, however, certain variations on these homespun prayers, songs and chants emerged. Variation gave way to distinctive musical texts, forms and melodies, which were the antecedents of Christian music during the following centuries.

Although the New Testament does not record melodies, rhythms or other such musical elements, it does offer some information about the content and performance of emerging Christian music. For example, a number of short, lyrical praise formulas appear in the New Testament, such as the doxology sung by the angels at the birth of Jesus (Luke 2:14). These probably were employed as a conclusion to vocal prayer or preaching. Based on Jewish models, such doxologies eventually led to the development of Christological doxologies [quotation 21]. The New Testament also contains a significant number of lyrical fragments borrowed from Judaism but given a distinctively Christian treatment [quotation 22]. Hymns to Christ and other large lyrical forms also were based on Jewish models [quotation 23]. Though lyrical texts are not the same as musical settings, their consistent appearance throughout the New Testament confirms that the followers of Jesus embraced the lyrical heritage of Judaism and carried it with them into an urban and Gentile world.

Paul's words about public worship are helpful in understanding the form and style of early Christian singing [quotation 24]. Though Paul recognizes a place for solo expression in worship—such as the gift of

Quotation 24. *Therefore, one who speaks in a tongue should pray for the power to interpret. For if I pray in a tongue, my spirit prays but my mind is unproductive. What should I do then? I will pray with the spirit, but I will pray with the mind also; I will sing with the spirit, but I will sing praise with the mind also. Otherwise, if you say a blessing with the spirit, how can anyone in the position of an outsider say the "Amen" to your thanksgiving, since the outsider does not know what you are saying? For you may give thanks well enough, but the other person is not built up. I thank God that I speak in tongues more than all of you; nevertheless, in church I would rather speak five words with my mind, in order to instruct others also than ten thousand words in a tongue.* I Corinthians 14:13–19

tongues—his overriding concern is for the engagement and prayer of the whole community. His emphasis that all gifts should serve the common good would extend to the musical elements of worship as well. This suggests a preference for responsorial rather than solo forms, a leaning toward dialogue rather than monologue in worship and a constant respect for the community's "Amen." Paul's emphasis also implies a preference for a style of liturgical-musical leadership more akin to that which would be found in the synagogue than to that of the temple. Although talented musicians undoubtedly performed in the early community, they did not dominate the lyrical landscape of first-century worship, which strove for single-voiced praise.

Summary

Each place for Jewish worship made a distinctive contribution to the musical life of Israel and influenced Christian song, which appears to be variations on borrowed material. The synagogue especially left its mark on Christianity. The liturgical-musical style found there served the word and engaged the community. This model, played out in the domestic worship of the first-century community, shaped Christian music for the next three centuries.

BOOKS

Torah occupies the central place in the life of Judaism. "Torah" usually refers to the first five books of the Bible, which also are called "the Law." Ancient belief holds that on Mount Sinai, God revealed the Law to Moses, who wrote down this revelation in five books [quotation 25]. By the middle of the second century CE, this belief further developed that God communicated an oral revelation to Moses in addition to the written Law. These written and oral parts together constitute the full Torah. The oral Torah, passed on from generation to generation, was most perfectly captured in those great written works of the rabbis of the fifth and sixth centuries, the Palestinian Talmud and the Babylonian Talmud. Though the development of the Torah is not so simple as this tradition describes, nor Moses' role so well defined, the Law embodies a living covenant stretching back to the time of the Exodus.

Quotation 25. *Moses came and told the people all the words of the LORD and all the ordinances; and all the people answered with one voice, and said, "All the words that the LORD has spoken, we will do." And Moses then wrote down all the words of the LORD.* Exodus 24:3–4

In the fluid tradition of the Torah, Christianity was born. The influence of this rich heritage goes far beyond the acceptance of the Hebrew Scriptures that Christians call the Old Testament. From this tradition, Christians learned that reverencing, proclaiming and even studying the word are acts of worship. They learned to surround the public proclamation of the word with blessing and song, to embody

11. An Essene manuscript from about the turn of the era (BCE to CE) measuring 27 feet long, written on animal skin, containing at least 66 columns of text.

their own oral traditions in written texts and to see the books inherited from Judaism and their own books as the word of God.

Synagogue

Though some evidence suggests that scriptural texts were read publicly at worship in the temple, these readings were neither regular nor continuous. Through the synagogue, especially, reverence for the Torah in its written and oral forms was communicated over the centuries. It is not clear when the public reading of scriptures became a constitutive element of the synagogue service. Moses is remembered as having instituted an occasional public reading of the Law [quotation 26], but more probably, the weekly reading of scriptures in the synagogue dates from about the fourth century BCE. This practice recalls the scribe Ezra who helped restore worship in Jerusalem after the Babylonian Exile (587–516 BCE). As part of this restoration, Ezra established the regular reading of the Law as an act of worship [quotation 27].

The written texts that were cantillated and studied in the synagogue were not in what today would be called book form. Originally, these texts were written on sheets of papyrus—a kind of paper made from a river plant of the same name—or animal skin. The sides of papyrus sheets were glued together, or animal skins sewn, to form a scroll that could be rolled up. A scroll ordinarily would be 25 or 30 feet

Quotation 26. *Then Moses wrote down this law, and gave it to the priests, the sons of Levi. . . . Moses commanded them . . . you shall read this law before all Israel in their hearing.* Deuteronomy 31:9, 11

Quotation 27. *[Ezra and the Levites] read from the book, from the law of God, with interpretation. They gave the sense, so that the people understood the reading.* Nehemiah 8:8

long and about ten inches high. The text typically was written in five- or six-inch-wide columns, which were exposed as the scroll was unrolled from right to left [illustration 11]. Jesus no doubt used such a scroll when he read from the prophet Isaiah in the synagogue in Nazareth [quotation 28]. These scrolls were kept in the synagogue in a special niche or cupboard, which sometimes was elaborated into a beautiful shrine or ark [illustration 12]. Some scrolls were beautifully decorated and became the treasures of the synagogue.

Besides the various scrolls of the Law and the Prophets, ancient Israel knew no other "books" for prayer. Although the Mishnah and the Talmud, as well as various other writings, contain many examples of Jewish prayer, they were not composed as prayer books. The first extant example of a prayer book or *siddur* was compiled by Amram Gaon (d. 871 CE). The late development of the *siddur* is one more reflection of the Jewish community's reluctance to confine their prayer to written forms. Lawrence Hoffman suggests that the slow evolution of a common book of prayer is testimony to the enormous variation that occurred in synagogue worship until this period. Only the special genius of eighth- and ninth-century scholars called *geonim* made the emergence of the *siddur* possible. Unlike scholars of previous generations, the *geonim* were able to answer liturgical questions in a clear and decisive manner. Their answers allowed for no variation in the ritual, which made a fixed prayer book possible. Until this period, however, the Jewish community employed no written texts for their prayers, which they passed on orally and improvised from generation to generation.

Emerging Christianity

The early Christian community seems to have employed books much like those used in the synagogue. The tradition of publicly cantillating the Law and the Prophets probably was continued by the Jewish followers of Jesus in their own gatherings. In the Christian synagogues of the late first and early second century, the ancient practice of lyrically proclaiming the word may have been continued. Public readings from the Law and the Prophets also may have been part of the worship enacted by the Gentile Christian communities before 80 CE.

The number of quotations from the Jewish scriptures in the New Testament demonstrates that these were very familiar and were valued by the community. Frederick Crowe has noted that after the resurrection, the early followers began to believe that the Jewish scriptures pointed to Jesus. Paul's letter to the largely Gentile community at Rome, for example, declared that the Jewish scriptures were a proclamation of the new gospel of Jesus [quotation 29]. Luke, also writing for

Quotation 28. *The scroll of the prophet Isaiah was given to [Jesus]. He unrolled the scroll and found the place where it was written: "The spirit of the Lord is upon me. . . ." And he rolled up the scroll and gave it back to the attendant, and sat down. Luke 4:17–18, 20*

12. Niche in the wall facing Jerusalem in the Dura Europos synagogue (c. 245 CE), believed to have been the repository for the Torah scrolls.

Quotation 29. *Paul, a servant of Jesus Christ, called to be an apostle, set apart for the gospel of God, which he promised beforehand through his prophets in the holy scriptures, the gospel concerning his Son . . . Romans 1:1–3*

Quotation 30. *Then beginning with Moses and all the prophets, [Jesus] interpreted to them the things about himself in all the scriptures. Luke 24:27*

Quotation 31. *Until I arrive, give attention to the public reading of scripture, to exhorting, to teaching. 1 Timothy 4:13*

Quotation 32. *We constantly give thanks to God for this, that when you received the word of God that you heard from us, you accepted it not as a human word but as what it really is, God's word, which is also at work in you believers. 1 Thessalonians 2:13*

Quotation 33. *Give my greetings to the brothers and sisters at Laodicea, and to Nympha and the church in her house. And when this letter has been read among you, have it read also in the church of the Laodiceans; and see that you read also the letter from Laodicea. Colossians 4:15–16*

Gentiles, depicted Jesus sanctioning such a perspective [quotation 30]. These insights about the Law and the Prophets probably emerged in the Jewish-Christian communities that continued the Jewish tradition of scripture study. Through people such as Paul, this perspective spread to the Gentile communities, which learned to value this important heritage. The First Letter to Timothy likely reflected the tradition of proclaiming the Jewish scriptures in a Christian assembly composed of both Gentiles and Jews [quotation 31].

Aside from the ritual reading and study of the Jewish scriptures, sections of what came to be called the New Testament also may have been read in the assemblies of the faithful. This suggestion finds support in some sections of the New Testament that equate the Christian message with the "word of God" [quotation 32]. If there existed a tradition for publicly reading the "word of God" in any form in Christian assemblies, it would be difficult to imagine that the message of Jesus as the "word of God" would not similarly be proclaimed. The proclamation of this word, however, does not presume that it existed everywhere in written form. From the beginning, the good news was a preached event that required oral, rather than written, transmission. Although some collections of the sayings of Jesus and a few narratives existed earlier, only toward the end of the first century did written forms of the gospels appear.

One form of the Christian message that was written for the early community was the letter. Many of these letters, while intended only for a particular community such as the Galatians or Ephesians, were circulated among the various churches to be read at worship [quotation 33]. Thus began a tradition that continues to the present.

Summary

The devotion of the Jewish community to the Law and the Prophets greatly influenced Christianity. In borrowing this tradition, the Christian community also extended and adapted it to the message of Jesus. This, too, came to be venerated as the word of God and acquired a written form. Christian books or scrolls, however, did not materialize overnight. When they did appear toward the end of the first century, it is not clear that they immediately became the new Torah for the Christian community. These written forms originally may have prepared communities to hear the good news of Jesus preached to them, but as the community moved further in time and space from the events of Jesus' life, the written forms took on more importance in the life and ritual of the community.

VESSELS

Just as the temple was not the Jewish institution that most influenced the music, architecture and books used in the earliest Christian worship, the same is true of ritual vessels. The temple did possess exquisite cups and other utensils of precious metals, many of which were looted during the various campaigns against Israel and later replaced [quotation 34]. But the vessels of the temple were not the models for those used by the emerging Christian community in its rituals. Nor did the synagogue influence the vessels used in Christian worship. Because the services that took place in the synagogue did not include food or drink, the synagogue did not possess vessels for ritual eating or drinking.

It was in the home that Jews celebrated their ritual meals, and it is there that the types of vessels used by the first Christians for their ritual meals are found. The most important vessels were those that held bread and wine. Understanding the kinds of bread and wine common to the Jewish household will help in understanding the vessels in which they were stored and served.

Bread and Its Vessels

Daily bread in the Hellenistic world often was baked in round loaves. Examples of such loaves were preserved in the ruins of Pompeii, destroyed by the eruption of Mount Vesuvius in 79 CE. These loaves, leavened and made of wheat, were approximately eight inches in diameter and weighed almost one pound [illustration 13]. Similar loaves still are made in the Mediterranean world today.

Barley was the most common grain used by the Jews for bread, but barley was not allowed to be used in the temple. Unleavened bread or *matzah* was prepared for religious services. Some rituals required a certain type of unleavened bread, known as a cereal offering, made of wheat ("choice") flour, oil and frankincense [quotation 35]. The showbreads set out in the sanctuary of the temple every week and consumed by the priests also were unleavened [quotation 36].

Unleavened bread also played an important role in the yearly Feast of Unleavened Bread, which marked the beginning of the barley harvest. During this spring festival, it was traditional to eat bread prepared only with the new grain, without flour, leaven or any ingredient from the previous year. These flat barley cakes were eaten during the seven days of the festival. The Passover celebration was the result of this ancient feast combining with an even earlier feast of nomadic origins, which included the sacrifice and consumption of a

Quotation 34. *King Belshazzar made a great festival for a thousand of his lords, and he was drinking wine in the presence of the thousand. Under the influence of the wine, Belshazzar commanded that they bring in the vessels of gold and silver that his father Nebuchadnezzar had taken out of the temple in Jerusalem, so that the king and his lords, his wives and his concubines might drink from them.* Daniel 5:1–2

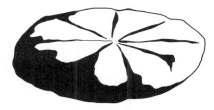

13. Bread from Pompeii, preserved by the eruption of Mount Vesuvius in 79 CE.

Quotation 35. *When anyone presents a grain offering to the LORD, the offering shall be of choice flour.* Leviticus 2:1

Quotation 36. *You shall take choice flour and bake twelve loaves of it. . . . You shall put them in two rows, six in a row, on the table of pure gold.* Leviticus 24:5–6.

young lamb, possibly as a ritual offering for good pastures in the coming year.

The New Testament writers agree that Jesus' Last Supper occurred within a Passover context [quotation 37]. Given the ritual requirements of this feast, Jesus and his disciples probably ate the flat barley cakes of the Passover festival at their last meal together. The New Testament does not attach any significance to the use of unleavened bread, and little evidence exists that the early community continued to use such bread in their eucharistic gatherings. More probably, the barley bread eaten at daily meals became the staple for eucharistic meals as well.

Bread was customarily kept in baskets, both in the temple [quotation 38] and in people's homes [quotation 39]. First-century sources give little evidence that fragments were saved after the eucharistic breaking of the bread; later sources indicate that bread from the celebration was sent to those not present.

Wine and Its Vessels

Although water was the usual drink of Jews at the time of Jesus, wine was served on many festive occasions, including the celebration of marriage, the Sabbath meals, Passover and other festivals. Wine often was kept in the home for such occasions, as well as for medicinal purposes [quotation 40]. Many kinds of wine were available in Palestine, though red seems to have been preferred. The wine usually was thinned with water because it was too strong to drink undiluted.

Wine often was stored in a covered pitcher or jar. Smaller pitchers would rest on a table or shelf, while larger, more stationary vessels would sit on the floor. These containers were often earthenware, though some were made of stone and, less often, of metal. More portable containers made of goatskin [quotation 41], which came into use before the appearance of earthenware containers, still were in use at this time.

Individual drinking vessels were a familiar commodity in Jewish society, though it is not likely that individual cups were available to all the family members or guests at a meal. A communal cup frequently was used. Vessels for drinking wine and other liquids were made from a variety of materials. A cup for ordinary use often was made of clay, though precious materials were used for drinking goblets for the wealthy. During the first century, glass was a common material for cups in the Hellenistic world. Simple glass beakers [illustration 14] and bowls with or without a base served as drinking vessels. Very seldom would a stem or node separate the base from the bowl.

Quotation 37. On the first day of Unleavened Bread, when the Passover lamb is sacrificed, [Jesus'] disciples said to him "Where do you want us to go and make the preparations for you to eat the Passover?" Mark 14:12

Quotation 38. Take . . . unleavened bread, unleavened cakes mixed with oil, and unleavened wafers spread with oil. You shall make them of choice wheat flour. You shall put them in one basket and bring them in the basket. Exodus 29:1–3

Quotation 39. Breadbaskets—their measure is with loaves of bread. A papyrus basket for which one made reeds below and above for strengthening is clean. [If] one made for it handles of any sort, it is unclean. Mishnah, Kelim 17.3

Quotation 40. [If he said,] "Qonam be wine, because it is bad for the belly," [and] they told him, "But isn't old wine good for the belly?" he is permitted to drink old wine. And not old wine alone is permitted. But all wine [is permitted]. Mishnah, Nedarim 9.8

Quotation 41. And no one pours new wine into old wineskins; otherwise, the wine will burst the skins and the wine is lost, and so are the skins, but one puts new wine into fresh wineskins. Mark 2:22

14. Roman drinking glass (First to second century CE).

The simple glass cup is probably the vessel Jesus used during the various ritual meals in which he participated, including the Last Supper. The New Testament notes that the Last Supper was celebrated in the company of a large number of disciples. These accounts also point out that Jesus passed his own cup to the disciples [quotation 42].

As already noted, the early community sometimes gathered for the breaking of the bread in the houses of wealthy believers. During the earliest decades after the resurrection, these gatherings would have included a meal with the eucharist. Though various drinking vessels may have been used during the meal, the use of one communal cup probably was typical of the eucharist that followed. Paul seems to imply the use of one cup in his discussions of eucharist. A hallmark of these eucharistic discourses is Paul's emphasis on unity and oneness in the breaking of the bread and the sharing of the cup [quotation 43]. His insistence on the unity of the body of Christ in the eucharistic action, as well as the precedent established by Jesus at the Last Supper, suggest the use of one common cup from the very beginning.

Summary

More than architecture, music or books, a discussion of vessels demonstrates the influence of domestic Judaism on first-century Christianity. In one sense, Christianity was born around the domestic table. The mealtime traditions of Israel and the instinct always to bless God at the breaking of bread is the context from which specific Christian rituals emerged; this is the best example of the Christian genius to borrow and change a tradition. As for specific vessels, Judaism had few that it would consider sacred to the domestic rites. Similarly, the vessels of first-century Christianity were of a decidedly nonsacred nature. A cup, a pitcher and a basket served the bread and wine which, in turn, served the unity of the community. In this time, it is not the things—not even the bread and wine—that are important, but the community. The believers more than any single food are the body of Christ.

Quotation 42. *Then he took a cup, and after giving thanks he gave it to them, saying, "Drink from it, all of you; for this is the blood of the covenant which is poured out for many for the forgiveness of sins."* Matthew 26:27–28

Quotation 43. *The cup of blessing that we bless, is it not a sharing in the blood of Christ? The bread that we break, is it not a sharing in the body of Christ? Because there is one bread, we who are many are one body, for we all partake of the one bread.* 1 Corinthians 10:16–17

JACOB AND RUBEN

Jacob splashed water on his face, shook the dust from his robes and hurried to greet his guests. He had hoped to arrive home earlier, but camel trading was an unpredictable business. A dispute with an old customer over the price of two small dromedaries delayed him. After finally arriving at an acceptable price, Jacob excused himself, bolted out of the bazaar and raced through the back streets of Jericho, praying as he ran that he would arrive home before Ruben and the others.

Ruben was brother-in-law to the great preacher, Paul of Tarsus. Like Paul, Ruben traveled from city to city telling the story of Jesus of Nazareth. He sometimes preached in the streets, but more often he would go to a local synagogue and there proclaim this "good news." It was at the synagogue in Jericho that Jacob first met him. Ruben had been asked by the president of the synagogue to say a few words after the reading from Ezekhiel. Ruben began by announcing that Jesus was the fulfillment of every prophecy and was the one true messiah. The synagogue erupted into a holy brawl. Some wanted to hear more, but most rushed forward to refute the heretic.

As the assembly turned into an angry mob, Jacob knew that he had better act quickly or Ruben, who stood his ground, could end up hurt or dead. Jacob worked his way through the crowd, grabbed the unwelcome prophet by the back of his tunic and pulled him like a reluctant camel through the chaos. Once outside the synagogue, Jacob maneuvered Ruben through the back streets, finally dragging the prophet into his home.

Ruben was furious that he had been denied the opportunity to preach his message and to answer the objections of his detractors. To calm Ruben down—and to satisfy his own curiosity—Jacob invited Ruben to share the evening meal with Jacob's family and to tell his stories to them. It was a dinner none of them would ever forget.

As he prepared for dinner, Jacob mused that his children would be a formidable challenge for Ruben. Though he loved them dearly, Jacob knew they were a quarrelsome brood whose penchant for misbehavior was amplified by the presence of guests. Had Abraham experienced such difficulties with Isaac? To spare his guests the experience of his squabbling offspring, Jacob usually ate alone with his guests. Tonight, however, he welcomed all ten of his offspring to the table, hoping that they would keep Ruben occupied for the duration of the meal.

To Jacob's surprise, his lone guest mesmerized the children. How quiet they were as Ruben unfolded the stories of Jesus curing a boy with palsy, mending relationships between quarreling spouses, multiplying bread and fish for thousands and sharing a final meal with his inner circle of friends. They sat transfixed as Ruben whispered the story of Jesus' trial, crucifixion and burial. The events of the third day were astonishing to them—but also most believable. Jacob's skepticism was muted by the simple assent of his own offspring.

Then Ruben did something quite unexpected. He took a piece of bread and offered a blessing in the memory of Jesus. Then he shared the bread with the children, saying, "If you eat this, you too become part of the story, for this is the very body of Jesus." Jacob's youngest passed the bread to her father, who ate in silence. Then Ruben took his cup, spoke another blessing and passed the cup to the children, saying, "By drinking from this cup, you drink from the heart of Jesus who died that we might live, for this cup is an invitation to a new covenant sealed in his blood."

That was 17 years ago. During the interim, Jacob's camel trade has flourished, his children have given him grandchildren, and Ruben has become a frequent guest. In the early years, after the children had gone to bed, Ruben would spend long nights with Jacob exploring the Jesus story. Jacob began to invite a few close friends for marathon dinners that often ended with the simple ritual of bread and wine. Over the years, the company began to expand. Jacob's grown children often returned for dinner when Ruben came to town. Their children and friends became part of an ever-growing crowd. Jacob never knows who will show up for dinner these nights. Even when Ruben is not present, these followers of the new way still gather around Jacob to hear him repeat the stories, the invitations and the rituals. Many times, Jacob has broken the bread with his family and friends, repeating the words that Ruben taught him. But for tonight, he will simply play the host, welcoming the old prophet and newfound friends who will again come to recognize Jesus in their midst through the breaking of the bread.

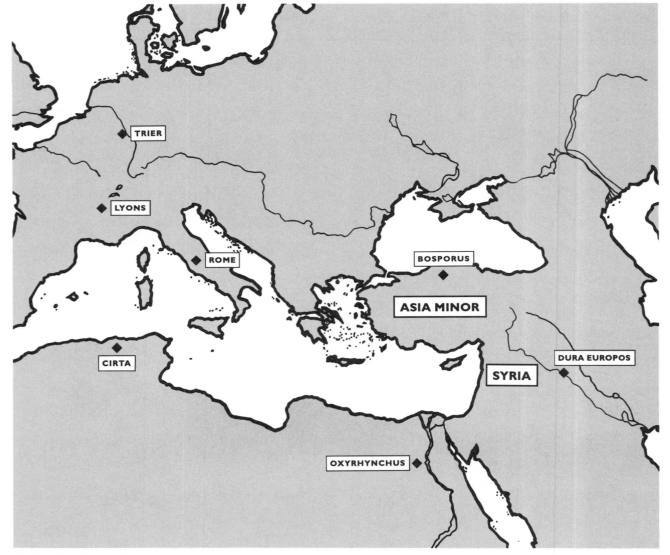

15. Map for Chapter Two.

CHAPTER TWO

The Domestic Church:
100 to 313

The Christianity of much of the first century could be considered a movement within, rather than a religion distinct from, Judaism. During the second and third centuries, however, Christianity established itself as a separate religion. This is evident not only by its separation from Judaism but also by Christianity's expansion independent of Judaism, a developing pattern of conflict with the Roman government and the emergence of a distinctive structure, theology, cult and canon of sacred texts.

During the first century, the Jewish community took steps to expel Christians from the synagogues and, eventually, the Christian community sought to distance itself from Judaism. This separation—rooted in the different views that these two groups had of Jesus—often was conscious and deliberate. For example, early Christian writings indicate that Jewish fast days were intentionally abandoned by Christians [quotation 44]. Similarly, Sunday, rather than the Sabbath, was kept by Christians as the primary day for public worship.

More than the simple assertion of a new identity, these distinctions were symptomatic of a growing adversarial attitude toward Judaism. Anti-Semitism may have been, in some cases, a survival tactic employed by Christians wanting to distinguish themselves from the Jews, who were becoming increasingly unpopular in the Roman Empire and increasingly hostile toward those who identified themselves as Christians. The first and second Jewish revolts against Rome in the years 66–70 and 132–135 CE generated enormous contempt for the Jews in the empire. Christians were motivated by these events to distinguish themselves from their Jewish forebears as the Christians moved throughout the Mediterranean.

During the first century, Paul already had carried the gospel from Palestine into modern-day Syria, Turkey, Greece and Italy. The empire's network of roads connecting the city-states provided a useful system for the spread of Christianity. By the second century, Christian

Quotation 44. Do not keep the same fast days as the hypocrites. Mondays and Thursdays are their fast days, but yours should be Wednesdays and Fridays. Didache 8 (early second century)

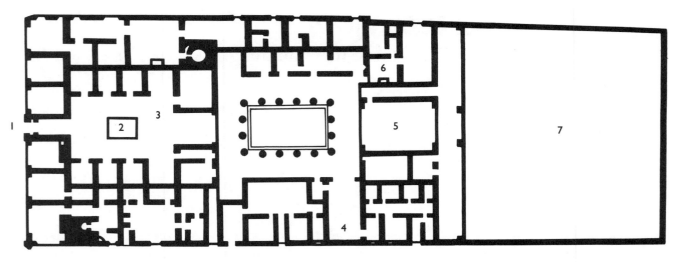

1. Main entrance
2. *Impluvium*
3. Atrium
4. Dining room *(triclinium)*
5. Reception room *(oecus)*
6. Kitchen
7. Garden

16. Plan of House of Pansa, Pompeii, second century BCE. (After Gardner, p. 174.)

Quotation 45. *To eliminate the suspicion that he himself had set the fire, the emperor diverted it to the Christians, who were hated because of their misdeeds.* Tacitus (d. 120) Annals, 14.44

Quotation 46. *Philip, after a reign of seven years, was succeeded by Decius. Through hatred of Philip, he started a persecution against the churches, in which Fabian found fulfillment in martyrdom at Rome.* Eusebius (died c. 340), History of the Church, 6.39.1

communities could be found along the North African coast, scattered throughout Asia Minor and as far north and east as modern-day Trier and Lyons [illustration 24]. By the following century, those borders stretched from India to the British Isles. From a handful of disciples, Christianity grew to almost 20,000 adherents by the end of the first century and to at least 7 million by the year 300. In an empire of 50 or 60 million inhabitants, this was a significant minority.

Christianity's expansion also led to a growing conflict with the Roman authorities; this conflict occasionally erupted into persecution. The first persecution of Christians by Roman authorities occurred under the emperor Nero (d. 68) in the year 64. In his search for a scapegoat for the great fire of Rome—which many suspected Nero himself had set—the emperor blamed the Christians [quotation 45]. Other short-lived persecutions occurred under Domitian (d. 96) in Rome, Trajan (d. 117) in Asia Minor and Marcus Aurelius (d. 180) in Lyons. Decius (d. 251) believed that Christianity was a threat to the state, and he persecuted Christians throughout the empire [quotation 46]. This brief but intense persecution was similar to the longer ones that occurred under Diocletian (d. 305). These persecutions, though sporadic and often separated by long periods of peace, chart the progressive visibility of Christianity.

These external signs of growth were matched by internal developments within the church. The period between the years 100 and 313 saw the emergence of basic ecclesial structures, worship forms and dogmas. During this period, the roles of bishops, deacons and many other ministries were delineated. Christians still follow an outline for worship formed by the middle of the second century [quotation 47]. This was the time when the divinity and authority of Christ were defined, the New Testament canon was identified and Greek philosophy was first employed in the service of a Christian theology. In short, it was a time when one could recognize a church: urban, Gentile and Hellenized. Lacking a central government, pluriform in practice and belief, more familial than institutional, the years 100–313 might be called the era of the domestic church.

ARCHITECTURE

During the era of the domestic church, the community gathered primarily in borrowed spaces, the most important of which was the house. The catacombs in which Christians buried their dead also were significant places in the evolution of Christian worship. A third architectural structure, the basilica, emerged toward the end of this period as a replacement for the house church. This development, however, is more characteristic of the next period and will be discussed in the following chapter.

The House Church

During the first century of the Christian era, as noted in chapter 1, borrowed rooms and believers' houses were important gathering places for the Christian community. The destruction of the Jewish temple and the separation of the Christian community from the synagogue led to the emergence of the house church as the primary place for community worship.

In the Roman Empire at this time, the building of homes was an important architectural concern. Large homes for the wealthy—usually four-sided structures built around a square, open courtyard—were found in virtually every urban center of the empire [illustration 16]. Their large dining rooms (well suited for eucharist), as well as the pools in the atria (adaptable for baptism), made them serviceable buildings for Christian worship. Structurally, this type of house faced inward with rooms that opened onto the courtyard at the center of the building. The resulting interior provided shelter from the commotion of the street and from the disapproving gazes of the pagan neighbors and the authorities.

The first house churches were family dwellings, which suggests that some spatial limitations were encountered by the worshiping community. Permanent structural changes in a home might have disrupted the family's life, so the community probably limited its modifications to

1. Assembly room with dais at east end
2. Room for baptisms
3. Open courtyard

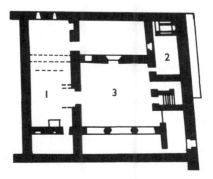

17. Plan of the house church at Dura Europos. (Jones p. 481.)

rearranging the furniture to accommodate worship. In the dining room, for example, a single table could have been employed for eucharist, with a chair for the host or bishop who led the worship. As the size of the community increased and the limits of ordinary rooms were strained, a community might have looked for a larger home in which to gather. During the long periods of religious toleration in these centuries, some communities acquired permanent places for worship. Several sources document the ownership of such houses by Christian communities. One account even records that the Roman emperor sold a house for use as a place of Christian worship rather than allow it to be converted into a tavern [quotation 48].

These permanent places for worship were more likely to undergo structural changes to accommodate the community than were the family homes that had been used for Christian gatherings. Evidence of such changes appears in a home in the ancient fortress town of Dura Europos in eastern Syria. Built about the year 200 and converted into a church around 232, this house is a typical four-sided structure built around an open courtyard [illustration 17]. Tearing down a wall and joining two rooms created one large room—about 16½ feet by 43 feet—which was large enough for the community's eucharist. A basin with a canopy was built in another room; frescoes in the room, for example, Christ walking on the water, suggest that the space was used for baptisms. Although few other examples are as well preserved as the house at Dura Europos, its arrangement is believed to be typical of Christian house churches in the second and third centuries.

Catacombs

Few places of the ancient Christian cult have captured the imagination as much as the catacombs. They often are depicted in epic movies and historical novels as subterranean hideouts where Christians gathered for worship during constant persecutions. This scenario is more fanciful than truthful. In fact, persecutions were a sporadic occurrence and did not have a lasting effect on the worship spaces of the early community. Christian places of worship not only were above ground but often were well known [quotation 48]. When there were persecutions, the authorities often knew what buildings the Christians used for their worship [quotation 49]. Besides, the size and shape of the catacombs could not accommodate large gatherings.

The catacombs were a network of subterranean cemeteries that existed in many cities of the empire from as early as the second century. More than 40 such cemeteries were dug outside the walls of Rome, where the law required all burials to take place. Often consisting of three or four stories of passageways, the narrow corridors of the

Quotation 48. When the Christians took possession of a certain place, which had previously been public property, and the keepers of an eating-house maintained that it belonged to them, Alexander rendered the decision that it was better for some sort of a god to be worshiped there than for the place to be handed to the keepers of an eating-house. The Writers of Augustan History: Severus Alexander (d. 235) 49.6, translated by David Magie.

Quotation 49. When he came to the house in which the Christians gathered [for worship], Felix the high priest and supervisor [of the colony of Cirta] said to bishop Paul, "Give me the scriptures of the law and whatever else you have here as ordered so that you may be able to comply with [this] order. Paul said, "The lectors have the scriptures, but what we have here we give. . . . two chalices of gold, six chalices of silver, six silver jars, a silver dish, seven silver lamps, two torches, seven short bronze candlesticks with their candles, eleven bronze lamps with their chains. . . . Afterwards the book chests [armaria] in the library were found to be empty. From the Acts of Munatus Felix (19 May 303) as cited in the Acts of Zenophilus

18. Small chapel, sometimes called the Crypt of the Popes, in the Roman catacomb of Callistus, as it appeared at the time of its discovery in 1854.

catacombs stretched for miles. Niches were cut from the floor to the ceiling to receive the bodies of the dead. Occasionally, these passageways opened into small chapels or burial chambers for the more notable deceased [illustration 18], but these never were meant to accommodate large groups of worshipers.

The catacombs of Rome were the site of tens of thousands of Christian burials. Some of the more important of these catacombs were those of Saints Callistus, Domitilla, Pancras and Priscilla. After the period of persecution, these and others became favored places of burial for Christians who wished to be interred near the saints. This honor could be afforded to many because the same niche or alcove often was used for a series of burials over the centuries as the bodies of those previously buried there decayed.

After the collapse of the empire in the fifth century, the inhabitants of Rome retreated within the old city walls for refuge. The Christian citizens, now in the majority, took the bodies of many saints from the catacombs and placed them in churches within the city. Because the bodies of many saints were removed, the catacombs were abandoned as burial sites in the sixth century and forgotten altogether by the Middle Ages. The catacombs were rediscovered accidentally in 1578.

Although the architecture of the catacombs did not influence the development of Christian worship, the cult surrounding the bodies of the martyrs did. These cemeteries became places of great reverence and veneration. Churches commemorating specific saints often were built over or near their tombs [illustration 19]. Eventually, this cult of the saints was disconnected from the original place of burial, and relics were divided and dispersed throughout Christendom. Originally, however, the catacombs were unspoiled places for burial and veneration of the dead.

Summary

The house church was the primary architectural symbol of the second- and third-century church. Although the worship in these spaces often was well regulated [quotation 50], the spaces themselves symbolize a church that was more a collection of small communities or extended families rather than an international organization. As these homes—often renovated specifically for Christian worship—became more prominent in the community, they took on new significance in the Christian consciousness. One of the results of moving from borrowed rooms to permanent worship structures was the transference of the name traditionally given to the community, *ekklesia,* to the building itself. While this change in terminology did not indicate that the community no longer considered itself the true *ekklesia* or foundation

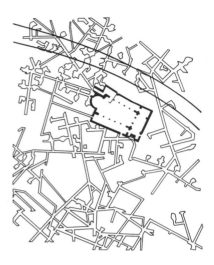

19. Rome, the catacomb of Domitilla (off the Via Ardeatina, south of the city), in use as a Christian cemetery since ca. 200 CE; plan of the section under the modern street called Via delle sette chiese. The church was raised over the tombs of Sts. Nereus, Achilleus, and Domitilla, ca. 580–90. (After Kostof, p. 249.)

Quotation 51. *The Truscans, certainly, make use of the trumpet in their wars, the Arcadians the syrinx, the Sicilians the pektis, the Cretans the lyre, the Lacedaemonians the aulos, the Thracians the horn, the Egyptians the tympanum and the Arabians the cymbal. We, however, make use of but one instrument, the word of peace alone by which we honor God.* Clement of Alexandria (died c. 215), *The Tutor*, 2.4, translated by McKinnon

Quotation 52. *And when he has been made bishop, all shall offer the kiss of peace, greeting him because he has been made worthy. Then the deacons shall present the offering to him; and he, laying his hands on it with all the presbytery, shall say, giving thanks: The Lord be with you . . .* Hippolytus (died c. 236), *Apostolic Tradition*, 4.1–3, translated by Jasper and Cuming.

Quotation 53. *A reader is appointed by the bishop giving him the book, for he does not have hands laid on him.* Hippolytus, *Apostolic Tradition*, 11, translated by Jasper and Cuming

of living stones, it did anticipate a time when such consciousness would be lost among the baptized. Eventually, only the building would be recognized by the vast majority of believers as "the church."

MUSIC

As a distinctive Christian cult emerged within the setting of the house church, so did a distinctive Christian song emerge. The fragmentary information about worship in this period allows only the broadest sketch of what ritual elements might have been sung. Because instrumental music almost certainly was not ordinarily allowed in Christian worship [quotation 51], this section will concentrate on vocal music. Besides suggesting what was sung, how it was sung and who did the singing, reflections on the possible form and style of this singing also will be offered.

Prayer and Readings

It is impossible to distinguish clearly between song and speech in the worship of this period. Public prayers and readings especially had a certain tunefulness about them.

Some prayers, such as early eucharistic prayers, were improvised by the leader. Like improvised synagogue prayer, these were offered in such a way that the community members could make it their own adding their "Amen." These prayers probably were cantillated. By the third century, a written model for a eucharistic prayer appeared [quotation 52]; the Jewish forms of chanting employed for grace after meals may have provided models for singing this great thanksgiving. As Christian prayer developed a separate identity from its Jewish precedents, the chanting most likely did the same.

The tradition of public reading, already detectable in first-century sources, became an constitutive element of Christian worship by the second century. Justin Martyr notes the central role of the readings in the Christian assembly [quotation 47]. Approximately 75 years after Justin's account, Hippolytus (d. about 225) offered information about the appointment and installation of readers for Christian worship [quotation 53]. At first, the readings probably were cantillated in the same manner as they were in the synagogue. As the Christian understanding of the word of God evolved and distinguished itself from that of Judaism, however, the cantillation of these readings developed its own style.

Biblical and Nonbiblical Psalms

Although it is traditional to speak of the psalter as the Christian prayer book, little evidence exists that Christians sang psalms in first-century worship. The Pauline admonition to sing psalms [quotation 54] cannot be taken as proof that the psalms of David were an ordinary part of early Christian worship. Psalms, in this context, simply means a Christian song, and no precise differentiation is possible between the three genres of songs that he mentions.

The first certain reference to the singing of psalms in Christian worship appears in the apocryphal *Acts of Paul* written about the year 190 [quotation 55]. Soon after this, the North African writer, Tertullian (d. about 225), notes that psalms were sung as part of the liturgy of the word [quotation 56]. Psalm singing was probably an ordinary part of Christian worship from at least the third century. Besides biblical psalms, many pieces, also, were written in imitation of the psalms. Some of the earliest examples of these nonbiblical psalms, or *psalmi idiotici*, are the *Odes of Solomon*, written in the first or second century [quotation 57]. Scholars such as James Charlesworth believe that this collection is the earliest Christian hymnbook.

While some prayers and readings were chanted by a single voice, biblical and nonbiblical psalms could have been sung in their entirety either by a soloist [quotation 58] or by the whole assembly. They also may have been divided between a soloist and the congregation [quotation 59], between various segments of the assembly or even between a number of singers and the assembly. A preference for the responsorial form is detectable in the constant concern that the community would be able to join their "Amen" to the prayer. The underlying message in this era about the centrality of the assembly and the call to accommodate all ministries to the needs of the community further underscore this bias for responsorial forms.

Hymnody

Christian hymnody, already anticipated in the New Testament, continued to develop during this time. One illustrative text from the early second century notes that the Christian community sang hymns to Christ [quotation 60]. Only from the mid–second century on, however, are compositions found that can be accurately described as hymns. Two distinguishing features allow this definition: one textual, the other musical. Textually, these first Christian hymns are new works of metrical poetry and not imitations of biblical prose. The texts are shaped into stanzas of two or more lines. Each stanza employs the

---

Quotation 54. *With gratitude in your hearts sing psalms, hymns, and spiritual songs to God.* Colossians 3:16

Quotation 55. *And each shared in the bread and they feasted . . . to the sound of David's psalms and hymns.* Acts of Paul, 7.10

Quotation 56. *The scriptures are read and psalms are sung, sermons are delivered and prayers offered.* Tertullian (died c. 225), On the Soul, 9.4

Quotation 57.
*I extended my hands and hallowed
    my Lord,
For the expansion of my hands is his sign.
And my extension is the upright cross.
Hallelujah.*
Odes of Solomon, Ode 27, translated by James Charlesworth

Quotation 58. *After the ritual hand washing and the lights, each one is invited to stand and sing to God as he is able: either something from the holy Scriptures or of his own making.* Tertullian, Apologeticum 39.18

Quotation 59. *When they recite psalms, all shall say, "Alleluia."* Hippolytus, Apostolic Tradition, 25, translated by Jasper and Cuming

Quotation 60. *They were accustomed to meet on a fixed day before dawn and sing alternately among themselves a hymn to Christ as to a god.* Pliny's Letter to Trajan, 10.96 (c. 112)

20. The Oxyrhynchus papyrus 1786, from the end of the third century, showing the end of a hymn written in Greek vocal notation. (*New Groves Dictionary of Music and Musicians,* 4:368. Modern transcription by H. Stuart Jones as found in *Musik in Geschichte und Gegenwart,* s.v. "Fruehchristliche Musik.")

Quotation 61.
King of Saints, Almighty Word
    of the Father, Highest Lord.
Wisdom's head and chief,
Assuagement of all grief;
Lord of all time and space
    Jesus, Savior of our Race.
Hymn to Christ, Clement of Alexandria, translated by W. L. Alexander

same meter, rhyme scheme and number of lines. Music is composed for the first stanza, and each succeeding stanza is sung to the same music. These are true hymns. In contrast, psalms are not structured in stanzas of similar meter, rhyme and length. In psalms, the music changes, however slightly, from line to line to accommodate the varying meters and accents of the text.

The first Christian hymns were composed by Gnostic writers in the second century. Under their influence, Clement of Alexandria (d. about 215?) composed his hymn to Christ the Savior [quotation 61]. The earliest fragment of a Christian hymn text with a primitive form of musical notation, called the "Oxyrhynchus hymn," dates from this same era. It is named after the place in Egypt where it was found [illustration 20].

Hymns probably were sung in their entirety by the assembly. This is suggested by the structure of the hymn, which presumes the repetition of poetic and melodic units. This makes the hymns accessible to an entire assembly. The common singing of hymns by the whole assembly also could be suggested by the continuous concern for unity in the community. Unity for Christians referred not only to the bond that existed between Christians and Christ but also among Christians themselves. Joseph Gelineau believes that singing with one voice is one privileged way of expressing this unity. This has been true since the

Quotation 62. *Therefore it is fitting that you should live in harmony with the will of the bishop, as in deed you do. For your justly famous presbytery, worthy of God, is attuned to the bishops as the strings to a harp. Therefore, by your concord and harmonious love, Jesus Christ is being sung. Now do each of you join in this choir, that being harmoniously in concord you may receive the key of God in unison, and sing with one voice through Jesus Christ to the Father.* Ignatius of Antioch (died c. 107), *Letter to the Ephesians,* 5.1–2, translated by Kirsop Lake

time of Ignatius of Antioch (d. about 107) who urged the community to live the way they sing: in unison through Jesus Christ [quotation 62].

Summary

During the second and third centuries, identifiable Christian music developed. Increasingly distinctive in text and tone, this music still was closely connected to the lyricism of the first century. This was true not only in music's contribution to the unity of the community but also in its integration into the ritual. Thus it was difficult to consider music as a separate element in the Christian cult of this time; it was, rather, the aural aspect of that cult. The intimate relationship between prayer and song is further reflected in the absence of references to special singers, psalmists or cantors in this period. There is no separate liturgical musician. The whole of worship was musical: To the extent that the worship belonged to the entire assembly, so did the music belong to them.

BOOKS

Though it later became possible to condense all the official rites of the church into a few bound volumes, the worship of the second and third centuries was not prayer by the book. Worship was, rather, a largely improvised and auditory event, similar to the worship of the synagogue. Yet just as Christians began to develop distinctive architectural and musical forms appropriate to their worship, they also began to develop their own books. The first of these was the New Testament, which was combined with the Hebrew Scriptures to form the Christian Bible. Besides this book, which was read in worship, books also appeared that were used to prepare for worship. These auxiliary liturgical books reappear in various forms throughout the history of Christian worship. Early examples are sometimes called church orders. Because Christianity contributed to the transition from the scroll to the codex, the physical appearance of these books, as well as their role and content, will be considered.

The New Testament

The scriptures were an integral part of early Christian worship: the Jewish Law and the Prophets at first and then increasingly the letters of Paul. To these were joined what have come to be known as the gospels, and other letters and narratives. Originally, there were many more than the 27 books that the Christian churches today consider part of the

The Gospel of the Nazaraeans	The Book of Thomas the Athlete
The Gospel of the Ebionites	The Gospel according to Matthias
The Gospel of the Hebrews	The Gospel of Judas
The Gospel of the Egyptians	The Apocryphon of John
The Gospel of Peter	The Apocryphon of James
The Gospel of the Four Heavenly Regions	The Gospel of Bartholomew
The Gospel of Perfection	The Questions of Mary
The Gospel of Truth	The Gospel according to Mary
The Sophia Jesu Christi	The Genna Marias
The Dialogue of the Redeemer	The Gospel of Cerinthus
The Pistis Sophia	The Gospel of Basilides
The Two Books of Jeu	The Gospel of Marcion
The Gospel of the Twelve Apostles	The Gospel of the Apelles
The Gospel of the Twelve	The Gospel of Bardesanes
The Memoria Apostolorum	The Gospel of Mani
The (Manichean) Gospel of the Twelve Apostles	The Protoevangelium of James
The Gospel of the Seventy	The Infancy Story of Thomas
The Gospel of Philip	The Gospel of Nicodemus
The Gospel of Thomas	

21. Partial listing of New Testament Apocrypha according to Hennecke and Schneemelcher

Quotation 63. *Blessed is the one who reads aloud the words of the prophecy, and blessed are those who hear and keep what is written in it; for the time is near.* Revelation 1:3

New Testament. Many works now considered apocryphal were publicly read and revered in Christian communities [illustration 21]. During the middle of the second century, a move was under way to define the authentic books of the new religion. The four gospels and the 13 epistles attributed to St. Paul were central; other letters and books eventually were added to this group. A fragmentary list from the late second century—called the Muratorian canon after its discoverer, L. A. Muratori—represents the widespread consensus of the orthodox churches regarding the New Testament canon. This list is very similar to that promulgated by the Council of Trent in 1546. Although the first complete list of the books eventually accepted by the church appeared in the writings of Athanasius (d. 373), the second and third centuries were pivotal for the establishment of the New Testament canon.

As a New Testament canon developed, a special group of people emerged who read the scriptures at worship. Allusions to this function already appear in the New Testament [quotation 63]. The office of reader developed in some places by the end of the second century. Hippolytus included a rite for appointing readers in his *Apostolic Tradition* at the beginning of the third century [quotation 53]. Further evidence for the office of lector is found in the various lists of clergy that circulated after the third century [quotation 64].

Even when they were not being read, the scriptures came to be venerated in the early Christian community. In Judaism, when the Torah scrolls were not in use, they were stored in a place of honor in the synagogue [illustration 12] and were cared for by specially appointed people [quotation 65]. Similarly, Christians often designated special places for their books of scripture. The previously cited report of a church under persecution in North Africa [quotation 49] noted that the scriptures were kept in special book chests *(armaria)* in the house church library. In this instance, the books had been removed from these chests and transported to safety before the officials arrived. The account further confirms that particular people were entrusted with the care of the scriptures. Many stories are told about lectors who were martyred because they refused to surrender the scriptures to pagan officials.

Church Orders

During this period, auxiliary books for worship also appeared. A handful of these pastoral handbooks survive from this era. Though not exclusively concerned with worship, they often contained instructions about various aspects of the community's prayer. The *Didache* or "Teaching of the Lord to the Gentiles through the Twelve Apostles" was a compendium of regulations and instructions, probably dating from the early second century. It included information about fasting, baptism, the Lord's Prayer and possibly the earliest example of a eucharistic prayer. The *Didascalia Apostolorum* or the "Catholic Teaching of the Twelve Apostles and Holy Disciples of Our Redeemer" is from the early part of the third century. More developed than the *Didache*, this church order included liturgical instructions about the consecration of bishops, the celebration of baptism and the place and manner of gathering for prayer [quotation 50].

The *Didache* and the *Didascalia Apostolorum* were but two examples of various handbooks, guides and church orders that circulated throughout the early church. Many of them originated in a particular community but were shared with others—not unlike the letters of Paul written to a specific church but circulated to others. These church orders were the forerunners of the auxiliary liturgical books containing instructions and rubrical details that would appear at a later time. Eventually, these books of instructions would merge with collections of prayers to form the mixture of prayers and rubrics typical of today's liturgical books. Like Jewish prayer, however, Christian worship was originally improvised according to accepted patterns. Auxiliary books of instruction never were meant to eliminate improvisation but only to safeguard the traditional patterns of such improvisation.

The Codex

Until the dawn of Christianity, the basic form of all books was the scroll. During the second century, evidence appeared of another book form that would become universal by the fourth century, the codex. A scroll was composed of papyrus sheets glued together or animal skins sewn end to end so that they could be rolled together into a bundle [illustration 11]. A codex also was composed of papyrus sheets or animals skins, but these were bound together along one side so that a single sheet of information could be exposed more easily [illustration 22]. It is not known whether the codex originated with Christianity, but the majority of Christian manuscripts from the second and third centuries were codices. Virtually all extant pagan manuscripts from that time are scrolls.

Judaism began to use codices for many purposes by the fifth century, though it continues to use scrolls for the Torah to this day. Christianity's preference for the codex may have been purely functional: Having more than one book of Scripture on a scroll may have become too unwieldy. Some books of the Hebrew Scriptures, such as the Book of Kings, were divided into two books because they could not fit on a single scroll. Some scholars speculate that Christians may have employed the codex to bind the four gospels together. Whatever the reason, Christianity adopted a form of book that further separated it from its Jewish roots and prepared the way for unforeseen yet significant developments.

Summary

Despite the emergence of some written liturgical documents in this period, Christian worship was not dominated by the book in the second and third centuries. This was a time of great freedom and improvisation. As Christianity grew, the natural tendency to regulate and record traditions, teachings and worship developed. Thus a New Testament canon took shape, models for eucharistic prayers emerged and pastoral handbooks for community life and worship appeared.

As with the architecture of this period, these material changes contributed to changing perceptions. Just as both the community and the building came to be called *"ekklesia,"* so, too, not only the spoken word but also the written word began to be identified as "gospel." During persecutions, not only were Christians martyred but buildings were destroyed and books were burned. These objects and buildings

22. Depiction of the evangelist Matthew with a codex, writing tools and a box filled with scrolls, from the bema of San Vitale in Ravenna (547).

23. A reconstruction of a piece of goldglass from the Roman catacombs, demonstrating its appropriateness for use as a paten in the eucharists of the early community. (After Kraus I:479.)

served the community in prayer, but they also began to take on identities of their own.

VESSELS

The development of separate spaces, music and books for an increasingly defined Christian cult found a parallel in the development of specific Christian vessels. Of particular importance were those employed in eucharist, the central and distinguishing ritual of Christianity. From this period, documentary and iconographic evidence appears of vessels for both bread and wine.

Bread and Its Vessels

Throughout both Eastern and Western Christianity during this period, people used the same kind of bread for eucharist that they baked and consumed at home. Although the tradition recalled that Jesus shared unleavened bread with his disciples during the Last Supper, this detail had no apparent impact on the primitive Christian eucharist. The memory of Jesus sharing himself through bread and wine, rather than a memory about the specific kind of bread and wine, shaped this unfolding ritual.

VESSELS FOR USE DURING THE EUCHARIST: As in the first century, homemade baskets likely were used to hold the bread for the Lord's Supper. Glass patens may have been used as well. Fragments of goldglass from the catacombs of the period demonstrate that glass was used for dishes appropriate for eucharistic use [illustration 23]. Liturgical symbols on some of these surviving fragments support this hypothesis. A sixth-century source reports that a third-century bishop of Rome named Zephyrinus (d. 217) issued a directive about glass vessels for the eucharist [quotation 66]. The same source notes that another bishop of Rome, Urban I (d. 230), donated silver patens to various churches [quotation 67]. Although the historical accuracy of such passages is not certain, a wide variety of materials including glass, precious metals, wood, pottery and bone probably were used to make vessels for the eucharistic bread.

Quotation 66. *[Zephyrinus] made a regulation for the church that there should be glass patens before the priests in the church and assisting ministers while the bishop was celebrating Mass. Book of the Popes, 16*

Quotation 67. *[Urban] established sacred vessels all of silver and donated 25 silver patens. Book of the Popes, 18*

VESSELS FOR USE OUTSIDE THE EUCHARIST: From very early on, bread from the community's celebration of the eucharist was sent to members who could not be present. As already seen in the writings of Justin Martyr, the eucharist was sent through the deacons to those who could not share in the Sunday celebration [quotation 47]. Frescoes in

Quotation 68. *When a certain woman with unclean hands attempted to open her arca, in which the body of the Lord was contained, she was prevented by a flame which flared up from it.* Cyprian (d. 258), *Concerning the Lapsed*, 26

the catacombs of Callistus, dating from the second century, show wicker baskets that may have been used for this purpose [illustration 24]. A third-century fresco from the catacombs of Peter and Marcellinus in Rome depicts a small box, possibly used for the same purpose. These little boxes—sometimes called *arcae* or chrismals—were worn around the neck or kept in people's homes. Cyprian, bishop of Carthage (d. 258), tells of a woman who attempted to open her own *arca* after she had denied her faith during a persecution [quotation 68]. Evidence in the sixth century exists that the eucharist was carried by acolytes in linen bags. It is quite possible that this practice reaches back to the earliest Christian centuries.

More permanent places of reservation during this period may have included cupboards, closets and chests. The eucharist often would be wrapped in a cloth or placed in an *arca* before being stored in a cupboard or closet.

Wine and Its Vessels

Quotation 69. *You know, however, that we have been warned. In offering the chalice, the Dominical tradition is to be observed so that nothing may be done by us other than what the Lord first did for us. The chalice which is offered in commemoration of him is offered mixed with wine. For when Christ says, 'I am the true vine,' the blood of Christ is, indeed, not water but wine.* Cyprian, *Letter 63 to Caecilius* (253)

Since the time of Jesus, Christians have celebrated the eucharist with bread and a cup of wine. Whenever various groups have rejected the use of wine and substituted water, stern warnings have reminded the faithful to use only wine as Jesus had done [quotation 69]. Some ritual situations called for a cup of water and a cup of milk and honey to be present along with the cup of wine, most notably the eucharist following baptism [quotation 70], but this eventually became unacceptable and only wine was allowed on the eucharistic table [quotation 71].

Tertullian is one of the first writers after the New Testament to mention the cup or chalice in connection with eucharist. He also notes that some chalices were decorated with images [quotation 72].

Quotation 70. *And then let the offering be brought up by the deacons to the bishop: and he shall give thanks over the . . . cup mixed with wine for the antitype . . . of the blood which was shed for all who have believed in him; and over milk and honey mixed together in fulfillment of the promise which was made to our fathers in which he said "a land flowing with milk and honey" . . . and over water as an offering to signify the washing that the inner man also, which is the soul, may receive the same things as the body.* Hippolytus, *Apostolic Tradition*, 21, translated by Jasper and Cuming

Quotation 71. *If any bishop or presbyter used any other things in the sacrifice at the altar except what the Lord ordained, that is, either honey or milk or a strong beer instead of wine . . . let him be deposed.* Apostolic Canons (third century), canon 3

24. Baskets holding eucharistic bread from the catacomb of Callistus, second to third century.

Quotation 72. *Perhaps that shepherd whom you picture on the chalice will favor you. Tertullian, On Purity, 10.2*

Quotation 73. *Sources report that three chalices of glass are prepared with white vinegar to which white wine is added. Epiphanius (d. 403), The Panarion, 34.1, drawing on a report from Irenaeus of Lyons.*

Quotation 74. *Be eager to celebrate one eucharist, for there is one flesh of our Lord Jesus Christ and one cup of unity in his blood, one altar as there is one bishop together with the presbyters and deacons. Ignatius of Antioch, Letter to the Philadelphians, 4*

Although Tertullian says nothing about the material or shape of the cup in question, other sources confirm that glass, precious metals, wood, bone and certain stones such as onyx were used in the fashioning of these cups. The second-century theologian, Irenaeus of Lyons (flourished around 170), was remembered as having criticized the heretic Marcus, who celebrated an unacceptable eucharist with a glass chalice [quotation 73]. It does not seem, however, that the use of glass had anything to do with the unacceptability of the eucharist.

Precious metals were used for Christian ritual vessels with increasing frequency over the centuries. The testimony about Urban I bestowing a gift of silver vessels and patens on the church at Rome [quotation 67] and the inventory of vessels in the account of the fourth-century persecution of the church in North Africa [quotation 49] bear this out. Although these examples would multiply dramatically in later years, the tradition of fashioning eucharistic cups out of precious metals seems firmly established by the third century. Glass, stone, wood and bone chalices, however, continued to be used well into the Middle Ages.

Because a single cup was used during eucharist in this era [quotation 74], the size of such a cup would have been proportional to the number of believers who gathered for worship. Chalices large enough to serve 100 people or more would have been needed in some of the larger house churches, while some of the smaller gatherings could have used a simple, stemless cup or even a bowl. Joseph Braun believes that double-handled cups probably were used for the eucharist during this period. Although no examples of this type of eucharistic cup exist from this time, Braun offers this conjecture based on examples of double-handled chalices from a later period and on surviving examples in secular use from the pre-Constantinian period [illustration 25]. Braun also notes the practicality of this form of cup for communal use.

Summary

In this era of the domestic church, the vessels for eucharist originated as domestic elements. A wicker basket and a wooden bowl would have sufficed in many situations. Because the large homes of the wealthy also were used by the Christian community during this time, the precious goblets and trays of those households probably also were used. The acquisition of special buildings for worship and the evolution of special ministers and storage places for the various objects employed in worship suggest a development in the things themselves. In a specially constructed or renovated building for worship, it would not be surprising to find vessels fabricated especially for eucharist, often of the finest materials. The vessels could be said, however, to reflect the size, means and needs of the community that they served.

25. Example of a secular, two-handled drinking cup from the pre-Constantinian Roman empire.

JULIA

Voices from the atrium woke Julia from a sound sleep. At first, she was confused by the commotion outside her window. Then she remembered that it was Sunday. This morning there was to be another gathering at her parents' villa in Antioch.

Julia was used to large crowds at the villa. When she was very young, her parents often hosted elaborate parties that lasted long into the night. Her father's important friends, visiting dignitaries and sometimes a famous charioteer would dine for hours, debating issues unresolved in the city council or listening to the odes of Antioch's newest poet. Julia had often watched the crowds from her room overlooking the atrium, wishing that they would all go home so she could go to sleep. But ever since she was eight years old, no noisy night gatherings have been held at the villa. That was the year she and her parents were baptized. Now large crowds come to the villa only on Sunday mornings.

Julia would like to have stayed in bed a little longer this morning, but now that she was 12 years old, her parents thought it was important for her to greet the guests. As Julia combed her hair, she wondered who might join them today. There were always old friends to greet and strangers to welcome. Some were from important and wealthy families, while others were very poor. Julia's mother had taught her that it was important to treat everyone the same, even their servants.

The ritual this morning would be a familiar one. After friends and strangers have been welcomed, the community will gather in the garden with Anicetus, their bishop. The meeting begins with news of other communities of believers from around the provinces. Sometimes there is sad news about some who have

been arrested or even put to death because of their belief. Other times there are stories of wonderful conversions or healings. After these stories of faith, Anicetus calls the community to prayer. Then they sit on the ground and listen to the prophetess Cara.

Julia knows well the story of how Cara met the apostle Peter when she was a little girl. She had been blind from birth, and many thought that Peter would restore her sight. But Peter told Cara that it was not her eyes but her voice that would give glory to God. From that day forward, Cara listened to the stories about Jesus and to the letters of instruction written by his followers. By the time she was Julia's age, Cara had memorized all the stories and letters. Julia's favorite letter is the one from Peter. She especially likes the part in the middle about baptism that Cara always sings.

After Cara's message, Anicetus asks if there are any in the community who, having heard the instruction, would like to be baptized. If there are, the bishop takes them to the pool in the garden and asks about their faith. If enough people testify about the faith and virtue of these people, Anicetus baptizes them right there. Others are not ready for baptism. The bishop embraces them and assures them that they always are welcome to return, but they are not allowed to remain for the rest of the gathering.

After all the unbaptized are escorted out of the garden and the gate is locked, the community prays for those in need. After these prayers, everyone shares the kiss of peace. Some men bring a table into the garden, and Julia's mother places bread and wine on the table. Anicetus steps forward and prays over the community and the gifts. Julia's father and mother assist at the table and help Anicetus break the bread and share the wine with all present.

After the holy banquet, the bishop inquires about those who are missing from the assembly. Philip and his wife Romana record the names of those who are absent and see to it that the sanctified bread is brought to them and that their other needs also are taken care of. Often, at the end of the service, Cara breaks out into song that the community takes up until all are dispersed.

Sunday is Julia's favorite day of the week.

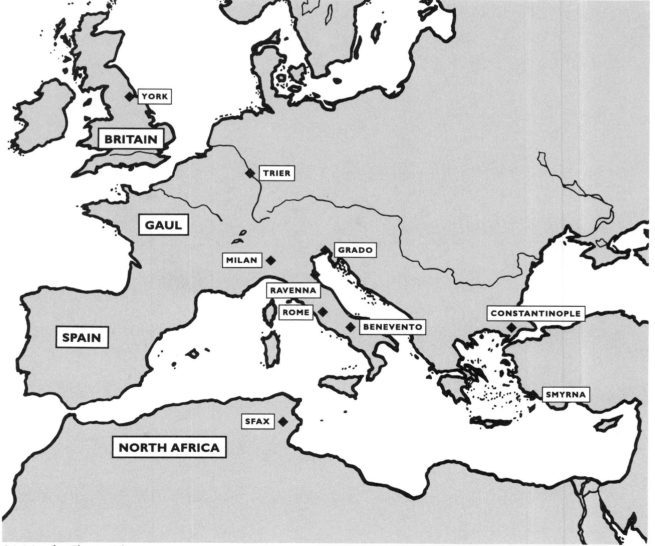

26. Map for Chapter Three.

CHAPTER THREE

The Rise
of the Roman Church:
313 to 750

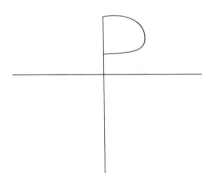

27. Christian symbol that Constantine placed on his soldiers' shields. (Jedin I:411.)

Few individuals have influenced the development of the church as much as the Roman emperor Constantine (d. 337). Son of the emperor Constantius (d. 306), Constantine became one of the two rulers of the West when his father died. (In 293, the Emperor Diocletian divided the empire into East and West to increase the stability of his government. In each division of the empire, he appointed a primary emperor, or "Augustus," and an assistant emperor, or "Caesar.") Constantine became the sole emperor of the West by defeating Maxentius, his Caesar, in 312. History records [quotation 75] that before the battle with Maxentius, Constantine was instructed in a dream to place a Christian symbol on his soldiers' shields [illustration 27]. The ensuing victory sealed his commitment to Christianity. With his coemperor Licinius, who was Augustus of the East, Constantine recognized the right of all religions to exist in the year 313 and granted special privileges to the church. During the next 25 years, Constantine increasingly became involved in the church, intervening in various doctrinal controversies and even calling church councils. Constantine was baptized after Easter in the year 337 and died on Pentecost that same year.

Although the depth of Constantine's conversion may be debated, the effect of this conversion is difficult to overestimate. It meant the end of the church of the martyrs and the beginning of the Christianization of society throughout the empire. Instead of an illegal sect, Christianity became the preferred religion of the empire, the politically advantageous religion to profess. Christian initiation, which had been a somewhat perilous commitment made by a believing adult, evolved into a familial act of christening infants. Christian identity became, over time, more an accident of birth than a result of conversion.

The expansion of the church and its growing status in society brought with them the external trappings of imperial favor. Bishops were granted various honors and wore the insignia of civil magistrates, which caused some people to criticize the bishops for their new positions of privilege [quotation 76]. Spectacular buildings for Christian worship were constructed, and amateurism in liturgical ministry became unacceptable. Corps of specialists emerged to carry out this princely form of worship. This was fitting for what would become the official state religion under the emperor Theodosius (d. 395) in 380.

Constantine also exerted a long-range influence on Christianity by moving his government from Rome to the ancient city of Byzantium on the Bosporus, renaming it Constantinople [illustration 26]. By doing so, Constantine gave the Eastern empire a fitting capitol, one which was geographically well situated for controlling the eastern part of his empire. Constantinople's rise foreshadowed the political collapse of Rome during the following century.

After Constantine's death in 337, the empire was divided among his three sons. Though briefly reunited under Emperor Theodosius, the eastern and western parts of the empire eventually separated permanently. As the East grew, the West declined: Barbarian tribes invaded from the North, overrunning Britain, Gaul, Spain and North Africa. When the Visigoths invaded Italy, the Western emperor Honorius in desperation moved his capital from Rome to the more secure city of Ravenna in 404. Rome was plundered by the Visigoths in 410 and again by the Vandals in 455. The last Roman emperor, Romulus Augustulus, was deposed in 476 and the German leader, Odoacer, became the first barbarian ruler of Italy. Throughout this decline in the West, the church grew, becoming the one stable element in Rome during the barbarian invasions. Significantly, it is not the Roman emperor Valentinian III, but Pope Leo the Great (d. 461), who is remembered as having met Attila the Hun in 452 outside of Rome at Attila's camp in Mantua and having persuaded him to accept a

1. Altar
2. Column of Trajan
3. Entrance from forum
4. Forum of Trajan
5. Library
6. Tribunal for judges and assessors

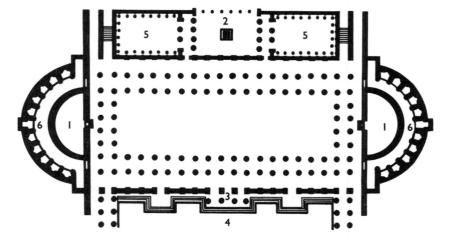

28. Basilica Ulpia. (After Gardner, p. 190.)

29. Trier Basilica.

payment of tribute and spare Rome. This story highlights the growing influence of the church and its leadership in the wake of the Roman Empire's collapse.

ARCHITECTURE

The transformation of the church of the martyrs into an imperial church meant a dramatic change in the setting for Christian worship. Although some house churches continued to exist into the fourth century, Christianity's growth in membership and stature called for a new type of worship space, the basilica. Separate buildings for baptism and for honoring martyrs also came into being during this period.

Basilica

"Basilica" is a Greek word that means "hall of the king." These rectangular structures were built by the Romans for use as royal audience halls, law courts, business offices and a variety of other civic purposes. Often gigantic in proportion, basilicas were monuments to the power and glory of the Roman Empire. The Basilica Ulpia was one such building [illustration 28]. Constructed around 112 CE, it dominated the northwest quadrant of the Roman Forum. This imposing structure was 426 feet long and 138 feet wide, with a spectacular enclosed space

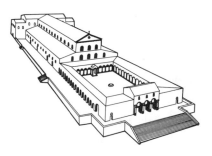

30. Old St. Peter's. (After Gardner, p. 217.)

Quotation 77. *First of all the building should be oblong, directed toward the rising sun, with sacristies on each side toward the east, so that it resembles a ship. Let the throne of the bishop be placed in the middle, the presbytery to sit on either side of him, and the deacons to stand nearby, neatly dressed in their full garments, resembling the sailors and officers of a ship. Relative to them the lay men are to sit toward the other end in complete quiet and good order, and the women are to sit along and they too are to maintain silence. In the middle the reader is to stand upon something high and read the books of Moses.* Apostolic Constitutions (late fourth century), 2.57.3–7, translated by McKinnon

under a huge vaulted ceiling. Each of the two shorter sides of the building included a semicircular structure called an apse. This multi-functional building housed law courts, administrative bureaus and business offices. It also was the site of various civic services.

Christians borrowed this style of building for their worship. Although some simple Christian basilicas had been built before the fourth century, after the triumph of Constantine and the legalization of Christianity, the basilica became the preferred model for Christian churches. Rather than employing the double-apse basilica style, like the Basilica Ulpia and others, Christians adopted the single-apse style that had been used for imperial audience halls [illustration 29]. In this design, one of the apses was removed and replaced by a main entrance. The result was a dramatic longitudinal path, sometimes flanked by columns, leading to the apse. As Richard Krautheimer notes, "The Christian basilica, both in function and design, was a new creation within an accustomed framework."

One of the first great Christian buildings was old St. Peter's [illustration 30], constructed around the year 333 over what was believed to be the burial place of the apostle Peter. In addition to the rectangular design of the imperial audience hall, old St. Peter's included a large atrium outside the church for the gathering of the people, a double colonnade on either side of the nave and short transepts, resulting in a rudimentary cross shape. Christian Norberg-Shulz hypothesizes that this cross shape is a hallmark of churches dedicated to the apostles, recalling that the apostles were the first to take up the cross of Christ. This architectural design also distinguished these churches from secular basilicas, which did not have transepts.

The basilica functioned as a kind of enclosed path. Originally, little in the body of these churches interrupted the movement from the atrium to the apse. The bishop's throne often was placed in the center of the apse and was surrounded by the college of presbyters, who sat on a long, low bench [illustration 31]. The congregation stood in the nave, often with the men separated from the women [quotation 77]. The altar was a freestanding wooden structure situated in front of the apse and around which the people could gather [quotation 78]. As the centuries progressed, wooden altars were replaced by stone altars, often massive in size. These altars were moved away from the people, into the apse, which came to be called the "sanctuary." By the fourth century, women were excluded from the sanctuary in some places [quotation 79]. Further evidence shows that in Rome, at least by the fifth century, the sanctuary and the pathway that led to it were open only to the clergy and to the choir that participated in the procession [illustration 31].

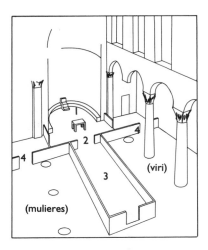

31. An early Roman chancel arrangement. (After Thomas Mathews.)

1. Presbyterium—place in the apse for the throne of the bishop and benches for presbyters

2. Sanctuarium (sanctuary)—site of the altar, set off by a low barrier from the body of the church

3. Solea-schola—processional area set off by a pair of low walls. This area was used principally in the ceremonies of pontifical entrance and exit, but was also used for the reading of scripture.

4. Senatoreum and Matroneum—areas set off by barriers and used for the presentation of the gifts in the offertory procession and for the reception of eucharist by the laity: men (viri) and women (mulieres)

Quotation 78. *Consequently, the table, like the fountain, lies in the middle in order that the flocks may surround the fountain on every side and enjoy the benefit of the saving waters.* John Chrysostom (d. 407), Second Baptismal Instruction, translated by Harkins

Quotation 79. *Women should not approach the altar.* Council of Laodicea (mid-fourth century), canon 44

The people were further distanced from the altar when Gregory the Great (d. 604) raised the floor of the apse of old St. Peter's above the level of the nave so that the altar could be directly over what was thought to be the tomb of St. Peter [illustration 32]. The ambo, which probably had originated as a wooden platform, also was moved into the sanctuary at the same time.

Baptistries and Martyria

Besides the basilicas, there arose during this time what Spiro Kostof calls "occasional buildings." Especially important were the places for baptism and those for memorial rites for martyrs. Although the longitudinal layout of the basilica could have been used for these structures, as it was in the martyrium of St. Peter, occasional buildings generally employed a central-plan construction.

The Anastasis in Jerusalem [illustration 33] is one of the most famous of these central-plan buildings. Erected sometime during the middle of the fourth century, this round structure occupied the western end of a long complex of buildings and courtyards on Golgotha. It was thought to have housed the tomb of Christ. The pagan tradition of building round burial mausoleums inspired this mausoleum for Jesus' tomb, which was an important model of this style and ensured the continuance of central-plan structures in Christianity. Martyrs, who were venerated for imitating the death of Christ, often were honored with similar central-plan buildings over their tombs that were called martyria.

Quotation 80. *Just as Christ was truly cru-cified, buried, and raised again . . . you are considered worthy to be crucified, buried and raised with him in likeness by baptism.*Cyril of Jerusalem (d. 386), *Catechetical Sermon*, 3.2, translated by Yarnold

The Christian belief in baptism as a participation in the death and resurrection of Christ [quotation 80] contributed to the architectural similarity between martyria and baptistries. This can be seen today in an eight-sided baptistry, dating from the fifth century and restored in 1925 [illustration 34], in the ancient town of Grado. The baptistry stands adjacent to a sixth-century cathedral. The octagonal shape is a reminder of the "eighth day," a symbol of resurrection and eternity in Christian thought.

Longitudinal Versus Central Plan

Although central-plan buildings continued to be constructed in the West, the basilica form was preferred. This was due, in part, to the ability of the basilica design to support liturgical processions, which became increasingly important in the imperial worship of this period. In later centuries, a central plan often was integrated into a basilica-style building in the West, in imitation of buildings from the East. This was accomplished by adding a central dome to a cruciform building or by connecting a central-plan structure to the apse end of a basilica.

As the West came to prefer the rectangular design of the basilica, the East embraced central-plan, domed churches such as San Vitale in Ravenna, Italy. This church was completed about the year 548 after the city had been taken from the Ostrogoths and united to the Byzantine Empire. It consists of two concentric octagons with a dome surmounting the inner one [illustration 35]. San Vitale was not the first central-plan Byzantine church—that distinction belongs to Saints Sergius and Bacchus in Constantinople—but this important church in the new seat of Byzantine government in Italy greatly influenced church design in much of the Byzantine Empire. Peter Cobb suggests that the preference for the central plan in the East and for the longitudinal plan in the West indicated a growing distinction between the ecclesiology of East and West. The central-plan churches, he contends, contributed to the

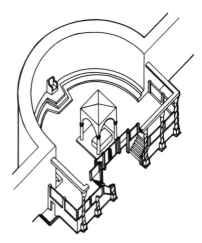

32. St. Peter's in Rome, c. 600, with altar raised over tomb of St. Peter. (After J.B. Ward-Perkins as cited in Jones, p. 483.)

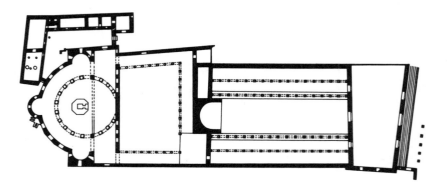

33. Fourth-century basilica and Anastasis on Golgotha in Jerusalem. (After Krautheimer, #27b.)

34. Interior of fifth-century baptistry at Grado, an eight-sided building, showing a six-sided font inside.

survival of the communal understanding of the church in the East, whereas the longitudinal-plan churches of the West emphasized the hierarchical nature of the church.

Summary

Great diversity existed in the architectural developments of the years 313 to 750 and a pervasive flexibility allowed the community to shape its space according to its needs. Within such diversity and flexibility, however, a few trends can be detected.

Shortly after the ascent of Constantine to the imperial throne, Christian worship moved from the house to the palace. Simple rooms or renovated houses that could accommodate 25, 50 or even 100 people gave way to enormous enclosed spaces that could accommodate thousands. Churches were constructed as basilicas, whose long paths lead to the apse, where the throne of the emperor was replaced by the bishop's chair. Auxiliary buildings, however, generally were designed on a central plan; this shape became the preference for churches in the East by the sixth century.

As the tradition of large basilicas developed in the West, so did the tendency to restrict certain parts of these buildings to the clergy and other officials. Eventually, all the laity were excluded from the sanctuary, which became the privileged domain of the clergy. In buildings of imperial scale, presiders began to look like court officials, and the iconography began to depict Christ more as King than as Good Shepherd. In this context, the word "church" came no longer to designate the community of faith, but only the building that housed it.

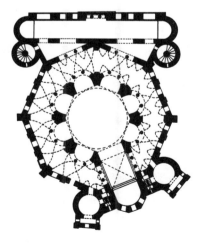

35. San Vitale in Ravenna. (After Gardner, p. 235.)

MUSIC

Music is shaped by the space in which it occurs. Moving worship from the house church to the basilica meant not only a change in the architectural space but also in the acoustic space.

Prayers and Readings

The fourth century resembled the previous centuries in that there was no public speech that was not musical to some degree. This was especially true in the proclamation of a text, such as a reading or an oration. To the extent that presiders publicly proclaimed orations and prayers—especially in the spacious basilicas of the era—such texts were chanted. This also was true of the readings; the tradition of cantillating readings, which Christians borrowed from the synagogue, continued uninterrupted.

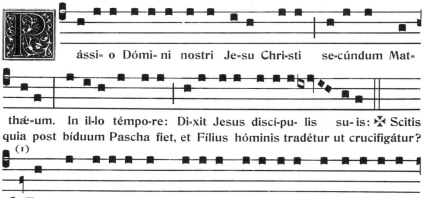

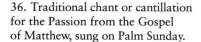

36. Traditional chant or cantillation for the Passion from the Gospel of Matthew, sung on Palm Sunday.

Quotation 81. *Unless sounds are remembered, they perish because they cannot be written down.* Isidore of Seville (d. 636), *Etymologies,* 3.15

Quotation 82. *At times a child was already designated a lector, and only when he reached the age of thirty was he entrusted with the task of acolyte or subdeacon. . . . If one began as an adult, the first ministry often was that of lector or exorcist. After two years . . . he was eligible to be an acolyte or subdeacon.* Kenan Osborne, p. 197

Quotation 83. *No one shall sing in the assembly except the canonical singers who ascend to the ambo and chant from parchment.* Council of Laodicea, canon 15

The exact style of cantillation in the fifth to the seventh centuries is difficult to ascertain. Because musical notation did not develop until a later period, cantillation patterns—like all melodies—had to be memorized [quotation 81]. Though the living memory of the chant from this era has been lost, later examples of psalm tones exist that might suggest how some readings of this time were cantillated [illustration 36].

Various nonmusical developments also offer hints about the chanting of the readings at this time. For example, the role of the lector became a relatively fixed ministry by the fifth century. Individual lectors served in this ministry for many years [quotation 82], which could have enabled them to develop distinctive cantillation patterns. These patterns may have been handed on from one generation of lectors to the next within a particular community. Architectural evidence also acknowledges the special function of the lector. Early church buildings included a cleared space in the midst of the assembly that could have been employed for the proclamation of the word [illustration 31]; later churches provided a special structure, the ambo, for this action. Documentary evidence for the ambo exists from the fourth century [quotation 83], and archaeological evidence exists from at least the sixth century [illustration 37]. It is improbable that such ministerial, legislative and architectural developments would have occurred without parallel musical developments at the same time.

Biblical and Nonbiblical Liturgical Chants

During the period 313 to 750, the eucharistic liturgy acquired many of the musical elements that are familiar today. The biblical psalms were central. They were chanted at the entrance, with an alleluia refrain

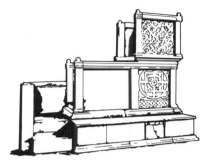

37. Ambo of the type common in the sixth century, reassembled in the eleventh century from old material.

Quotation 84. *The readers and singers have no right to wear the* orarium *or to read or sing thus vested.* Council of Laodicea, canon 23

Quotation 85. *I decree that the psalms before the other readings are to be sung by the subdeacons or, if necessary, by those in minor orders. It is decreed that in this see, those who serve the holy altar [i.e., deacons] will not serve as cantors. Their sole duty at Mass is to proclaim the gospel reading.* Gregory the Great (d. 604)

Quotation 86. *Choirs of laymen or girls are not allowed to sing songs nor prepare meals in church for it is written, "My house will be called a house of prayer."* Synods of Auxerre (561–605), canon 9

before the gospel, and at the offertory and communion. The psalm between the readings, as noted in chapter 2, seems to have originated at an earlier time.

Many familiar nonbiblical texts originating in the East were introduced into the West at this time. The *Kyrie* was adapted from the processional litanies of the East and introduced into the West by the fifth century. The *Gloria,* originating in the daily office in the East, appeared in the West by the sixth century, though originally it was used only in the bishop's Mass. The *Sanctus,* which probably originated in synagogue worship, was adopted by Eastern Christians at an early date and appeared in the West by the fifth century. The *Agnus Dei* was introduced into the West by Pope Sergius I (d. 701). Though the *Sanctus* and perhaps the *Gloria* were congregational songs from the start, the other musical parts of the Mass were divided between the congregation and the professional leaders of music.

Professional musicians increased in number and kind during these years. The first evidence of a specially appointed singer who alone led the chants came from the East during the fourth century [quotation 83]. The first distinctions between "reading" and "singing" also began to appear in Christian writings at this time [quotation 84]. Choirs appeared in both East and West, although little evidence supports the legend that Pope Gregory the Great founded a choir school *(schola cantorum)* at Rome. Gregory did, however, restrict the ministry of chanting psalms and other readings to subdeacons or others in minor orders [quotation 85].

This growing number of specialists became the primary musicians in the imperial liturgy. The assembly joined in many refrains and responses, especially because the worship was celebrated in the language of the people, but their musical role in the liturgy was becoming increasingly restricted. The physical distance of the people from the center of the liturgical action was a visible sign of their musical distance. Women, who were the first to be prohibited from entering the sanctuary, also were prohibited from assuming leadership roles in music [quotation 86].

It is difficult to know exactly how the music of this time sounded. Many liturgical centers in the East and West—such as Milan, Constantinople and Benevento—developed their own style of chant. A body of chant known as Old Roman chant, which developed in the context of the imperial Roman liturgy, most likely was used in Rome at this time. Although the earliest manuscripts for this music date from the eleventh century, such music could have developed as early as the sixth century [illustration 38]. Gregorian chant probably was not used at Rome during this time, nor is it believed to be the work of Gregory the Great.

38. Old Roman chant. Introit from
Midnight Mass of the Nativity. (Apel,
Gregorian Chant, p. 488.)

Hymns

During the years of peace that followed Constantine's recognition of
the church, Christian hymnody flowered. This was due, at least in part,
to the congregational nature of hymnody, which called for a relatively
popular compositional style. Ambrose of Milan (d. 397)—sometimes
called the father of Western hymnody—knew the attraction of this
kind of music [quotation 87]. He divided his hymn texts into short
stanzas, each following the same pattern (number of lines, meter and
rhyme scheme) as the previous one [illustration 39]. In so doing,
Ambrose established basic principles for hymn writing that have been
followed for centuries. Though the music for Ambrose's hymns does
not survive today, Richard Hoppin suggests that these early hymns
may have been sung to well-known secular tunes. Whether this is true
or not, the music probably was as simple and engaging as the texts,
qualifying it as true folk music.

Popular Latin hymnody arose at a time when the assembly was
being distanced from the central liturgical action. Some hymns were
sung at Mass, but they never made an impact on the structure of the
Mass or became a constitutive part of it. Hymns remained peripheral
to the eucharist, just as the people were to become peripheral to the
action of the priest. Official attempts to ban nonbiblical hymns from
the liturgy [quotation 88] had little effect on their popularity. Many
Latin hymns eventually were incorporated into the liturgy of the hours.

*Quotation 87. They also say that the peo-
ple are led astray by the charms of my
hymns. Certainly, I do not deny it. Sermon
Against Auxentius, 24, translated by
McKinnon*

*Quotation 88. It is decided that except
for the psalms or other parts of the canonical writings of the old and new testament no poetic composition may be sung
in church. First Council of Braga
(563), canon 12*

Summary

The transition from a domestic church to an imperial church heralded
a series of dramatic changes, many of which were to exert their full
impact in a later age. With the continual refinement of the liturgy and
the introduction of new liturgical chants, specialists begin to dominate
the music of worship. The people sang refrains and certain central texts
such as the *Sanctus,* but the people's role gradually was reduced in size
and importance. As a balance to this development, people cultivated

Ae-ter-ne re-rum con-di-tor, Noctem di-em-que qui re-gis, Et tempo-rum das tem-po-ra, Ut al-le-ves fa-sti-di-um.

39. Three melodies for the hymn *Aeterne rerum conditor* by Ambrose of Milan.

and enjoyed forms of religious music that were not essential to the celebration of the eucharist, such as hymns. In all of these developments, the emphasis still was on vocal, unaccompanied music. Instruments had no place in Christian worship yet.

BOOKS

After Constantine, the liturgy became more complex. Large assemblies, throngs of clergy and specialized ministers processed, sang and prayed in monumental spaces. The etiquette of the imperial court influenced Christian worship, resulting in elaborations in vesture, personnel and gesture previously unknown in the liturgy. With these many elaborations came the need for new books to outline the complex rituals and to assist those who directed them. Besides the quantity of new books, the quality of manuscripts produced in this period also changed. Many liturgical books from this time are true works of art and are valued for their appearance as much as for their content.

Types of Liturgical Books

The categories that contemporary scholars use for cataloging medieval books did not exist in the Middle Ages. Consequently, these books assumed a variety of forms and were called by many names. This section will employ standard names for these books and describe them in their purest forms while acknowledging that they were not always found in such forms.

ANTIPHONARIES AND CANTATORIES In Rome, a series of books developed that contained the chant texts for Mass. The antiphonary *(antiphonarium)* contained the texts of the antiphons that were sung between the verses of the psalm during the introit and communion.

Quotation 89. *St. Gregory ordered the English churches to celebrate the summer ember days as it is set forth in his antiphonary and missal during the week after Pentecost. Such observances were not only present in our antiphonary, but I also saw them with my own eyes in the Roman books in the churches of Peter and Paul themselves.* Egbert of York (d. 766), On the Catholic Foundation, 16

Quotation 90. *It seems appropriate to request from your excellency that you make 50 codices of the sacred scriptures—which you know are very necessary for the church—elegantly written on magnificent parchments by experts thoroughly versed in the ancient arts.* Letter of Constantine to Eusebius cited in Eusebius's Life of Constantine, 36

Quotation 91. *Musaeus, a presbyter of the church of Marseilles, at the request of the holy bishop Venerius, excerpted from the holy scriptures suitable readings for feast days during the entire year. He also did the same for the responsories and psalms that suited the seasons and their readings.* Gennadius of Marseilles (died c. 505), On Ecclesiastical Writers, 79

The cantatory *(cantatorium)* contained chants sung by a soloist, including the gradual, tract and alleluia verses. Certain evidence exists that such collections circulated outside of Rome by the early eighth century [quotation 89]. The Frankish name for the cantatory was the "gradual" *(graduale)*. No music was included in the early version of these books for notation did not exist yet. These books were used by those in charge of the music rather than by the singers, who memorized their music.

BIBLES, GOSPEL BOOKS, EPISTLE BOOKS AND LECTIONARIES   Readings from the Old Testament, the epistles and the gospels were traditional elements in the celebration of eucharist. Originally, the readings were proclaimed from a codex of a complete Bible. Marginal notes or a list called a "capitular" *(capitularia)* indicated what sections were to be read for a given liturgy. Constantine reportedly commissioned 50 manuscripts of the Bible for liturgical use [quotation 90]. Individual books of the gospels (evangeliaries) and epistles (epistolaries) emerged by the fifth century [illustration 40], and finally lectionaries developed. These contained the biblical pericopes that were selected for each day of the liturgical year. The first documentary evidence of a lectionary comes from the end of the fifth century [quotation 91], and manuscripts survive from the sixth century.

CALENDARS AND MARTYROLOGIES   Christian calendars developed as aids for remembering and venerating the dead. Polycarp of Smyrna was one of the first to be widely venerated after his martyrdom on February 23 in the year 155. Lists noting the dates and places of the deaths of martyrs began to develop after this time. One of the earliest lists, the *depositio martyrum* [illustration 41], dates from 354. As these early liturgical calendars expanded, they became martyrologies, combining lists of martyrs, other saints and feasts celebrated throughout the year.

LIBELLI MISSARUM AND SACRAMENTARIES   As worship became more formalized, the practice of improvising public prayer decreased, and books containing prayers for the presiders appeared. Initially, these booklets *(libelli missarum)* contained the orations and the preface for a single feast. Collections of these booklets existed in certain parts of Christendom by the end of the fourth century. Although individual examples do not survive, a collection of them remains from the end of the sixth century. This collection, called the *Leonine Sacramentary*, is actually neither a sacramentary nor the work of Leo the Great (d. 461) but, rather, a private collection of formularies and prayers, haphazardly collected for various feasts throughout the year. This collection

40. Panel of a binding for a copy of the gospels, 402.

was falsely ascribed to Leo in the 1735 edition of the work by F. Bianchini. A true sacramentary contains all the prayers that the presider (and only the presider) needs, especially for the celebration of Mass. The first authentic sacramentary that survives is the *Old Gelasian Sacramentary,* which was compiled in Rome during the seventh or early eighth century.

ORDOS   Complex Christian worship required written directions for its enactment. These directions were not included in the books of prayers or music but were collected in a separate volume known as an ordo. Like *libelli missarum,* ordos *(ordines)* originally were small booklets or sometimes even a single page of instructions. Eventually, these were gathered into collections. The earliest collection known is from seventh-century Rome.

Reverence for the Book

Gestures of respect were common for the first liturgical book, the Bible, which people guarded with their lives during times of persecution. During the post-Constantinian era, signs of reverence for liturgical books increased. Architecturally this meant providing not only special places for proclaiming the word (the ambo) [illustration 37], but also special cupboards *(armaria)* for storing the scriptures when they were not in use [illustration 42]. Only specially designated people were allowed to read and care for ritual books. Lectors, who from ancient times were guardians of the scriptures, eventually were replaced by higher ranking clergy, with deacons responsible for the gospel and subdeacons responsible for the epistle [quotation 85]. A description of a seventh-century papal Mass notes that after the proclamation of the gospel, the gospel book was kissed by all the clergy in the sanctuary [quotation 92]. Moreover, when the book was carried by anyone other than a deacon, that person's hands were covered.

The ritual books came to be great works of art. Although this was especially true for the scriptures, it became increasingly true for other liturgical books as well. Vellum (calfskin) and parchment (lambskin) became the preferred materials. These were better than papyrus for writing and also for illustration or illumination. The earliest illuminated book of the gospels dates from the sixth century. On rare occasions, the parchment was dyed purple, and gold or silver was used as ink. Many book coverings also were magnificent works of art [illustration 40]. Besides those few books that have survived from this time, various mosaics from this period attest to the priceless codices owned by the church [illustration 43]. During this period, liturgical books began to be given as gifts.

December 25	VIII Kal. Ianu.	Natus Christus in Bethleem Iudeae.

— Mense Ianuario —

January 20	XIII Kal. Feb.	Fabiani in Calisti et Sebastiani in Catacumbas.
January 21	XII Kal. Feb.	Agnetis in Nomentana.

— Mense Februario —

February 22	VIII Kal. Mart.	Natale Petri de catedra.

— Mense Martio —

March 7	Non. Mart.	Perpetuae et Felicitatis, Africae.

— Mense Maio —

May 19	XIIII Kal. Iun.	Partheni et Caloceri in Calisti, Diocletiano VIIII et Maximiano VIII cons. [304].

— Mense Iunio —

June 29	III Kal Iul.	Petri in Catacumbas et Pauli Ostense, Tusco et Basso cons. [258].

— Mense Iulio —

July 10	VI Id.	Felicis et Filippi in Priscillae; et in Iordanorum Martialis, Vitalis, Alexandri; et in Maximi, Silani; hunc Silanum martyrem Novati furati sunt; et in Praetextati, Ianuari.
July 30	III Kal Aug.	Abdos et Sennes in Pontiani, quod est ad Ursum piliatum.

— Mense Augusto —

August 6	VIII Id. Aug.	Xysti in Calisti, et in Praetextati, Agapiti et Felicissimi.
August 8	VI Id. Aug.	Secundi, Carpophori, Victorini et Severiani in Albano; et Ostense VII ballistaria, Cyriaci, Largi, Crescentiani, Memmiae, Iulianae et Smaragdi.
August 9	III Id. Aug.	Laurenti in Tiburtina.
August 13	Id. Aug.	Ypoliti in Tiburtina et Pontiani in Calisti.
August 22	XI Kal. Sept.	Timotei, Ostense.
August 28	V Kal. Sept.	Hermetis in Bassillae, Salaria vetere.

— Mense Septembre —

September 5	Non. Sept.	Aconti in Porto, et Nonni et Herculani et Taurini.
September 9	V Id. Sept.	Gorgoni in Labicana.
September 11	III Id. Sept.	Proti et Iacinti in Bassillae.
September 14	XVIII Kal. Octob.	Cypriani Africae, Romae celebratur in Calisti.
September 22	X Kal. Octob.	Bassillae, Salaria vetere, Diocletiano XIIII et Maximiano VIII cons. [304].

— Mense Octobre —

October 14	prid. Id. Octob.	Calisti in Via Aurelia, miliario III.

— Mense Novembre —

November 9	V Id. Nov.	Clementis, Semproniani, Claudi, Nicostrati in comitatum.
November 29	III Kal. Dec.	Saturnini in Trasonis.

41. *Depositio Martyrum.* (Denis-Boulet, pp. 53–54.)

42. Example of a cupboard *(armarium)* with the four gospels. These cupboards stood in the sacristy adjoining the apse of the basilica. Based on detail from a mosaic in the so-called mausoleum of Galla Placidia, Ravenna, c. 450 CE

Quotation 93. *When one serves at the altar, prayer is always directed to the Father. Whoever borrows prayers for himself from another place must not use them unless he first submits them to the more learned brothers [of his own church].* Council of Hippo (393), canon 21

Quotation 94. *It is decided that the prayers, orations, Masses, prefaces, commendations and imposition of hands which were examined in council may be celebrated by all. No others whatsoever may be used in church—neither those strongly against the faith, nor thought composed by the ignorant, nor those written by the less zealous. Exceptions to this rule are those employed by the more skilled or those sanctioned in synod.* Council of Carthage (407), canon 10

Standardization of Content

The post-Constantinian period was a time of transition from improvised prayer to standardized liturgical texts. Although the content of the Bible was relatively fixed by about the year 200 CE, liturgical prayers still were evolving. The first written example of a eucharistic prayer did not appear until the early third century. Bishops, who ordinarily were the only presiders in fourth-century worship, retained their right to improvise prayer. Because of the growing complexity of worship as well as the many theological controversies of the time—especially those surrounding the issue of Christ's divinity—a new concern for orthodoxy in public prayer developed. Consequently, various local synods attempted to regulate the content of the liturgical prayers and the books that contained them. A synod in Hippo, attended by St. Augustine, required that prayers at the altar should be directed to the Father and that prayers borrowed from other places could not be used until they had first been examined [quotation 93]. A later North African council tried to impose a collection of prayers that had been prepared with hierarchical approval [quotation 94]. Although examples of such legislation are few in this period, they bear witness to a growing concern for controlling the content of liturgical books. This move toward standardization eventually spread throughout the church.

Summary

Generally speaking, the liturgy of the years 100 to 313 knew only one liturgical book: the Bible. After the conversion of Constantine, a whole library of liturgical books emerged. These confirm both the growing complexity of worship as well as an increased concern about the theological content of public prayer at a time when the church was shaping the basic tenets of the faith. New attention to the content and etiquette of ritual meant new restrictions concerning both the books and the people who used them. Care for the content of the books was matched by concern for the appearance of the books, which often became magnificent works of art. The growing reverence for liturgical books—initially dictated by their content, later by their artistic value as well—prepared the way for a later time when objects such as liturgical books would be treated as more important than the people they would serve.

43. Four bishops, each carrying a rich jeweled gospel codex, from the apse of St. Apollinare in Classe, Ravenna, sixth century.

VESSELS

The eucharist always was central to the life of the Christian community, but to a certain extent this became even more true after Constantine. Initially celebrated only on Sunday, eucharist soon came to be celebrated on the other days of the week. Communal worship such as morning and evening prayer diminished in importance for ordinary people and increasingly became the domain of the numerous religious communities that developed during this time. Although many devotional practices evolved, none became more important than the eucharist, which dominated Christian piety. In the wake of this expanding eucharistic piety, a variety of eucharistic vessels developed, especially for the bread.

Bread and Its Vessels

The tradition of employing ordinary leavened bread for the eucharist continued during this period [quotation 95]. Since at least the third century, it had been customary for people to bring gifts of bread and wine from their homes for the eucharist. Because of this custom, Ambrose had to explain to the newly baptized that although eucharist looked like ordinary bread, it really was the Body of Christ [quotation 96]. Various texts and artistic renderings show that eucharistic bread took various forms during this period. Sometimes the bread was a flat disk [illustration 44]; sometimes it was braided into a circle called a

Quotation 95. Epiphanius [d. 403] criticized the Ebionites because, unlike the rest of orthodox Christians, *"They annually celebrate certain mysteries in which they employ unleavened breads and for the other part of the mystery pure water."* The Panarion, 2.30.16

Quotation 96. *Perhaps you say: "My bread is ordinary bread." In fact before the sacramental words this bread is simply bread. But when the consecration occurs it changes from bread to the body of Christ.* Ambrose, About the Sacraments, 4.14

crown [quotation 97]; often the bread was a small round loaf, marked with a cross [illustration 45].

BASKETS   Given the sizes and shapes of the bread in this era, baskets continued to be the usual containers for the eucharistic bread [illustration 46]. Jerome (d. 420) noted the appropriateness of baskets for this purpose [quotation 98]. Besides baskets, other common containers were used to hold the eucharistic bread. A description of the papal Mass at Rome in the seventh century, for example, notes that the bread collected from the faithful was put into linen sacks, and the consecrated bread was carried in linen sacks back to the people for communion [quotation 99].

PATENS   In this period, special dishes or patens were produced for use at eucharist. With increasing frequency, these were made of precious metals. Patens originally were relatively large vessels used to hold small loaves, crowns or disks of leavened bread. A description of the papal Mass at Rome noted that the paten was carried by two acolytes, indicating its substantial size. According to a sixth-century source, Constantine donated many gold and silver patens, each weighing at

Quotation 97. *The priest said, "It is not customary for me to appear ungrateful to this man who was so very helpful to me. It is necessary for me to bring him a gift. Thus he brought with him two crowns of bread (coronas) as an offering. . . . The man sighed with distress and said, "Why do you give this to me, Father? This bread is holy and I am not able to eat it."* Gregory the Great, *Dialogues*, 4.55

Quotation 98. *Nothing costly for the one who carries the body of the Lord in a wicker basket.* Jerome (d. 420), *Epistle to Rusticus*, 20

Quotation 99. *The regional subdeacon receives the offerings from the pontiff and presents them to the next subdeacon, who places them in the linen bag, which two acolytes hold. . . . The subdeacons, with the acolytes who are carrying the bags, come to the right and the left of the altar and while the acolytes extend their arms with the bags. The subdeacons stand forward so that they may prepare the open sacks for the archdeacon to place the offerings in, first in the right one and then in the left one.* Roman Ordo I, 71, 101

44. Oldest extant example of a stamp for eucharistic bread, measuring about 6½ inches in diameter, from Djebeniana (present day Sfax) in North Africa. The inscription reads *"Ego sum panis vivus qui de celo descendi"* (I am the bread of life come down from heaven). Dating from the sixth century. (After: Righetti III:483–484.)

Quotation 100. *[Constantine] offered the following gifts to the Constantinian basilica [St. John Lateran] . . . seven golden patens each weighing thirty pounds, sixteen silver patens, each weighing thirty pounds.* Book of the Popes, 34

45. Detail of loaves from side of sarcophagus (350–380 CE) in Arles, in a presentation of loaves and fishes prefiguring the eucharist.

Quotation 101. *Nothing may be placed upon the altar except the capsa with the remnants of the sancta . . . or the pyx with the body of the Lord for viaticum for the sick.* Leo IV (d. 855), On Pastoral Care

Quotation 102. *And after all have taken part in communion, let the deacons carry what remains to the sacristy.* Apostolic Constitutions, 8.13.17.

Quotation 103. *Basil, having called upon a goldsmith, asked him to make a dove of pure gold in which he placed a portion of the body of Christ. He suspended the dove over the holy table as a figure of the sacred dove that appeared at the Jordan over the Lord during his baptism.* Life of St. Basil, attributed to Amphilochius of Iconium (d. after 394)

least 30 pounds, to the Lateran Basilica in Rome [quotation 100]. Extant patens from the sixth century measure almost 24 inches in diameter. Even the smaller examples from this period indicate that ordinary leavened bread was being used [illustration 47].

PYX   Besides vessels for bread during the eucharist, vessels for holding the holy bread after eucharist continued to develop. A variety of names were employed: *arca,* chrismal and pyx were the most common names. (Because the term "pyx" is most familiar, it will be used here.) The pyx was usually a small, cylindrical vessel shaped so that it could hold a small round loaf of bread [illustration 48]. Examples exist from the fourth century. These small, portable cases were employed, at least sometimes, for carrying communion to the sick [quotation 101]. Evidence also exists that people carried the eucharist with them in small cases or sacks around their necks as talismans against evil and for giving themselves communion.

TABERNACLE   Besides portable containers, certain evidence in this period indicates that stationary containers also were used for the eucharist. Although these were known by a variety of names, here they will be gathered under the general heading of "tabernacle." The fourth-century Syrian church order, *Apostolic Constitutions,* gives the first account of what appears to be eucharistic reservation within a church [quotation 102]. The evidence for primitive tabernacles increases over the centuries. Basil (d. 379) seems to have known a vessel shaped like a dove that was used for reserving the eucharist [quotation 103]. Other documents from Italy during the sixth and seventh centuries indicate that the eucharist sometimes was kept in a small case that was then placed in a closet or a cupboard in the sacristy.

Wine and Its Vessels

The tradition from the beginning was the use of grape wine—common throughout the Mediterranean countries—diluted with water for Christian eucharist. Red wine seems to have been preferred, at least in part because it well symbolized blood. Like the bread, wine for the eucharist was brought by the people from their homes.

CHALICES   The large number of people that filled the Christian basilicas after the conversion of Constantine required larger vessels for communion. Since the earliest times, the symbolism of one bread and one cup required that a single cup sufficiently large to hold wine for the whole community would be used. Often these chalices were large, vase-shaped vessels attached to a round base, sometimes with handles

46. Christ depicted with seven jars of wine and seven baskets of bread. Panel from the door of S. Sabina, Rome, 422–430.

Quotation 104. *The pope goes down to the senatorium and . . . accepts the offerings of the noblemen in order of their rank. After him the archdeacon accepts the flasks of wine* (amulae) *and pours them into the main chalice* (calice maiore) *held by the regional subdeacon. Roman Ordo I, 69–70*

attached to the side to aid in drinking. Examples of much smaller chalices from this period exist as well [illustration 49]. The material for these vessels—large or small—was more often a precious metal than glass, wood or bone. Examples in amber, onyx and ivory also survive from this time.

The size of a chalice generally indicated the size of the community that used it, because everyone present for the celebration of the eucharist would have drunk from the chalice. Certain evidence shows, however, that for a brief period in Rome, two different types of chalices were used at the same Mass: a large chalice on the altar for consecrating the wine [quotation 104] and smaller chalices, filled from the main chalice, for communion of the people. Though unique to the church of Rome, this distinction in vessels is further testimony that communion under both forms was presumed for the assembly during this period.

47. Sixth-century paten of silver gilt from Riha in Syria, 9½ inches across.

48. The so-called Berlin pyx from the fourth century, made of ivory and measuring approximately 4¾ inches high and 5⅛ inches in diameter. (After Righetti I:451.)

CRUETS   The evidence from this period indicates that special vessels were employed for carrying the wine and water before they were poured into the chalice at eucharist. Undoubtedly, people originally brought their gifts of wine to the church in ordinary containers. During the early fourth century, however, the inventory from the church at Cirta noted that six silver jars *(urceola)* [quotation 49] had been confiscated. This may be the first evidence of a special vessel for wine before its consecration. With the elaboration of the offertory and its processions in the post-Constantinian church, evidence for these special vessels increases. In a late fifth-century document from Gaul, *urceola* are mentioned as part of the ordination rite of an acolyte

49. Late fifth- or early sixth-century chalice from Syria, measuring 7½ inches high and 6 inches in diameter.

Quotation 105. *When an acolyte is ordained . . . he receives an empty* urceolum *for carrying the wine of the blood of Christ in the eucharist.* Ancient Statutes of the Church (late fifth century), canon 6

[quotation 105]. In the papal Mass of the seventh century, the wealthy, at least, seem to have brought their gifts of wine in a special vessel *(amula)* [quotation 104]. Such vessels at first were large. As the number of people who received communion from the cup diminished, so did the size of these vessels [illustration 50].

Summary

Significant changes occurred in the number, size and quality of vessels for the bread and wine after the conversion of Constantine. What is most striking is the transition from household utensils to liturgical vessels. The ordinary wicker, pottery and wood vessels that had long been used to hold the bread and wine before and after their consecration became less and less common. Gold and silver became the preferred materials, the hand of the artisan was more evident and the sacredness of the vessel itself was emphasized. This was true not only for vessels used during the eucharist but also for those used before and after the Mass. During the next period, 750 to 1073, these vessels, and the special people who crafted and cared for them, will be set apart from the assembly that they were supposed to serve.

50. Example of an early Christian amula (After Kraus, I:517.)

FELIX

Felix is convinced that he has the best grandfather in all of Rome. Felix never knew his father, and he hardly remembers his mother, who died when he was three. Felix's grandfather has been his whole family for almost as long as he can remember. They do everything together. When grandpa gets up, Felix gets up. When grandpa goes to the market, Felix goes to the market. And when grandpa goes to work making sandals in his little shop on the slope of the Esquiline Hill, Felix goes to work and makes sandals. When he was younger, Felix just pretended to make sandals, playing with scraps of leather and a wooden knife. But now that he is eight, he is learning how to measure a foot with chalk on the stone floor of the shop and how to choose the right leather for the different parts of the sandals. Soon his grandfather is going to teach him how to cut the leather. In the meantime, Felix is in charge of dyeing the straps for the sandals and setting them in the sun to dry.

But today there is no work. Today is Sunday and there is going to be a great worship service at the Church of St. Mary on the hill. Felix remembers the stories he has heard about the old days when Sunday was a workday. But then the emperor who believed in Jesus closed the law courts on Sunday. Pretty soon, everyone who believed in Jesus took Sunday as a free day. Felix thinks that Constantine must have been a very great man.

Although they are not going to work today, Felix and his grandfather rise before dawn because they want to get a good spot inside the church before the service begins. They eat their bread as they walk through the narrow streets that lead to St. Mary's. A crowd already is streaming into the church when they arrive. There also are many people inside, singing

hymns and responding to the litanies, but Felix and his grandfather manage to work their way through the crowd and arrive at the barrier that creates a passageway to the altar. Felix likes this spot because the barrier is low enough that he can rest his arms and chin on it and hold himself up during the long service. If he stands on his toes and cranes his neck, Felix can look down the open passageway to watch the movement around the altar. Right now, the area behind the altar is filled with bishops and presbyters singing and praying with the people, while deacons scurry everywhere.

The crowd behind Felix and his grandfather is so thick that they cannot see the back of church, but grandpa always seems to know when something is about to happen. He has been going to the bishop's liturgy for almost 50 years now, and he knows the worship inside and out. Grandpa whispers that all of the bustle in the back and the movement in the sanctuary must mean that the saintly Bishop Leo has arrived.

Sure enough, in a few minutes one of the subdeacons, accompanied by an acolyte, winds his way through the crowd. The acolyte is carrying a beautiful book in front of him on a white cloth. As they pass, Felix can almost reach out and touch the book, its gold cover and precious stones gleaming. Felix stretches himself over the barrier to watch them carry the book into the sanctuary and place it on the altar and then return back through the crowd. A few minutes later, the singers who were standing at the side of the altar leave the sanctuary. Grandpa says they are going to join the procession that now is forming in the back of the church. When the singers leave, the singing of the assembly dies down as the people sense that the procession is about to begin.

A song erupts from the back of the church, *"Introibo ad altare Dei"*—"I will go to the altar of God." First intoned by a few strong voices, the refrain soon is picked up by the whole congregation, whose voices echo throughout the vast hall. The choir of men, accompanied by boys not much older than Felix, sings alternating texts as they make their way through the crowd and form an honor guard inside the barrier. Felix squirms along the railing, trying to see through the choir members who stand in two rows inside the passageway, men on the outside and boys on the inside. Finally, Felix finds a spot about ten feet away from grandpa, right on the end of the barrier, where he has an unobstructed view of the passageway—and just in time. A cloud of incense announces that the main procession is reaching the front of the church. After the man with the incense passes, seven torchbearers follow, their faces all red from the blazing torches. Then come the subdeacons and the deacons. One of them, Marcus, lives down the street from Felix and his grandfather. At the end of the procession is the bishop.

Although he is an old man with a long beard, the bishop moves steadily through the crowd, greeting the people, and often leaving behind the archdeacon, who walks to his right. Felix is transfixed as the old man approaches. As the crowd parts to let him into the passageway, the bishop spies Felix leaning on the edge of the barrier, reaches out and gently pats him on the head as he passes.

It was a long service, but Felix doesn't remember any of it. He doesn't remember the splendid singing of the gospel, the collection of gifts by the deacons or the solemn prayers. He doesn't even remember drinking from the gold chalice. What Felix does remember, and one day will tell his own grandson, was the moment when the saintly Bishop Leo reached out and blessed him.

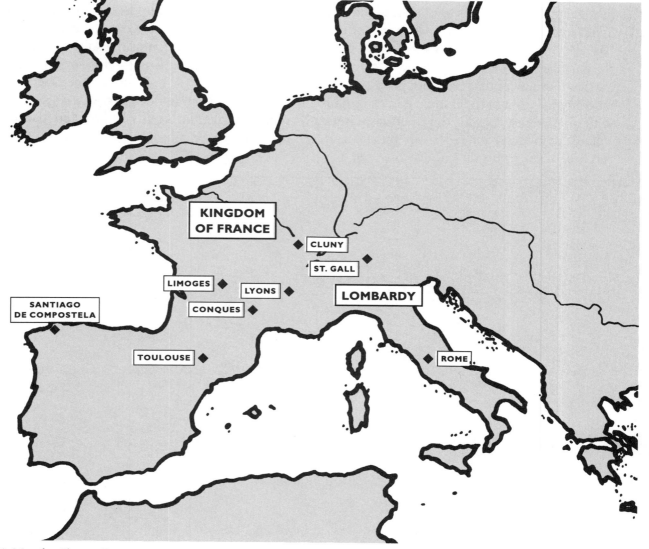

51. Map for Chapter Four.

Frankish
Domination:
750 to 1073

By founding Constantinople in the year 330, Constantine was able to establish a geographically central capital for the empire. He also was able to construct a Christian center for his empire. This shift of political power to the East prepared for the dissolution of the Roman Empire in the West and the ultimate division between the churches of East and West. Separated from the strongholds of the East, weakened by internal corruption and beaten down by the barbarian invasions, Roman civil government collapsed by the end of the fifth century. Though the ecclesiastical government remained intact, its influential ties with the emperor of the East began to wane. Eventually, the alliance forged between the Roman church and Constantine, which had produced the Roman liturgy, gave way to a new political and liturgical partnership between Rome and the Frankish kingdoms [illustration 51].

Since the conversion of Clovis (d. 511), king of the Franks, in the year 498, an important Christian kingdom had existed north of the Alps. The Merovingian kingdom, named for Clovis's grandfather Merowig was severely weakened during the seventh century through a series of internal power struggles. The church in the kingdom of the Franks experienced a similar decline in this period.

The ultimate victor in the internal political struggles of the Franks was Charles Martel (d. 741). His son, Pepin III (d. 768), and Pepin's sons, Carloman (d. 771) and Charlemagne (d. 814), established the Carolingian empire and brought about a new wedding of church and empire. Together they signed an alliance with Pope Stephen II against the Lombards, who threatened the security of Rome. In return, the pope anointed them kings in 754.

The major challenge to this newfound dynasty was the reform and unification of the kingdom. To no small degree, this was achieved by first reforming the church that had experienced such decline in the seventh century and then employing it as an agent of unification for the realm. A first step in the reunification of the kingdom was the establishment of a unified liturgy. Thus Pepin and Charlemagne attempted to impose the Roman liturgy on the Frankish church. To achieve this goal, liturgical books and personnel were imported from Rome. Anglo-Saxon missionaries who had strong ties to Rome, such as Boniface (d. 754), assisted in this venture. The incompleteness of the Roman books, combined with the significant differences between the Roman and Frankish temperaments, resulted not so much in the imposition of the Roman liturgy as in the emergence of a new genre of liturgy. This hybrid form of worship, mixing the sobriety of the Roman style with dramatic Frankish elements, has been called the Franco-Roman liturgy. This form, eventually adopted even by Rome, came to be the predominant liturgy of the Latin church during the late Middle Ages.

ARCHITECTURE

In the centuries following its legalization, Christianity used various types of buildings for its worship. Eventually, a single style of building, based on the basilica form, became common in the West. This multifunctional type of building had to meet sometimes contradictory ritual requirements, such as providing places for both public and private Masses. The architectural solution to this problem was the subdivision of the building into various sections each with a different ritual focus.

The predominant architectural style of this period often is called "Romanesque." This nineteenth-century term acknowledges the similarities between buildings of this era and those of ancient Rome. As the "Holy Roman Emperor," Charlemagne sought to revive the spirit of the fourth century, when Christianity and empire became one. This included a return to the architectural style of Constantine's Rome.

Charlemagne's architectural projects provided order and direction for his liturgical reforms. His concern was to replace local worship with "official" Roman worship. At the same time, he sought to replace local architecture with an idealized version of the architecture of Constantine's Rome. Charlemagne's buildings, like those of Constantine, were monumental in size and geometrically constructed.

Carolingian architecture also expanded the "westwork" of the church building. In many churches, the sanctuary was located in the east end of the building, which served as a kind of divine precinct in the structure; the west end served as an architectural and political counterpoint, symbolizing the emperor's claim to authority over the church. This westwork often consisted of an elevated space that included

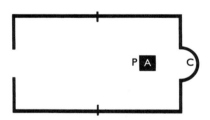

52. Arrangement of presider (P), chair (C) and altar (A) in basilica with apse facing east.

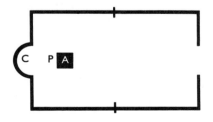

Arrangement of presider (P), chair (C) and altar (A) in basilica with entrance facing east.

towers, chapels and sometimes a second apse, anterior to the main part of the church.

Carolingian architecture extended from the late eighth century to the late ninth century. Ottonian architecture—the architecture of Germany during the rule of the Ottonian emperors that continued to develop and refine the Carolingian style—appeared in the last half of the tenth century. Romanesque architecture, properly speaking, is an eleventh- and twelfth-century phenomenon. While Carolingian and Ottonian architecture might be characterized as imperial, Romanesque architecture appeared as a more popular phenomenon reflecting the spirit of the age. With the new political stability on the continent, a new optimism arose. The ascendancy of the middle class, a new economic promise and the general relief that the world had not come to an end at the turn of the millennium all contributed to the positive outlook of the eleventh century. In this optimistic age, Christians were on the move, crisscrossing Europe on pilgrimage. The pilgrim centers were beneficiaries of booming economies that developed around the relics that were the focus of these pilgrimages. It was around such relics that many of the great Romanesque churches of Europe were built.

As Spiro Kostof notes, no typical Romanesque church exists; these churches varied according to region and to the needs of the community. It is possible, however, to enumerate some characteristics of this style, many of which were anticipated in Carolingian and Ottonian buildings. These include the use of basic geometric shapes, especially the round arch; an increased emphasis on vertical construction, particularly through high vaulting and the addition of towers; the employment of thick, load-bearing walls; and the even subdivision of the walls into sections or bays, resulting in a rhythmic undulation of the building.

1. Raised gallery
2. Presbytery
3. Main altar
4. Choir
5. Tower

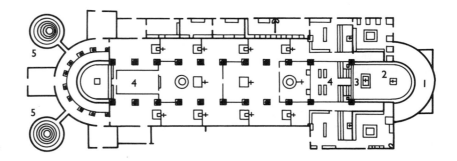

53. Church from a monastic plan from c. 820, now in the library at St. Gall, Switzerland. The church shows 14 altars in the main body of the structure, with more altars in the towers and the crypt, bringing the total number of altars to at least 20. (After Gardner, p. 285)

Main Altar

A basilica is a type of enclosed path, and every path leads someplace. That someplace in the post-Constantinian Christian basilica was the apse. As the focal architectural point, it naturally became the focal liturgical point. Initially, the apse was the place for the bishop's throne. Adapted by monasteries and parish churches, the apse became the place for the altar.

Originally, the altar was a movable wooden table, often placed in the body of the church so that the community could gather at least around three sides of it. The presider stood on whichever side of the altar allowed him to face east, the place of the rising sun and a symbol of the resurrection. If the apse pointed toward the east, then the presider stood on the same side of the altar as the community and faced the same direction that they did. If the entrance to the basilica pointed toward the east, then the presider faced the community across the altar [illustration 52]. The second arrangement was more common in the West after the time of Constantine until the period of Frankish domination. During the eighth century, the first arrangement, with the priest facing away from the people, became more common. Over time, the altar was pushed farther into the apse until it ended up against the back wall. In this position, the back of the altar began to be embellished. Eventually, more emphasis was placed on the back embellishment, called the reredos, than on the table itself.

Another change was in the material used for altars. Stone altars, already mentioned by John Chrysostom in the fourth century, were mandated in some places by the sixth century [quotation 106] and for the whole empire by Charlemagne in 789. As the altar became more closely connected with relics, its shape changed from a table to a sarcophagus. The growing distance between the people and the altar was underscored by the development of special rites for the dedication of an altar during this period. Previously, the only essential act for dedicating an altar was the celebration of eucharist. Specific rites requiring the deposition of relics and the anointing of the altar appeared by the eighth century [quotation 107].

Secondary Altars

One major difference between Western churches of this period and those of the previous period was the inclusion of more than one altar within a church. Although some evidence suggests the existence of secondary altars before the seventh century [quotation 108], it was after the seventh century in Gaul that the number of altars increased significantly. This was due, in part, to the growing importance of relics

Quotation 106. *Altars may not be consecrated unless they are made of stone.* Council of Epaon (517), canon 26

Quotation 107.
Almighty God,
in whose honor we consecrate this altar
   through the invocation of your name,
graciously hear and answer our prayers
so humbly and respectfully offered
so that the offering on this altar
may be acceptable to you,
may be pleasing to you,
and may always be rich and overflowing
   with the gift of your Holy Spirit
so that at every time in this place
when supplication is offered to you
   from your family
you may relieve our anxieties,
cure our afflictions, hear our supplications,
accept our promises, confirm our desires
and yield to our requests.
   Prayer for the blessing or consecration
   of an altar, *Old Gelasian Sacramentary*
   (seventh or eighth century), 694

Quotation 108. *The presbyter Leuparicus, who brought us your fraternal greetings, informed us of your church constructed in honor of the blessed apostles Peter and Paul and also the martyrs Lawrence and Pancratius. We have learned that in that church there are 13 altars, four of which are yet to be dedicated.* Gregory the Great, *Letter to Bishop Palladius of Santes* (c. 590)

54. Reconstruction of the interior of the third church at Cluny (begun in 1088) illustrating the enclosed choir set off from the nave by a solid wall, in front of which are altars for the services attended by the laity. (After Conant as cited in Norberg-Schulz, p. 171.)

in the post-Constantinian age. Important martyrs often were honored with a martyrium erected over their burial place. Because there were few important martyrs north of the Alps, churches in those areas began importing—or even stealing— relics. Each relic was a prized possession and deserved its own altar, which resulted in the multiplication of altars in any church possessing more than one significant relic.

The multiplication of altars also resulted from the increased demand for Masses. Originally, the eucharist was celebrated only on Sunday. By the sixth or seventh century, the practice spread to the other days of the week. Scheduling multiple eucharists on a single day was a response to requests that Masses be offered for the dead or for the fulfillment of a penance. Large numbers of monks began to be ordained priests, partly to fulfill these requests for Masses. As a result, multiple altars were erected, especially in monastic communities [illustration 53].

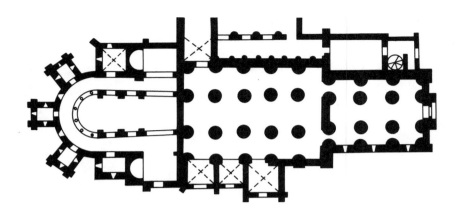

55. Church of St. Philibert in Tournus (950–1120) showing early form of ambulatory around apse, with main relics in far eastern chapel. (After: *Tournus: Abbaye Saint-Philibert.*)

A third reason for the multiplication of altars in this period was the attempt by churches north of the Alps to imitate the stational liturgy of Rome. This liturgy was held up as the ideal, and attempts were made to imitate it, especially as it was outlined in the papal books sent to Charlemagne during the eighth century. The papal liturgy was a roving liturgy that occurred in numerous churches throughout Rome. Various processions accompanied the celebration from one location to the next. Because the Christians of the north did not live in cities like Rome, with sprawling networks of urban churches that would have allowed them to repeat this stational liturgy, their individual churches and cloisters were turned into smaller versions of Rome. Numerous altars were erected as symbolic parallels to the Roman stations, first within Carolingian churches and later in Romanesque churches.

Choir Area

Evidence indicates that by the early fifth century, the laity was restricted from certain areas around the altar. The growing instinct to create a sacred precinct in the middle of the church prompted a number of architectural solutions. In the West, a low barrier often was constructed to contain the crowds, especially during the processions [illustration 31]. As monks and secular clergy took over the celebration of the Divine Office and came to provide music for the eucharist, the restricted space in front of the altar was shaped to meet their needs. Monastic and cathedral churches eventually were built to accommodate this choir of monks or clergy. The result was a hybrid basilica with an elongated apse and a large enclosed space for the monks or canons.

Screens or walls sometimes were built to demarcate the place of the monks or clergy from the place of the laity. By the eleventh or twelfth century, some of these walls were solid, presenting the laity with a visual obstacle to the divine service. Because of this, a second altar often was built for the people outside the boundaries of the choir [illustration 54].

Ambulatory

Quotation 109. *To clerics and monks . . . it is not proper that women should approach the altar.* Charlemagne, *General Admonition* (879), 17

The emphasis on relics in the new churches, combined with the increasingly restricted access to the main altar area, especially for women [quotation 109], led to an important development in Romanesque churches, the ambulatory. The ambulatory was an architectural solution for the problems that arose when large numbers of people tried to move through the pilgrimage churches. A church's most important relic was usually in the main altar, which, because of both canonical and architectural constraints, was inaccessible to the laity. A further problem was the throng of pilgrims surging through narrow side aisles or trying to squeeze into cramped corners where side altars or reliquaries sometimes were placed. The solution was a passageway behind the apse, which allowed pilgrims to circulate through the church while the monks or clerics were chanting the offices [illustration 55]. This also gave people access to relics located in a chapel off the ambulatory or in the main sanctuary. If the relics were located in the sanctuary, they could be viewed from the back through an opening in the wall of the apse. The ambulatory also provided room for more side chapels, which were common in the great pilgrimage churches of the Middle Ages, and processional routes for the monks or clerics to the principal relics.

Summary

Architecturally, this period saw the full flowering of trends begun in the previous period. The sanctuary area became definitely separated from the body of the church by legal and architectural barriers. The transition was made from a wooden table accessible to the assembly to a large stone altar, often in the shape of a sarcophagus, pushed up against a back wall and embellished with a reredos. A central choir space was carved out for monks or clerics, highlighting their place as the ecclesiastical and liturgical elite. And the number of altars multiplied. Because many of these developments occurred in the northern countries where the language of the liturgy was no longer the language of the people, they contributed to the separation of the community from the liturgical action.

MUSIC

The architectural subdivision of the church building serves as visual analogy for the musical developments in the West at this time. Architecturally, special places were allocated for the priest (sanctuary), the monks or clerics (choir) and the laity (nave and transepts). The music similarly was divided among the priest, the choir and the laity. The choir dominated the music of the eucharist. The priest gradually retreated into private or silent prayer, while the community came to be shut out of central musical action. Although many great diocesan music centers existed during this period, the musical development of the realm was lead by the monasteries.

56. Tunnel vaulting in nave of Cluny III, begun in 1088. (After Conant as cited in Norberg-Schultz, p. 171.)

Nos qui vivimus benedicimus Dominum ex hoc nunc et usque in saeculum.

57. Early form of polyphony (organum of the octave) in note-against-note style, c. 850. (Davidson and Apel, p. 21.)

Cunc-ti-po-tens ge-ni-tor de-us, om-ni-cre-a-tor, e-   ley-son. Chri-ste De-i splendor, vir-tus pa-tris-

que so-phi-a, e-   ley-son. Am-bo-rum sa-crum spi-ra-men, ne-xus a-mor-que, e-   ley-son

Example of free organum from eleventh century (Davidson and Apel p. 22.)

Choir

When Pepin III and Charlemagne after him mandated the use of the Roman liturgy throughout their kingdom, they also required that the official liturgical music of Rome be employed [quotation 110]. For eucharist this meant that the chants for the various proper and ordinary parts of the Mass were sung by musical specialists with occasional refrains or responses from the community. With the importation of these chants into the Frankish kingdom, where Latin was unknown by the laity, this resulted in the virtual exclusion of the congregation from the ordinary and proper parts of the Mass. One exception may have been the *Sanctus* that, even in the North countries, seems to have been sung by the people [quotation 111].

During this period, Gregorian chant emerged. Although the origin of Gregorian chant is still a matter of scholarly debate, it generally is agreed that this chant was not created by Gregory the Great. One of the most well-accepted theories suggests that Gregorian chant resulted from the fusion of imported Roman chant with local Gallican chants. At the time that Pepin and Charlemagne imported the Roman liturgy into Gaul, a local type of chant and liturgy known as Gallican already existed. The style of chant imported from Rome probably was Old Roman chant [illustration 38]. Because of the lack of notation, Roman chant was imported by borrowing books of texts and inviting Roman cantors who could teach the melodies. Over the years, these melodies

Quotation 110. To every cleric: All are to sing Roman chant in its entirety, which is to be properly executed both for the office and for Mass. This is to be accomplished according to the wish of King Pippin, our father of happy memory, and because of the peaceable alliance between Gaul and the holy church of God, accomplished in complete agreement with the apostolic see. Charlemagne, General Admonition (789), 80

Quotation 111. The priest with the holy angels and the people of God are to sing "Holy, Holy, Holy" with a common voice. Charlemagne, General Admonition (789), 70

58. Example of early stage of notation from c. 900, Manuscript St. Gall 359 (Apel, *Gregorian Chant,* plate I.)

began to fuse with the traditional liturgical chants already in use in Gaul. The result probably was what now is called Gregorian chant. This linear music sounded very good in the long, Romanesque churches—especially those with tunnel vaulting [illustration 56].

Besides Gregorian chant, professional musicians north of the Alps also developed polyphony, in which two or more lines of music sounded simultaneously. In its earliest form, known as "organum," a second line of music was matched note against note to an original chant line. The earliest forms of organum utilized a single text simultaneously sung on parallel pitches (parallel organum); later forms included the simultaneous singing of the same text on different pitches (free organum) [illustration 57]. The further development of independent musical lines and texts led to the obscuring of the liturgical texts. In contrast, Gregorian chant was word-centered music that supported the text. It continued something of the tradition of the earliest church music, although it was performed in a language ordinary people no longer understood. Polyphony, however, contributed to an ever-widening gap between music and the ritual texts.

In the monastic centers of the North, means for notating music developed. Until this time, only the chant texts could be recorded, while the music had to be memorized [quotation 81]. By the mid-ninth century, a relatively effective system of signs or "neumes" was developed to aid the singer in recalling a previously learned chant [illustration 58]. By the mid-eleventh century, the system was so accurate that music could be learned from a page alone [illustration 59].

The Laity

While choirs of monks and clerics dominated liturgical music almost to the exclusion of the laity, the people developed new kinds of religious songs. The song of the people had been a part of Christian worship since the very beginning. Initially, the people's songs were performed in the same language as the liturgy and were central to the worship. With the increasing number of liturgical professionals and the decreasing flexibility of the Roman liturgy and its chants, the first nonliturgical Christian songs developed. These vernacular songs sometimes were allowed during Mass—after the sermon, for example—but they were not integral to the rites, as the official chants were. For the first time, the vernacular song of the people not only was restricted but, to a large extent, was excluded from the eucharist. Vernacular song more commonly accompanied pilgrimages and other popular devotions and sometimes was used for religious instruction. Bede (d. 735), who wrote a celebrated history of the English church,

59. Example of eleventh-century notation, featuring notation in neumes as well as in letters. (Apel, *Gregorian Chant*, plate VI.)

Quotation 112. *In this monastery of Streanaeshalch, lived a brother singularly gifted by God's grace. So skillful was he in composing religious and devotional songs that, when any passage of scripture was explained to him by interpreters, he could quickly turn it into delightful and moving poetry in his own English tongue. These verses of his have stirred the hearts of many folk.* Bede (d. 735), *A History of the English Church and People,* 4.24

reported that such religious song existed in England, where missionaries had established the Roman liturgy and introduced Roman chant [quotation 112]. Evidence exists that vernacular religious song also developed in the Frankish kingdom. The *Ruf* (German for "call") and *Leise* (from *Kyrie eleison*) were two early forms of such song, dating from at least the ninth century.

The Priest

As the people's voice fell silent at eucharist, so did the priest develop a silent mode of prayer. At Masses with a congregation, the priest often chanted some of the parts, reminiscent of a time when no public speech could be rendered without music. But two developments contributed to the disappearance of the musical role of the presider and to the musical dominance of the eucharist by the choir. The first of these was the growing tendency to pray what had been vocal prayers silently at celebrations with a congregation. The most dramatic example of this is the complete silence of the priest during the canon of the Mass. Evidence from Gaul around the year 775 suggests that the presider

Quotation 113. And the pontiff begins the canon in a different voice so that it may be heard by only those standing around the altar. Roman Ordo XV (c. 775), 39

Quotation 114. And when the Sanctus, is finished the pontiff alone rises and begins the canon silently. Roman Ordo V (c. 850), 58

Quotation 115. Repeatedly we make this recommendation to all, so that every priest who desires can offer a reasonable and acceptable sacrifice to God. . . . When one celebrates Mass, first begin with a psalm and the Gloria Patri or antiphon followed by the Kyrie eleison. Similarly at communion, employ an antiphon and psalm, always adding the Gloria Patri, which is praise of the Holy Trinity. Roman Ordo XV, 155

changed his tone of voice when he began the canon so that only those standing around him could hear [quotation 113]. Toward the end of the ninth century, sources indicate that the canon became completely silent [quotation 114].

A second development that marked the disappearance of the sung role of the presider was the private Mass. In a private Mass, the priest assumed all the ministries, including the silent reading of chant texts that normally would have been sung by the choir. Evidence of priests saying Mass without a congregation may come from as early as the seventh century. Originally, certain elements such as the chant texts simply were dropped. Evidence exists that Masses for the dead in the ninth century were without chant texts from their beginning; they apparently originated as silent Masses without music. Evidence that priests began to recite chant texts comes from the ninth century [quotation 115]. From this period, therefore, one can first distinguish between a sung Mass *(missa cantata)* and a read Mass *(missa lecta)*.

Summary

Although musical specialists appeared in the time of Constantine, only during the period of Frankish domination did the congregation come to be excluded from the worship music. Even though the congregation often sang, this singing no longer was in the language of the liturgy nor was it generally considered integral to the worship. The one exception seems to have been the *Sanctus*. The congregational music that did develop often was more wedded to pilgrimage or other devotions than to the church's official liturgy. As the congregation lost its musical role, so did the presider begin to disregard the musical nature of his texts. Not only did presiders read what should have been sung, but they also changed from reading the texts audibly to reading them silently.

BOOKS

Two contradictory tendencies mark the development of liturgical books during this period. The first, continuing the trend of the previous period, was the creation of new books for the liturgy. A second, opposite tendency was the conflation of a number of liturgical books into a single volume. The result of this evolution was a new genre of self-contained liturgical books. Almost all of the previously mentioned books—the antiphonary, cantatory, Bible, gospel book, epistle book, lectionary, calendar, martyrology, sacramentary and ordo—continued. Only the *libelli missarum* disappeared. Of the existing books, the lectionary and the sacramentary underwent the most development in this period.

60. First page of a ninth-century
sacramentary, St. Gall 348. (After
Righetti, I:215.)

The Antiphonary for Mass and the Gradual

The various chant texts for the Mass existed in a number of different
books in Rome. As the Roman liturgy was imported into other parts of
the West, these books spread and changed. In the Frankish kingdom,
the various chants for Mass were gathered into a single book called the
"antiphonary for Mass" *(antiphonarius missae)* [quotation 116]. Another
type of antiphonary also existed at this time; it contained the chants
employed during the Divine Office. Eventually, the name "gradual"—
the Frankish designation for the Roman cantatory that contained the
gradual, tract and alleluia verses—was adopted as the name for the
book of Mass chants. In time, the distinction was made between the
book containing all the chants for the Mass (gradual) and that which
contained all the chants for the Divine Office (antiphonary).

Lectionary

After the time of Constantine, the lectionary began to replace the Bible
as a Christian liturgical book. A lectionary contains selected extracts
from the Bible, arranged for the various Sundays and feasts of the year.
Although there is some evidence for lectionaries in the fifth and sixth
centuries, it was especially after the eighth century that lectionaries
were in general use and displaced the Bible as a liturgical book. As
lectionaries became more common, they were combined with the
sacramentaries of this period. This eventually led to the development of
the full missal, which appeared by the tenth century.

Full Missal

One of the most significant new books of this period was the full
missal. This book combined materials from five other books: chant
texts from the antiphonary for Mass, readings from the epistle book,
the gospel from the gospel book, the priest's prayers from the sacramentary and rubrical instructions from the ordo. A number of factors
led to the emergence of the missal. One of these was the private Mass.
Numerous ministers meant numerous books, but in a private Mass the
priest assumed virtually all of the roles himself. A single book was
useful for this purpose. Another contributing factor was a changed
attitude toward the chants of the Mass. In the Christian West, liturgical
music was taken over by professionals. Even the priest began to lose his
role as a music maker. In some situations, however, no professional
singers performed the ritual chants that were beyond the ability of the
congregation. It was not appropriate to drop these chants altogether,
so the priest began to read them. A number of instructions directed

that chant texts—first in the absence of a choir and then even in their presence—were to be chanted by the priest [quotation 115].

Pontifical

Another book that developed during this period was the bishop's book, or "pontifical." Like the full missal, the pontifical combined a variety of books into a single volume. Although various combinations existed, most pontificals combined the rubrics proper to a bishop, which were contained in the ordos, with the corresponding prayers from the sacramentary. This was first done in smaller books, which then were gathered into a rudimentary kind of pontifical. The first pontificals appeared in the ninth century. The most important early form of

61. Cover of the Psalter of Charles the Bald, ninth century. The manuscript is purple vellum, with gold writing; the cover is a carved ivory scene, surrounded by gold and silver work encrusted with uncut precious gems. (After Righetti I:233.)

62. Example of an eleventh-century chalice with paten small enough to fit on top of the cup and large enough to hold the priest's host.

63. Eucharistic dove from Limoges, made of gold-plated copper and enamel. Twelfth century.

this book was the *Romano-Germanic Pontifical*. This book, which appeared around the year 950, contained a vast amount of material. Its versatility and importance led to its use throughout the Christian world: Eventually, it was even adopted in Rome. The development of a special book for the bishop demonstrated that the ordinary liturgical books no longer were intended for use by him. This occurred at a time when the bishop relinquished his role as the ordinary presider for the community; that role had been taken over by the priest. Most liturgical books were shaped for use by a priest. A special book for the bishop announced the end of his role as the primary leader of prayer for the Christian community.

Sacramentaries

Although the first sacramentaries appeared at the end of the previous period, during the time of Frankish domination, the number of sacramentaries increased dramatically [illustration 60]. Eventually superseded in the late Middle Ages by the full missal, sacramentaries were the predominant liturgical books of the early Middle Ages. The Frankish church definitively shaped the content and form of the sacramentary for Western Christianity. This process began when Charlemagne asked the Pope for authentic Roman books that could be used throughout the realm. In response to this request, Pope Hadrian (d. 795) sent Charlemagne a papal sacramentary around the year 785. This splendid looking book was missing texts for a large number of Masses, including those for the Sundays after Epiphany, funeral rites, penitential rites and a variety of votive Masses. The deficiencies of the so-called *Hadrianum* soon became apparent. Consequently, an extensive supplement was added to the *Hadrianum* at the end of the eighth century. This supplemented papal sacramentary played a pivotal role in the development of sacramentaries and the Roman Missal.

Summary

Books may be considered as an embodiment of the church's ecclesiology from which much can be learned about this period. First, materials for individual ministers, such as the liturgical chants for the singers, found their way into a single volume. Then the texts for a wide variety of ministers—the singer, lector, subdeacon, deacon—were condensed into a single volume for the priest. The bishop, who once was the ordinary presider for all Christian liturgy, came to require a special book for presiding. These developments summarized the consolidation of musical responsibilities by professionals; the centrality of the priest in Christian worship to the point that even the congregation could

Quotation 117. *The bread which is conse-crated into the body of Christ ought to be most pure without leaven or any other additive.* Alcuin, *Letter 90 to the broth-ers in Lyons* (798)

be eliminated; and the distancing of the bishop from the center of pastoral liturgy.

The liturgical books of the early Middle Ages continued to be illuminated, lavishly bound and presented as beautiful works of art [illustration 61]. Even in their artistry, however, they seem to indicate a distancing from the assembly from whom they came and whom they were supposed to serve.

VESSELS

Bread and Its Vessels

From the beginning of Christianity, the bread used at eucharist was similar to that used for ordinary meals. After the ninth century, however, unleavened bread became customary, and eventually mandatory, in the Christian West. Alcuin (d. 804), adviser to Charlemagne, offered one of the first testimonies for this change [quotation 117]. There was an ancient tradition for making eucharistic bread in the shape of flat disks. Bread stamps of the period [illustration 44] indicate that these disks were larger and thicker than the hosts of a later era. The new restrictions against the use of leaven and other additives eventually produced eucharistic bread that was round and flat.

The reasons for this change were many and complex. Contributing factors included an increased emphasis on the unworthiness of the laity. Unworthy people did not go to communion, nor did they bring gifts of bread and wine to the church as an offering. Consequently, the number of communicants declined significantly, and offertory processions were eliminated in many places. Where the offertory procession did survive, the people's gifts were not used in the Mass. Increasingly, the elements offered in the eucharist were prepared by monks or clerics. Furthermore, as the otherworldliness of the eucharist was emphasized, using bread that was different from ordinary table fare became appropriate. The image of the unleavened, specially prepared bread employed in Jewish temple sacrifices provided a biblical precedent for employing pure, specially prepared bread in the eucharist. Another factor in the use of unleavened bread was the widespread understanding of the eucharist as the reenactment of the life and death of Jesus. This view lent support to the use of unleavened bread for this is what Jesus is remembered as having used at the Last Supper. Thus at the turning of the millennium, ordinary table bread gave way to "hosts."

Increases in the number of private Masses and decreases in the number of communicants contributed to a reduction in the size of the host. The practice of placing the bread on people's tongues instead of in

64. A ninth-century ivory tablet, part of a book cover portraying early medieval episcopal worship. A chalice with handles stands upon the altar and three ring-shaped hosts lie upon the paten.

their hands, evident since the ninth century, also was a factor in this decrease in size. By the eleventh century, small hosts were prepared for the few remaining communicants.

PATENS   Changes in the bread brought about changes in the vessels that held it. Baskets disappeared as eucharistic vessels during this period. Patens, formerly large enough to hold a large piece of bread—if not all the bread—became smaller. Many small patens already were in use in the post-Constantinian period. In the early Middle Ages, however, they became the rule regardless of the size of the worshiping community. Because whatever bread that might be distributed to the assembly was reserved in the pyx, the paten needed to be just large enough to hold the priest's host. Thus the concave disk, small enough to rest on top of the chalice [illustration 62], already was in use by the tenth century. During this period, scattered directives about the materials for the paten appeared. The first requirements were prohibitive—forbidding the use of certain materials such as animal horn [quotation 118]. In general, however, few directives about the material for the paten appeared before the end of the Middle Ages. Much more legislation developed around the material for the chalice. In general, the paten was forged from the same elements as the chalice; gold and silver became common materials for both. These special vessels, distinguishable by their precious materials and reduced size, were further set apart by a special consecration [quotation 119].

PYX   As mentioned in chapter 3, the pyx—the vessel that held the eucharistic bread outside of Mass—assumed a number of forms. With the decreased size of the paten, the pyx also became the ordinary container for holding the small hosts for the laity during Mass. One early witness to this practice could be the handbook on church law and practice by the abbot Reginald of Prüm (d. 915). In this work, the abbot noted that the pyx was one of the vessels placed on the altar during the eucharist [quotation 120]. This quote makes it clear that the pyx was used for communion to the sick outside of Mass. It also attests to the placement of the pyx on the altar during the eucharist. This usage foreshadows a time when the pyx would commonly sit on the altar during eucharist. Eventually, the Mass-pyx would be called a ciborium. During this period, the pyx, like the paten, was consecrated before being used [quotation 121].

TABERNACLE   As in the previous period, evidence exists at this time that not only portable containers were used for the reserved sacrament but also stationary containers. For example, a pyx containing the eucharist sometimes was suspended above the altar [quotation 122].

Quotation 118. We prohibit making a chalice or paten for the sacrifice from the horn of an animal. Synod of Calechyt (787), canon 10

Quotation 119.
Lord,
deign to consecrate and sanctify this paten
*   through this anointing and our blessing*
*   in Christ Jesus our Lord*
who lives and reigns with you
*   and the Holy Spirit,*
one God forever and ever. Amen.
   Missal of the Franks (eighth century), 63

Quotation 120. If there is a pyx, it always may be upon the altar with the sacred offering for the viaticum of the sick. Reginald of Prüm (d. 915), *Book of Synodal Processes and Ecclesiastical Instructions,* 9

Quotation 121.
Almighty Triune God,
pour out the power of your blessing
*   into our hands,*
so that through our benediction
this vessel may be sanctified
and through the grace of the Holy Spirit
may become a new sepulchre for the body
*   of Christ.*
Through our Lord, Jesus Christ your son,
who lives with you and the Holy Spirit,
one God forever and ever. Amen.
   Missal of the Franks (eighth century), 68

Quotation 122. The holy Roman emperor Henry [d. 1024] . . . gave [to the Abbey of St. Vanne] an onyx pyx, hanging over the altar, in which the Lord's body is kept. Chronicle of Hugh, monk of Verdun and abbot of Flavigny, 1:8

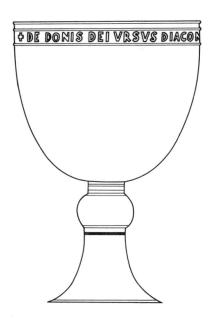

+ DE DONIS DEI VRSVS DIACON

65. An eighth-century chalice with a small node (After Braun, *Das christliche Altargerät*, p. 70.)

Quotation 123. *If the chalice with the paten is not from gold, it should be entirely of silver. If, however, some place is very poor, the chalice should at least be made of tin. Decretals of Gratian, part 3 ("Concerning Consecration"), distinction 1, canon 45*

After the ninth century, some of these hanging pyxes were shaped like doves [illustration 63]. Eucharistic doves became very popular during the late Middle Ages. Besides the hanging pyx, the eucharist also was stored in various church cupboards or closets. Often the sacrament was first wrapped in a cloth, put into a pyx and finally locked in one of these closets or cupboards. These cupboards or closets sometimes were found in church sacristies. Occasionally, they were set into a wall and specially decorated.

Wine and Its Vessels

Just as the laity no longer brought bread for eucharist during this period, so did they stop bringing wine. Eventually, only the kitchens of monks and clerics prepared the eucharistic bread and only their vineyards produced the wine. Like the vessels for bread in this period, the vessels for wine became smaller and were withheld from the laity.

CHALICES Evidence at this time suggests that large chalices, comparable in size to those of the previous period, were used. Continuing evidence also attests to the use of the traditional two-handled chalice [illustration 64]. Increasingly, however, chalices of this period were smaller than those of the previous era, largely because of a decline in the communion of the laity and the prevalence of private Masses. Even when the laity did receive communion, this seldom included drinking from the cup for fear that the precious blood would be spilled. A further change in the shape of the chalice was the inclusion of a node on the stem separating the base from the cup [illustration 65]. This design, which helped the priest more easily hold the chalice, eventually was mandated by church law.

Legislation concerning the material for fabricating chalices first appeared during this time. Initially, certain materials were disallowed, as had been the case with the paten [quotation 118]. Eventually, directives required that the chalice be made from gold or silver. The law was not consistent on this point, and various materials such as bronze or copper were permissible according to different synods or individuals. Exceptions also were made for poor churches that, for example, were allowed to use tin. Eventually, however, the preference that chalices should be made only of gold or silver was incorporated into the law of the church [quotation 123]. As chalices came to be forged from precious metals and held beyond the reach of the laity, their sacrality was further emphasized by the rites of consecration that appeared at this time.

TUBES   One of the more unusual utensils of this period was the tube *(calamus, fistula, pugillaris)* employed as a kind of straw when receiving communion from the cup [illustration 66]. The earliest evidence for this utensil comes from eighth-century Rome, where the tube was employed for the communion of the people during the papal Mass [quotation 124]. From at least the thirteenth century until the reforms of Vatican II, the tube was used on special occasions by the pope and his deacon and, less often, by bishops during a pontifical liturgy. The earlier sources, however, do not indicate that the pope or other clergy used the tube for communion. Some scholars suggest that because certain communion tubes were fashioned from gold, one could conclude that these were employed by the clergy. It also is conceivable, however, that silver and gold were used not because of the dignity of the communicant but because of the precious nature of the consecrated wine. In general, the tube was used for the communion of the laity. It served in the transition from the time when people drank directly from the chalice to a period when ordinary people did not receive the consecrated wine. Lay communion from the chalice disappeared in most places by the late thirteenth century.

Summary

The eucharistic vessels of this period underwent a reduction in their capacity for holding the eucharistic species, if not in their overall size. At the same time, insistence increased on the use not only of precious materials but specifically of gold and silver in the fabrication of these vessels. These phenomena symbolized the developments in the eucharistic theology of the period. During this time, the teaching and belief of the church increasingly focused on the presence of Christ localized in the bread and wine. This emphasis on Christ's presence under the eucharistic species virtually ignored the other modes of Christ's presence, especially his presence in the assembly. To a certain extent, the vessels that held the sacred species came to be considered more precious than the community itself. Vessels began to be consecrated at the same time that the people were increasingly restricted from receiving communion. Bread was no longer put in their hands, but on their tongues. Drinking through a tube replaced drinking from the cup, and eventually the cup was completely withdrawn from the laity. Beautiful chalices and patens came to replace the community as the primary vessels of the presence of Christ.

66. Communion tube.

BROTHER AELRED

Brother Aelred does not remember his age. Neither does anyone else in the monastery. The record of his entry into the abbey was lost in the great fire of 836. Now blind and lame, Aelred does remember that he was already a professed monk when the cornerstone for the new church was laid in 838. That was almost 80 years ago. Some of the young monks joke that "old Brother Aelred actually knew Saint Benedict."

Aelred does not have much contact with the young monks. He spends most of his days propped up near the big window in the infirmary, dozing in the sun. The infirmary on the second floor of the abbey overlooks the main cloister. Sounds from the abbey workshops, refectory and chapter room drift through the window into the infirmary. These sounds are Aelred's faithful companions.

Although he is unable to see the new dormitory wing or watch the processions through the cloister, the sounds of the monks at work or at prayer reassure him that his beloved abbey continues to thrive. The bells in the towers of the abbey church are special friends, calling the monks to prayer, to meals and to bed. Whether it is the bells, shouts in the cloister or chants from the church, almost everything that Aelred knows about the monastery these days he learns through hearing. This is appropriate for the monastery's former choirmaster.

It is late in the afternoon on the patronal feast of the monastery. Aelred had dozed off while listening to the monks chant the hour of None. He suddenly awakens to a strong arm beneath him and knows that Brother Accadam—or Brother Ox, as Aelred calls him—has arrived to carry him to bed. At least that is what Aelred presumes. But instead of carrying

him down the south corridor toward Aelred's cell, Brother Ox takes the main corridor into the central dormitory and then descends the stairway into the church. Brother Aelred is going to the afternoon's solemn Mass for the patronal feast.

The chants that rise from the abbey choir bring tears to the old monk's eyes. Unable to walk for almost a decade, Aelred seldom joins the monks in the choir anymore. Only on rare occasions does the prior give Brother Accadam permission to bring the old monk into the church. Maybe the prior thinks that this will be Aelred's last patronal feast with them. Aelred does not care about the reason as the Ox gently lowers him into an upper choir stall. Aelred is back in his beloved church.

Aelred knows all the chants by heart. The introit begins, and after the antiphon the choir erupts with Psalm 99, *"Iubilate Deo omnis terra, servite Domino in laetitia."* Although 80-plus voices join together on the psalm, Aelred easily picks out the uncertain voices of the novices sitting across from him on the left. They struggle through the seldom-employed solemn tone for this text. One young voice misreads the cantor's cue and instead of Psalm 99 sings the opening phrase from Psalm 65, *"Iubilate Deo omnis terra psalmum dicite nomini eius."* Aelred remembers his own years as postulant and novice, struggling to memorize all of the psalms before his profession of vows.

Over the years, he learned not only the psalms and their simple chants, but also hundreds of other tunes and texts. He learned them from Brother Romanus, who had trained as a cantor in the monastery of the Holy Apostles in the Eternal City. Aelred had been such a good student that Brother Romanus had asked him to tutor the oblates in the simple chants. And in the year that the new choir was dedicated, when Brother Romanus went to God, Aelred succeeded him as choirmaster in the abbey.

"Desiderium animae eius"—the opening phrase of the offertory chant draws Aelred out of his reverie. Father Abbot now must be at the altar, holding aloft the great silver paten and chalice that miraculously survived the fire.

Aelred smiles to himself as the antiphon rises from the voices of these sons of Benedict. What more perfect time and place to make the final offering? *"Posuisite in capite eius coronam de lapide pretioso"* chant the monks. "You placed on his head a crown of precious stones." The offertory verse becomes the old monk's final epithet. Before the last notes fades from the vault, Aelred accepts his own crown of glory.

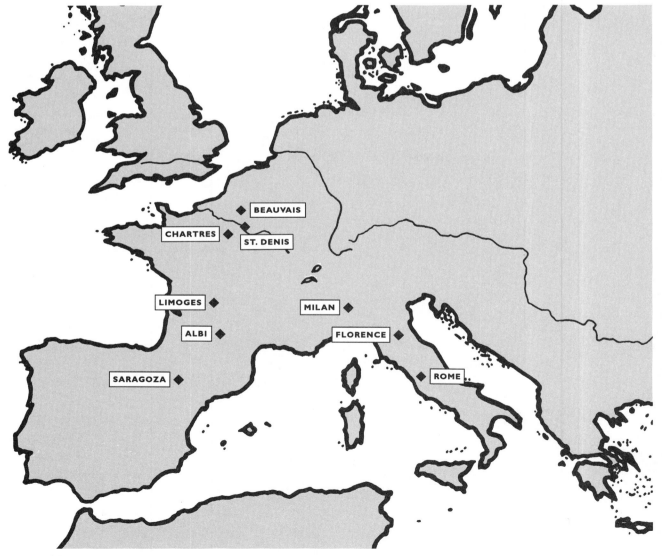

67. Map for Chapter Five.

CHAPTER FIVE

The Prelude
to Reform:
1073 to 1517

The innumerable political and social developments during this period make it difficult to generalize about Western Europe between the eleventh and the sixteenth centuries. Liturgically, however, a single, overarching direction occurs through these centuries: decline. At the beginning of this era, Rome attempted to reassert control over the church. A series of eleventh-century German popes—especially Gregory VII (d. 1085), who was elected in 1073—spearheaded the reassertion of papal authority and the centralization of ecclesiastical power in Rome. Among other things, this meant trying to reassert control over what could be called the Franco-Roman Mass.

Three centuries of Frankish influence on the liturgy could not be eliminated or ignored by Rome; it was embedded in the prayer texts and rubrics of Western Christianity liturgical books. These books were almost exclusively produced in the North countries where the Frankish influence was strongest. In the early Middle Ages, Rome had little capacity for producing liturgical books. Various stories report that the bishop of Rome sometimes offered gifts or privileges to Frankish monasteries in return for new liturgical books. These books introduced Frankish and other Germanic liturgical developments into the liturgy of Rome. Once incorporated into the practice of Rome, this hybrid liturgy was disseminated throughout Western Christianity by various religious communities, especially the followers of Francis of Assisi (d. 1226).

Out of reverence for the Holy See and for his own bishop—who already had introduced the ordo of the papal chapel into the diocese of Assisi—Francis charged his followers to celebrate according to the custom of Rome [quotation 125]. This directive was, in part, a reaction to the burdensome structures of monastic prayer, which would not have suited the mobile life-style Francis and his brothers practiced. As

Quotation 125. *The clerics are to recite the Divine Office according to the rite of the Roman Curia.* Francis of Assisi, *Rule of 1223,* chapter 3

the Franciscans and other religious groups like them spread throughout Western Christianity, they disseminated the rubrical and musical usage of the papal chapel throughout the Latin West.

Eucharistic controversies that originated in the Frankish realm in the ninth century also had a widespread effect during this period. For the first time, theologians wrote systematic treatises on the nature of eucharistic presence. The common inclination was a kind of gross literalism that taught that Christ's presence in the eucharist was literal and physical [quotation 126]. Although this cannibalistic approach was rejected by theologians such as Thomas Aquinas (d. 1274), it captured the popular imagination and piety. Stories of bleeding hosts and of appearances of the baby Jesus in the bread abounded. These contributed to an increased focus on the eucharistic bread apart from any communal action. The elevation of the bread after the consecration, evident by the year 1206 at Paris, and the exposition of the blessed sacrament were tangible results of these attitudes [illustration 68].

In this period of liturgical history, the laity was most decisively distanced from the eucharistic action. The celebration of the liturgy in a foreign language, a phalanx of intervening ministers, architectural barriers and the laity's own sense of unworthiness largely restricted its role to listening and watching. Because much of what the people heard was unintelligible, the visual elements of the liturgy became increasingly important. The elevation of the host became the high point of the Mass; for most of the assembly, this "ocular communion" substituted for receiving the sacrament. This preoccupation with seeing the host was reflected in the architecture. Many churches were constructed to function as large stone monstrances.

This stress on the visual was the culmination of a long development that systematically excluded the community from worship. This was an abandonment of traditional prayer styles in which the community not only watched but also participated by its words, actions and songs. Now the dialogue of praise was forgotten and the responsorial dynamic of an earlier age was put aside. Watching took precedence over hearing. In the process, eucharist became a thing, not an event—an object, not a relationship. The objectification of eucharist—that is, its reduction to bread without communion—contributed to a perspective that eventually allowed the sacrament to be both used and abused. Such developments prepared for the inevitable revolution known as the Reformation.

Quotation 126. *I, Berengarius . . . confess that the bread and wine which are placed on the altar are, after consecration, not merely a sacrament but rather the true body and blood of our Lord Jesus Christ, and that they are physically held and broken by the hands of the priest and crushed by the teeth of the faithful.* Confession of Berengarius before the Roman Synod of 1059

68. Fourteenth-century marble relief of the elevation from Milan.

ARCHITECTURE

Early in this era, the Gothic style of architecture was born in the North. Almost three centuries later, the Renaissance style emerged in Italy.

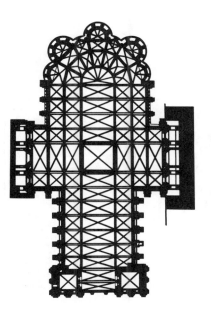

69. Groundplan of Chartres Cathedral, begun in 1145 and rebuilt after the fire of 1194. (After Norberg-Schulz, p. 195)

Quotation 127.
Whoever thou art,
  if thou seekest to extol the glory
    of these doors,
Marvel not at the gold and the expense
  but at the craftsmanship of the work.
Bright is the noble work;
  but, being nobly bright, the work
Should brighten the minds
  so that they may travel through
    the true lights,
To the True Light where Christ is
  the true door.
In what manner it be inherent in this world
  the golden door defines:
The dull mind rises to truth
  through that which is material
And, in seeing this light,
  is resurrected from its former submersion.
Abbot Suger (d. 1151), poem on the doors of St.-Denis, translated by Panofsky

These new styles signified more than a new type of arch, the addition of flying buttresses or a renewed interest in central-plan construction. In fact, many of these elements already had been in use before this time. Rather, the way such architectural elements were synthesized into these distinctive styles reflected a new way of viewing the world and the cosmos. They also embodied a particular view of the church, in which every person and ministry had an assigned place and role in a well-defined hierarchical order.

The Birth of Gothic

Gothic architecture differed from its predecessor, Romanesque architecture, in many significant ways. The masonry barrel-vault roof, typical of late Romanesque churches, exerted tremendous lateral stress, and the walls bore all the weight. Consequently, the walls of Romanesque churches often were very thick and had few windows. The few openings in the walls were made in the shape of rounded arches, which were relatively inflexible and did not greatly weaken the walls' load-bearing capabilities. In Gothic architecture, the weight from the roof was directed vertically to the piers by means of ribbed vaults. The webbing between the ribs consisted of lightweight masonry, which lessened the stress on the support system below and allowed the walls to be pierced with windows and galleries [illustration 69]. The Gothic building thus was a solid skeleton with huge open spaces filled with colored glass. This resulted in one of the basic characteristics of Gothic architecture: luminosity. In the medieval mind, light was a privileged and mysterious mediator of God. The Gothic cathedral, with its large stained-glass windows, became a symbol of the divine presence on earth [quotation 127].

Besides luminosity, another characteristic of Gothic was its embodiment of order. The twelfth and thirteenth centuries were times of great achievement in systematizing and organizing Western thought. Ageless examples of this are the theological compendiums or *Summas*—such as those of Thomas Aquinas and Bonaventure (d. 1274)—written during this era. As some Western minds were attempting a vast synthesis of the divine order on paper, architects were seeking the same thing in stone. The Gothic cathedral was, therefore, an architectural synthesis of late medieval understanding of the divinely ordered universe. The building itself was well ordered, with each part integrated into the whole [quotation 128]. Within the medieval universe, every person had a specific place and function ordained by God. The Gothic cathedral embodied this hierarchical vision. It acknowledged and accentuated the centrality of the priest and the mysteries he enacted within the sacred precincts of the sanctuary. If the Gothic

Quotation 128. *Like the High Scholastic Summa, the High Gothic cathedral aimed, first of all, at "totality" and therefore tended to approximate by synthesis as well as elimination one perfect and final solution; we may therefore speak of the High Gothic plan or the High Gothic system with much more confidence than would be possible in any other period. In its imagery, the High Gothic cathedral sought to embody the whole of Christian knowledge . . . with everything in its place and that which no longer found its place, suppressed. In structural design, it similarly sought to synthesize all major motifs handed down by separate channels and finally achieved an unparalleled balance between the basilica and the central plan type.* Panofsky, pp. 44–45

70. Interior view of the Cathedral of Beauvais. Begun in 1225, the vault collapsed in 1284. It was rebuilt over the next 40 years, reaching 158 feet at the height of the vault. The nave was never completed.

Quotation 129. *In the religious system of the Middle Ages, every phase of reality is assigned its unique place; and with its place goes a complete determination of its value, which is based on the greater or lesser distance which separates it from the first cause.* Ernst Cassirer, p. 39.

cathedral was the epitome of order, it also was the personification of liturgical exclusion. As Ernst Cassirer has noted, during the Middle Ages, a person's importance was demonstrated according to how close one was to the first cause [quotation 129]. In liturgy, this meant physical proximity to the altar where God became present. The distancing of members of the laity from the altar was a clear message about their lowly place in the church's power structure.

Gothic as the embodiment of order eventually evolved into Gothic as the embodiment of the extreme and the frantic. The flamboyant Gothic style of the late thirteenth century and the fourteenth century came to obscure the purity and order of early and middle Gothic.

Similarly, the liturgy of the time came to obscure the central action even further until—like the great vault of Beauvais [illustration 70]—it collapsed under its own weight.

While Gothic architecture flourished north of the Alps, Italy experienced something different. Gothic influence had made its way into Italy, but by the fifteenth century, architects in Florence and other great centers broke with Gothic and developed their own style called Italian Renaissance. Although this style of architecture put particular emphasis on centralized space and classical proportions [illustration 71], the Italian Renaissance style, like Gothic architecture, projected an image of the universe that was well ordered and logical. Thus it maintained—although to a lesser degree than Gothic—a distinct separation of the laity from the center of eucharistic worship.

Division of Space

Although some differences existed between the ways that Gothic and Renaissance architecture shaped the interiors of churches, many similarities marked ecclesiastical architecture during this period in the West.

MAIN ALTAR   The ultimate point of convergence in these buildings was the main altar. Raised on many steps, standing in the middle of the sacred precincts, often a great distance from the people and frequently crowned by a tabernacle or elaborate reredos, the main altar drew the attention of every worshiper. Most importantly, it was at the altar that Christ was made present and was raised up under the appearance of bread at the elevation of the Mass. The elevation became so significant in the late Middle Ages that everything possible was done to ensure

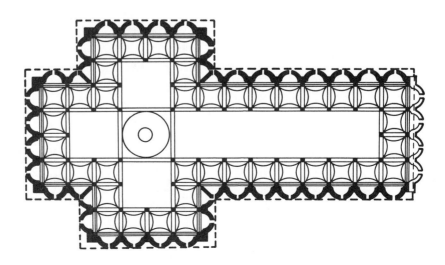

71. Church of S. Spirito in Florence by Brunelleschi; begun in 1436, completed in 1482; illustrating how a multitude of side altars with individual chapels are integrated into the design of a church; Brunelleschi intended to express the inclusion of so many side chapels externally, by articulating the exterior wall of each chapel with a semicircle; these were later concealed with a straight wall around the periphery of the building. (After Kostof, p. 383)

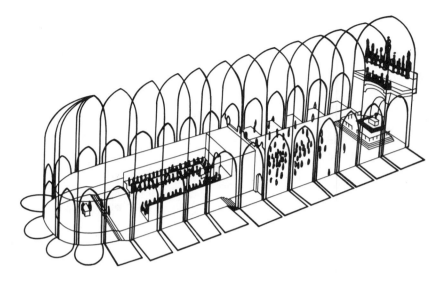

72. Schematic drawing of the cathedral at Albi, indicating the positions of clerics in the choir, the high altar, the rood screen, and the people outside the rood screen (After Quinn, p. 40.)

that the host might be seen. Sometimes a dark curtain was drawn behind the altar as a contrast to the white wafer. At other times, a special consecration candle was held aloft by a server to illuminate the bread. Often, bells were rung to signal this pivotal moment. The elevation became the ritual center of the liturgy celebrated at the architectural center of the church.

CHOIR AREA   The area where the monks or clerics prayed the offices and attended services became a permanent buffer zone between the assembly and the altar. This area often was separated by a wall or rood screen, which sometimes developed into an elaborate and impenetrable barrier [illustration 72]. These were so effective in blocking the people's view of the sanctuary that doors were constructed in the screen. These doors were opened during the elevation so that people could view the host. Pulpits sometimes were raised on top of these barriers so that the people could hear whatever preaching occurred. Behind the rood screens were magnificent choir stalls for the monks or clerics [illustration 73].

SIDE ALTARS   The popularity of the private Mass and the veneration of relics led to a multiplication of side altars within the churches of this era. In older churches, additional side altars were placed wherever an open space could be found. By the late Middle Ages, however, the need for multiple side altars influenced the design of a church. Gothic and Renaissance architects harmonized these altars with the rest of the building. Often, small chapels for these altars were arranged throughout the entire church building [illustration 71]. This contributed to the subdivision of sometimes massive spaces into a series of individual compartments. The church in effect became a series of private spaces gathered under the same roof, reflecting a privatization in the spirituality of the time.

PEWS   Since the beginning of Christian worship, allowances always were made for the seating of certain people. In the homes that served as the first gathering places, a bench often was placed along the wall in the dining room where Christians gathered. As the community changed from the Greco-Roman tradition of lounging while dining to standing—a symbol of resurrection—chairs were seldom provided for the whole community. Seats were provided for the bishop and, less frequently, for other ministers or elders. In the post-Constantinian period, seating also was provided for the emperor and other dignitaries. Soon benches were provided for the monks or clerics who occupied the choir area before the altar. From the Carolingian period, some evidence exists that scattered benches, mats or stools were provided for the laity. During the fourteenth and fifteenth centuries, this practice became more widespread. Churches filled with pews became common after the sixteenth century. These further contributed to the subdivision of the medieval church and helped confine the assembly to a secondary space where virtually no important ritual was enacted.

Summary

The historical and geographic proximity between the introduction of the elevation (early thirteenth century in Paris) and the birth of Gothic architecture (mid-twelfth century on the outskirts of Paris) is more than a coincidence. Rather, they are related events that affirmed both the predominance of the visual aspects of liturgy and the tendency to reduce the role of the assembly to that of spectator. Buildings and rituals no longer were shaped for the assembly's hearing or responding, for auditory intelligibility or for a corporate sense of worship. Rather, buildings were shaped to keep people at a distance while the buildings underscored the sacredness of the priest, who stood at the architectural and liturgical center.

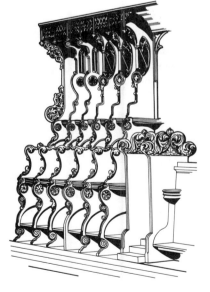

73. Choirstalls from Maulbronn, fifteenth-century carving (After Atz, p. 154)

MUSIC

By the late Middle Ages, the choir and, very occasionally, the priest sang during Mass. The people were entirely excluded from singing. The liturgical music of this era was largely the work of professional

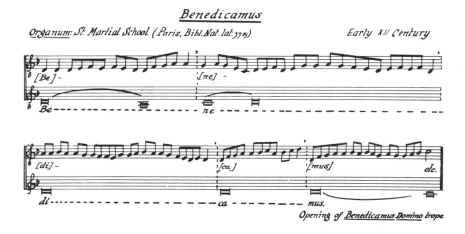

74. Two-part organum, with slow moving Gregorian melody in the lower voice and florid ornamentation in the upper voice. Early twelfth century. (Gleason, p. 30.)

singers and composers. The following section will consider two basic musical trends of the time: the addition of more than one line of music during a piece, and the textual changes that accompanied this musical development. Congregational music that was used outside the liturgy also will be considered.

Multiplication of Musical Lines

Polyphony appeared in the ninth century and grew to prominence during the late Middle Ages. The simple two-part works of organum were succeeded by three- and four-part compositions. As more musical lines were added to the compositions, they often became more florid as well. In some works based on Gregorian melodies, the chant was performed very slowly in the lower voice while ornate passages were sung in the upper voice(s) [illustration 74]. What had begun as a simple ornamentation of the plainsong began to supersede and obscure the chant, which often was reduced to an underlying drone performed on the primitive organs of the period. These melodic developments were matched by rhythmic advances such as the introduction of a repeated rhythmic pattern. This repeated pattern was one of the techniques thirteenth-century composers used for organizing their compositions [illustration 75]. The resulting music—marked with a new rhythmic coherence and verticality created by the many lines piled on top of each other—was much like the Gothic cathedral of the day with its soaring vaults and repetitive patterns of piers and buttresses. Both had a similar effect on the assembly as well: They exceeded the people's comprehension while invoking a sense of awe.

Early polyphonic composition was confined to the changeable or proper parts of the Mass. Renewed interest in liturgical composition in

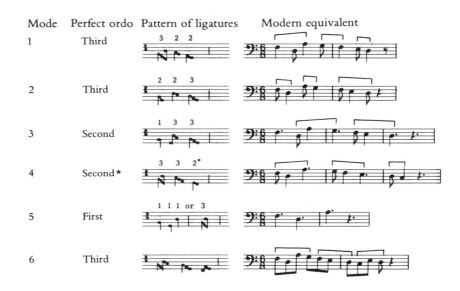

Mode	Meter	Musical equivalent
1	Trochaic: long short	
2	Iambic: short long	
3	Dactylic: long short short	
4	Anapaestic: short short long	
5	Spondaic: long long	
6	Tribrachic: short short short	

Mode	Perfect ordo	Pattern of ligatures	Modern equivalent
1	Third	3 2 2	
2	Third	2 2 3	
3	Second	1 3 3	
4	Second★	3 3 2*	
5	First	1 1 1 or 3	
6	Third		

75. The six rhythmic patterns known as "rhythmic modes" employed in organizing the rhythm of some late medieval music. (Hoppin, pp. 222, 224.)

the fourteenth century shifted composers' attention to polyphonic settings for the ordinary of the Mass. One reason for this shift was the awareness that settings of the ordinary could be more useful than propers, which generally were sung only once a year. It also is possible that the texts of the ordinary, which had been in use for many centuries, were considered a more venerable part of the ritual. For a long time, musicians thus were less inclined to depart from traditional Gregorian settings of the ordinary. During the late Middle Ages, however, Western music underwent significant artistic developments independent of the liturgy. In this context because of music's newfound independence from the liturgy and of the desire to push into new compositional territories, composers felt bold enough to apply polyphonic techniques to the ordinary of the Mass. The first complete Mass setting by a single composer was *La Messe de Notre Dame* by Guillaume de Machaut (d. 1377). Machaut and his musical contemporaries became some of the first composers to achieve fame for their individual achievements. This further indicated that music was assuming a life apart from

76. Example of a trope text sung in the upper voice *(Stirps Jesse)* against an original Gregorian *Benedicamus Domino.* Early twelfth century. (Gleason, p. 33.)

worship. This contributed to the composers' growing tendency to use the liturgy as a setting for their compositions, regardless of whether the assembly was prayerfully engaged.

Textual Changes

The addition of numerous lines of music to a single melody can be a thing of great beauty. The simultaneous sounding of independent lines of music in polyphony, however, makes it difficult—especially for the musically untrained—to identify or reproduce any of the melodies in a piece. While this was no doubt inspiring music, the obscurity of the various melody lines made it inaccessible to most people. One could not leave church humming a polyphonic work.

This melodic obscurity found a parallel in the obscurity of the texts in the liturgical music of the day. The propers and ordinary of the Mass developed out of a common textual stock: psalms, litanies and traditional hymns or prayers. Even if the people did not speak Latin, years of listening to the sung *Sanctus* or other chants allowed them to become familiar with these texts. The simultaneous singing of one text in two or three different rhythms or the singing of two or three different texts at the same time did not allow for such familiarization.

Various developments in polyphony contributed to a progressive obscuring of liturgical chants. In organum, a trope or second text sometimes was sung against the original text [illustration 76]. At times, only a fragment of the original text was employed in the lower voice. This type of composition was called a *clausula.* A Latin text eventually was added to the upper voice(s) of the *clausula,* thus creating the motet. In some motets, a second text in Latin or French occasionally was added [illustration 77]. The resulting polytextuality greatly obscured the texts. This was true not only for the uneducated congregations of the time, but for any who heard such music. Thus even the great

77. Motet based on gradual for Easter, *Haec Dies* (This is the day), with a Latin text *Virgo virginum* (Virgin of virgins) in the second voice and either a Latin text *O mitissima* (O Sweetest virgin Mary) or an old French text *Quant voi* (When I see returning the summer season) in the upper voice. (Davidson and Apel, p. 33.)

linguist Erasmus (d. 1536) could complain about the obscurity of the liturgical texts [quotation 130].

Vernacular Song

Although it is not possible to keep people from singing, it is possible to restrict when and where their singing is allowed. At no time in the history of Christianity was the song of the people completely ignored. During the late Middle Ages, however, this singing was effectively excluded from eucharistic worship. The last song to be sung by the people at Mass was the *Sanctus.* Literary evidence suggests that in some places this ancient text was considered a chant of the people as late as the twelfth century. Musical evidence also attests to a lingering conviction that the *Sanctus* belonged to the people. When composers began to apply polyphonic techniques to the ordinary of the Mass, they did not write complete settings that would have included a *Kyrie, Gloria, Sanctus, Benedictus* and *Agnus Dei.* Rather, they set individual pieces. The *Sanctus* was one of the last parts of the ordinary to receive polyphonic treatment. What appears to be the oldest complete polyphonic setting of the ordinary, called "the Mass of Tournai," for example, includes polyphonic settings for every Mass part except the *Sanctus,* which is set monophonically. This does not necessarily mean that the congregation was able to sing this simpler setting of the *Sanctus.* It does, however, at least attest to the living memory that congregations once sang this part.

Ordinary people developed their own devotional songs and hymns in many countries. Vernacular forms in Spain and Portugal *(cantigas),* France *(cantiques),* England *(carols),* Germany *(Gleisslerlieder)* and Italy *(laude)* flourished. Vernacular songs also moved farther and farther away from the heart of the church's worship. Although limited evidence suggests that in some places vernacular songs might have been sung after the sermon, this was not a general practice. Popular musical efforts most often found a place in the flourishing devotions of the period and not in official worship.

Summary

Theodor Klauser refers to this era as the period of "dissolution, elaboration, reinterpretation, misinterpretation." This unflattering assessment underscores the basic liturgical tendencies of this period and the growing estrangement between the liturgy and its music. From the end of the eleventh century, Rome enacted a series of reforms aimed at reasserting its control over the Mass and imposing its liturgical practice on all of Latin Christianity. During this period, as well, John XXII

Quotation 131. *Certain disciples of a new school . . . are turning their attention to new kinds of music. . . . For they trivialize the melody with a second or third line and sometimes they go so far as to burden it with additional secular texts. . . . By the sheer number of additional notes the plain-chant melodies—with their modest ascending and descending patterns by which the various modes are distinguished—are obscured.* John XXII (d. 1334), *Teachings of the Holy Fathers*

(d. 1334) issued one of the first authentic papal documents specifically dealing with music, *Docta sanctorum patrum* (1324–1325 CE), which challenged the introduction of many contemporary compositional practices into the liturgical music of the day [quotation 131]. These did little to give the music and the liturgy back to the people.

The silencing of the people at liturgy certainly was related to the emphasis on the visual in medieval worship. For the congregation, watching from a distance was considered sufficient. Music developed as a professional enterprise that took on a life of its own apart from the worship. Participation in or understanding of the music or the liturgy of the day was unnecessary. Watching the sacred action—especially the elevation—was of primary importance. Singing was ultimately dispensable, as was demonstrated by the private or read Mass, which eliminated it altogether. Ultimately, the read Mass, not the sung Mass, became the norm in the Roman Catholic Church.

BOOKS

By the early Middle Ages, the practice of combining materials from two or more liturgical books into a single volume was well established. The lectionary, for example, was a combination of the epistolary and evangeliary; consequently, it contained all the readings necessary for the celebration of Mass. The pontifical gathered together all the texts that a bishop would need for eucharist and other special ceremonies. This general trend of consolidating texts into a single volume continued during the late Middle Ages. Although individual books of chants or readings continued to be produced, they generally were superseded by the full missal. The various directions for celebrating the different Masses and feasts of the year were consolidated into a book called the ordinary. This penchant for self-contained volumes for the clergy eventually spawned similar volumes for the laity.

Full Missal

The full missal already had appeared in some places by the ninth century. This volume was a combination of five other books (Mass antiphonary, epistolary, evangeliary, sacramentary and ordo) and enabled the priest to celebrate Mass by himself. Though rare before the turn of the millennium, the full missal became one of the most frequently produced manuscripts of the late Middle Ages. As the full missal became more popular, the sacramentary diminished in popularity [quotation 132].

Quotation 132. *In the first half of the twelfth century, the sacramentaries were a small minority, in the thirteenth they were exceptional and in the fourteenth they were archaic leftovers.* Vogel, p. 105

In Die Sancto Pasche. Ad Matutinas primitus sonet classicum. Postea sonent campane duppliciter et non dicatur *Ad Dominum*. Sollempnitas ista sollempnitatum dicitur. Matutine hoc modo celebrentur. Primitus abbas incipiat *Domine labia mea* at postea dicatur *Deus in adiutorium* et *Gloria Patri*. Post Gloriam statim cantetur Invit. *Alleluya Surrexit Dominus vere* inter duo altaria a IIII in cappis. Ps. *Venite exultemus*. Remaneant cantores in choro et non cantetur Hy. set mox incipiat ebdomadarius Ant. super Ps. *Ego sum qui sum*. Ps. *Beatus vir*. Ant. *Postulavi Patrem*. Ps. *Quare*. Ant. *Ego dormivi*. Ps. *Domine quid multiplicati*. Ant. omnes dicantur sine neumate et per totam ebdomadam. V. *Surrexit Christus*. Prima Lc. a diacono alba dalmatica induto qui veniens stet ante abbatem et abbas benedicat incensum . . .

On the Holy Day of Easter. At Matins first ring the bell. After that sound the tower bells in doublets. *To the Lord* is not said. This solemnity is called the feast of feasts. Matins is celebrated in this way: First the abbot begins *Lord, open my lips* and afterwards is said *O God, come to my assistance* and *Glory be to the Father*. Immediately after the doxology the invitatorium *Alleluia, the Lord is truly risen* is sung by four cantors in copes standing between the two altars with the Psalm *Come, let us sing joyfully*. The cantors remain in the choir. The hymn is not sung. The leader next begins the antiphon before the psalm *I am who am*. Psalm *Blessed is the man*. Antiphon *I asked the Father*. Psalm *Why*. Antiphon *I slept*. Psalm *Lord, how many*. All the antiphons are said without modulation through the whole week. Versicle *Christ rose*. The first reading is read by a deacon robed in a white dalmatic. He stands before the abbot who blesses the incense . . .

78. Directions for celebration of Easter from early thirteenth-century ordinary from the abbey of St.-Denis outside of Paris. A Latin transcription and English translation follow in which the rubrics are in plain type and the prayer texts are in italics. (Foley, *First Ordinary of the Royal Abbey of St.-Denis in France*, figure 27.)

As noted in the previous chapter, the full missal developed for a number of reasons. Chief among these were the requirements of the private Mass, the tendency to reduce sung texts to read texts and the increased demand for portable books in an age of pilgrimage and mission. During the late Middle Ages, the second reason—the tendency to recite song texts—came to the fore. Evidence exists that in some places priests previously had been reading song texts in the absence of a choir [quotation 115] or even repeating song texts privately while the choir sang them. This practice spread, and by the mid-thirteenth century, legislation appeared directing that all chant texts must be read by the presider [quotation 133].

Quotation 133. *[After the priest has kissed the altar] the deacon places the missal on the right side of the altar and the sub-deacon the gospel book on the left side. . . . Then all the ministers, assembling at the missal and standing to the right of the priest (in order of their rank) say the* Introit *and the* Kyrie eleison. *[Then all are seated while the choir finishes singing]. . . . At the end of the* Kyrie eleison *the priest rises from his seat and, standing in the middle of the altar . . . begins the* Gloria in excelsis—*if it is to be said that day—with the other ministers arranged behind him according to rank, as previously noted. When the priest says "Deo" he joins his hands. Then, beginning with the priest and the others following, they move to the right side of the altar where the other ministers stand to the right of the priest according to their rank, as previously noted. When they have finished saying the* Gloria, *the priest and deacon remain there while the choir completes the singing of it.* The Dominican Ordinary of 1267

Ordinary

In the centuries following the conversion of Constantine, collections of rubrics developed to help ministers execute the increasingly complex Roman liturgy. The earliest collection of these ordos dated from seventh-century Rome. During the period of Frankish domination, these collections were widespread and well used. By the late Middle Ages, new influences led to the gradual expansion of these ordos. One such influence was the desire to include instructions for all the days of the church year and not just those for the special rituals outlined in the ordos. Another factor was the need to use Roman rubrics in places other than Rome. This necessitated further adaptations of these collections. In the process, the rubrics were combined with the opening few words of the relevant liturgical texts [illustration 78]. The result was a new genre of liturgical book called the "ordinary" *(liber ordinarius)*. Like the ordo, the ordinary never was used during worship but rather was consulted beforehand in the preparation process. The ordinary was, therefore, an auxiliary liturgical book that supplied texts and directions for celebrating the offices, the eucharist and a variety of other rites and devotions. The book was arranged according to the liturgical calendar and usually was drawn up for a specific church or religious community. The local character of these books was one of their chief assets because, in the midst of the diverse liturgical practices of the Middle Ages, they could clarify how specific rites were enacted in particular monasteries or cathedrals. Ordinaries appeared for the first time in the twelfth century, but they soon became obsolete. Two main factors contributed to their obsolescence. The first was the growing presumption that every liturgical book should include both texts and rubrics. Thus one of the special features of the ordinary—the rubrics—

79. Two pages from the *Taymouth Hours,* an early fourteenth-century book of hours written for a noblewoman of the time, probably Joan, daughter of Edward II of England. The reproduced pages show the last page of a liturgical calendar, which began the book, and a prayer said before Mass *(Oreison avaunt la messe)* along with an illustration, possibly of the noblewoman herself attending Mass. Though the prayer is for before the Mass, the illustration is of the most characteristic and important ritual moment of the Mass, the elevation. (Harthan, p. 46.)

was incorporated into all liturgical books. A second factor was the gradual standardization of liturgical books in the West. This development eliminated the need for descriptions of local rites and customs, which were characteristic of the ordinary.

80. Mid-fifteenth century ciborium from southern Germany, consisting of a typical pyx-shaped container on a stem.

81. A fourteenth-century monstrance.

Prayer Books

In the previous era, special liturgical books were developed for the various ministers, but none remained for the use of the laity. Song-books went to the singers, epistolaries to the subdeacons, evangeliaries to the deacons, and so forth. The laity often was restricted even from carrying such books, which were entrusted to clerics in minor orders. Having been completely restricted from even handling the official books of the liturgy, the laity began to develop its own books. This process is not unrelated to the musical trends of the previous era: The people were completely eliminated from the official song of the liturgy and consequently developed their own religious song for use outside the confines of official worship.

Although liturgical books generally were the property of worshiping communities, evidence suggests that after the conversion of Constantine, some individuals had books for their personal prayers. The great Christian prayer book was the psalter, and some individuals— especially the wealthy or the powerful—had personal copies for their prayer [illustration 61]. Previous to the Carolingian period, the laity had no need for books to aid in following the eucharistic liturgy because the liturgy was in a language and style that the laity understood. By the end of that period, however, the progressive distancing and ultimate exclusion of the laity from the liturgy created a climate appropriate to the development of prayer books for lay use during and outside of the eucharist. Many times, these books did not offer a translation or even the original Latin text of the prayers that the priest prayed at the altar. Rather, these books often contained various psalms, litanies and offices of the dead or the Blessed Virgin. They were called "books of hours," or in England "the prymer." Eventually, eucharist-related prayers and meditations were added to these books of hours [illustration 79]. Close parallels to the priest's prayers sometimes were included in these books for almost the entire Mass. At other times, meditations or allegorical interpretations of the Mass were offered, and the layperson was instructed to pray so many Our Fathers and Hail Marys for each part of the Mass. Regardless of the style of a particular book, the canon of the Mass and the changeable propers were seldom, if ever, printed either in Latin or in translation.

Summary

The subdivision of the late medieval church building into various segments for choir, priest and laity found an analogue in the liturgical books of the day. Each group had its own place in the building, and the priest's place was the most important. Similarly, particular books

Quotation 134. *The plenary missal is . . . the result of a new way of regarding the Mass. The eucharistic celebration ceases to be an actio liturgica [liturgical action] in which the celebrant, ministers, singers and people collaborate and have distinctive and cooperative roles to play. As a result, the priest-celebrant, as the sole actor in this liturgical process, will be provided henceforth with a new kind of book.* Vogel, p. 105

developed for each group. The book for the priest unquestionably was the most important of these; it incorporated within its covers material from almost every other liturgical book. As Cyrille Vogel has noted, the full missal was not just a new book, it also was a symbol of a new understanding of the Mass [quotation 134]. Eucharist was celebrated almost in spite of the laity. In partial response to this, some people created their own books. Although a useful prayer aid, these individual prayer books contributed to the growing isolation of individuals, not only from the action of the priest but also from each other. Watching, listening and now reading were the basic forms of participation available to the community during the eucharist. Because of the widespread practice of silent Mass, the inability of most laity to understand Latin and the complexity of the music that might have been performed, listening was the least important mode of participating. Thus the assembly was left to watch the liturgy or to read during it. Although these activities offered some satisfaction to the laity, they also contributed to the people's liturgical isolation.

VESSELS

During the late Middle Ages, two somewhat contradictory trends influenced the development of eucharistic vessels. The first was a continued increase in the number of vessels for the bread. Most important was the emergence of vessels for the display of the host. As the kinds of vessels for the bread increased, the number of vessels or utensils for the wine decreased. These trends witnessed to the increased rarity of communion by the laity. During this era, the cup was entirely removed from the people. Communion for the laity was given only under the form of bread. Theologically, this practice was supported by the theory of "concomitance," which held that when the bread was consecrated into Christ's body, the blood of Christ also was present. Eventually, an increased emphasis on the unworthiness of the laity and a style of worship that emphasized the visual led to a further decline in communion. The acceptable substitute for actual communion was ocular communion, or watching the host.

Bread and Its Vessels

By the eleventh century, the use of unleavened bread, first noted in the ninth century, became universal in the West. The practice of baking hosts of two separate sizes—a larger one for the priest and smaller ones for lay communicants—also become general practice. As early as the fourteenth century, the baking of hosts had, in some places, become a business that required ecclesiastical approval.

82. Example of wall tabernacle, thirteenth century, from San Clemente in Rome (After Righetti, I:436.)

83. A late medieval sacrament house from Austria. (After Righetti, I:439.)

Quotation 135. *[Blessed Dorothy of Montau] was accustomed to go before dawn to the Church of Corpus Christi, which lay outside of Gdansk, in order to see the sacrament of the eucharist which was openly displayed there in a monstrance.* From the *Life of Dorothy of Montau* by Johannis Marienwerder

Quotation 136. *The blessed sacrament was instituted as food, not as a showpiece.* Cardinal Nicolas of Cusa (1450)

CIBORIUM   In this era, vessels for carrying the eucharist outside of the church began to be distinguished from those for reserving the eucharist within the church. The pyx was that type of vessel used for holding the eucharist outside of church, especially for carrying the eucharist to the sick. Eventually, the pyx also became an ordinary container for holding the eucharist for the communion of the faithful. This occurred, in part, because of the reduced size of the paten, which was large enough only for the one large host to be consumed by the priest. The smaller hosts baked for lay communicants had to be held by another vessel. Consequently, a distinctive pyx developed for use during Mass. This Mass-pyx was shaped like an ordinary pyx—often round, with a conical lid surmounted by a cross—but attached to a stem [illustration 80]. The Mass-pyx came to be called a ciborium.

MONSTRANCE   No vessel is more symbolic of eucharistic theology in the Middle Ages than the monstrance. It developed in response to an increased theological and devotional focus on the bread and the consequent desire of the people to see the host. Reflecting this trend was the introduction of the elevation of the bread during Mass, the emergence of feasts such as *Corpus Christi* (The Body of Christ) and the growing number of processions with the sacrament. All of these developed during in the thirteenth century. Eventually, specific vessels were fashioned for a more permanent display of the host. The first clear evidence of such vessels comes from the life of Dorothy of Montau (d. 1394), who was later beatified and declared patroness of Prussia. Her biographer noted Dorothy's intense devotion to the Blessed Sacrament and described how she daily went to pray before the Blessed Sacrament displayed in a monstrance [quotation 135].

Some monstrances survive from the fourteenth century. Certain of these were modeled after reliquaries of the time, which held relics in a glass or crystal cylinder. This evolution not only was the result of a practical adaptation of one vessel for another use, but it also was an implicit acknowledgment that the eucharist was the ultimate Christian relic, and Christ was the supreme martyr.

Eventually, the monstrance developed into a distinctive vessel consisting of a stem with a node and a flat window for a large host. Monstrances often were crowned by designs similar to the surrounding architecture [illustration 81]. The prevailing custom of fashioning sacred vessels out of gold or silver continued with the monstrance. Although some objection was voiced to the popularity of eucharistic exposition [quotation 136], this practice and its accompanying vessels developed further in the coming centuries.

Quotation 137. *We decree that in all churches, chrism and the eucharist should be reserved under the reliable protection of lock and key.* Fourth Lateran Council (1215), chapter 20

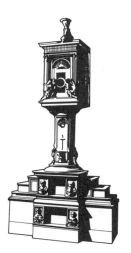

84. Sacrament house from Italy, which also allowed for permanent exposition of the sacrament.

85. Chalice, showing gothic architectural influence, with bells.

TABERNACLE   In many places, the eucharist continued to be reserved in a pyx suspended over the altar, in a special box or in a sacristy cupboard or closet. Eventually, more secure places for public reservation developed. Concern for the security of the sacrament prompted some councils of the period to suggest that, if possible, the eucharist should be kept under lock and key [quotation 137]. Permanent wall tabernacles began to be used in Italy by the twelfth century [illustration 82]. More common in northern Europe was the "sacrament house." These places of reservation were towering structures, resembling cathedral spires, often located within the sanctuary [illustration 83]. Some of these sacrament houses, as well as other tabernacles of the age, not only stored the sacrament but also allowed for its exposition [illustration 84].

CHALICES   While new vessels for the bread were developing, the number of vessels for the wine decreased. The chalice was a secondary vessel in terms of lay devotion, which was so influential in contributing to the development of other vessels. This was true because the cup was withdrawn from the people in most places by the twelfth century and was not an object of their devotion. Although it contained the blood of Christ, this species could not be seen during the liturgy nor easily reserved after it. Thus the eucharistic wine was not an object of intense veneration as the host was. Symptomatic of this was the belated introduction of the elevation of the chalice during Mass. Though some evidence suggests an elevation of the chalice as early as the thirteenth century, this was a rare occurrence. Rome made the elevation of the cup equal to the elevation of the bread only in the *Missal of Pius v* (1570).

Two-handled chalices fell into disuse during the late Middle Ages, and communion from the cup by the laity came to an end. The cup of a usual chalice of this period often was cone shaped and attached to a hexagonal or octagonal stem. The node often was enameled, carved with images or even shaped into an elaborate architectural design, reflecting the style of the surrounding building. Bells were added to some chalices, possibly to highlight their elevation [illustration 85]. The enlarged base of the chalice frequently was divided into six or eight compartments and adorned with enameled medallions. Various synods regulated the materials acceptable in the fabrication of chalices. Wood, glass and copper usually were forbidden. Tin was permitted, often as a concession to poor churches, while gold and silver were preferred [quotation 123].

Quotation 138. *Hold up, Sir John, hold up. Heave it a little higher.* Fortescue, pp. 341–42

Quotation 139. *Let all the faithful of both sexes, having arrived at the age of reason, alone faithfully confess all his sins to the appropriate priest at least once each year, and with all his strength he should try to fulfill the imposed penance, reverently accepting the sacrament of the eucharist at least during Easter.* Fourth Lateran Council, chapter 21

Summary

More than any other time in the Christian tradition, the late Middle Ages was a period when seeing was believing. Belief for most Christians was inspired and sustained by seeing the host; viewing the consecrated bread was the ritual high point of eucharistic devotion. It also was the context of enormous superstition. People believed that gazing on the host would prevent them from losing their eyesight that day and would keep them from starvation as well as from sudden death. Seeing the host was of such importance that priests were sometimes paid a special stipend for prolonging the elevation or inserting other elevations, for example, after the "Lamb of God." A story is told of a congregation in England crying out to the presider to lift the host higher if it could not readily be seen [quotation 138]. The vessels of the period reflected this preoccupation with the bread. Receiving the wine became unthinkable. Receiving the bread became dangerous and so infrequent that the church had to mandate yearly reception [quotation 139]. Seeing the bread became the ultimate substitute for receiving it.

CLOTHILDE

Although it was winter and she could feel the dampness of the stone pavement through her many layers of clothing, Clothilde never considered standing. She remembered being taught as a child that the raising of the host was the most sacred of all events; even the trees swayed in adoration at the elevation of the wafer. And, as her mother often reminded her, if nature in all its majesty was so responsive, then Clothilde, as one of the least of God's creatures, should kneel as well.

After the priest lowered the host to the altar and genuflected slowly, Clothilde struggled to her feet. This past winter her arthritis had worsened. She found it difficult to kneel and even more difficult to get up. Now that her children were grown with families of their own, Clothilde no longer had their help when she visited the cathedral. But this has never stopped her from making her daily pilgrimage to the great church at Chartres.

Clothilde walked away from the side altar of St. Martin, slowly working the blood back into her aching legs. She gazed into the vault as the sunshine exploded against the clerestory windows on the south wall of the nave. Although she had been there a thousand times before, Clothilde never ceased to marvel at the miraculous windows and their many moods in the shifting sunlight. Only God could have imagined so many shades of blue! As she watched the colors play against the stone, she thought of her husband who had worked on the cathedral for so many years. It was while he was working on the roof in the south transept that the accident occurred. The funeral in the unfinished cathedral seemed a fitting memorial to a man who had labored in this building his entire lifetime. Although it was almost 30 years since his death, Clothilde always felt a special closeness to him when she was in "their" cathedral.

As she lowered her eyes from the ceiling, Clothilde noted an unusual amount of movement within the great church that morning. There was always a flurry of activity within the cathedral, but this Sunday seemed to be an especially busy one. Dozens of small groups clustered around the innumerable altars in the church, attending Mass. All the while, scores of visitors from near and far roamed the cathedral, gaping at the stained glass or buying candles from one of the many stalls along the south aisles of the church. Some days, there seemed to be as many vendors as visitors, selling everything from herbal medicines to relics of the Three Kings. Clothilde herself had once owned a piece of cloth that had touched a relic of the true cross. She gave her little treasure to a friend whose child was sick with fever. After the child recovered, Clothilde left the relic with the family who now had a special devotion to the cross.

Like all of the townspeople of Chartres, Clothilde was proud of the cathedral. But more than the towers, the stained glass or the soaring vault, nothing was more prized than the veil of the Blessed Virgin. It was this mantle of the Mother of God that spurred the townspeople to build such a monumental edifice, and it was this precious relic that served as the focus for endless pilgrimages. Even now a large group of pilgrims was making their way around the ambulatory on their knees to the altar where the tunic was displayed.

Clothilde herself was thinking of making a visit to the Lady Chapel to view the relic when a bell rang, announcing the beginning of the bishop's Mass. Although she seldom attended the whole Mass, Clothilde did enjoy the opening flourishes of this ritual. From the side sacristy, she could see the long procession beginning. First out the door was a large young man carrying the bishop's cross emblazoned with his coat of arms. A stream of singers and minor clergy followed. Clothilde never could remember who among these was a priest, who was going to be a priest or who wasn't going to be a priest. She decided years ago that the simplest solution to this dilemma was to call all of them "Father." That way she never would be embarrassed and they never would be offended. After the real and would-be "Fathers" came the canons of the cathedral, wrapped in layers of purple and white. Their robes were certainly more beautiful than anything Clothilde had ever owned. Some of their garments were lined with fur—a luxurious antidote to the winter chill. At the end of the procession was the mitered archbishop. As he passed, the crowds knelt, receiving a blessing from the gloved hand adorned with a huge amethyst ring.

The music that accompanied the procession was glorious. The organ played a slow, simple tune that the choir embellished with melody upon melody. As the *Introit* ushered the archbishop into the sanctuary, the gates of the great screen closed behind him. She still could hear the music on the other side of the screen, but she no longer was able to watch the ritual. It was just as well, Clothilde thought to herself, for it was time to make her own pilgrimage to the Virgin's veil. Turning away from the barred sanctuary, Clothilde hurried to the Lady Chapel where she would join her friends in prayer. Even as she entered the ambulatory she could hear the invitation from the distance, *"Ave Maria, gratia plena . . ."*

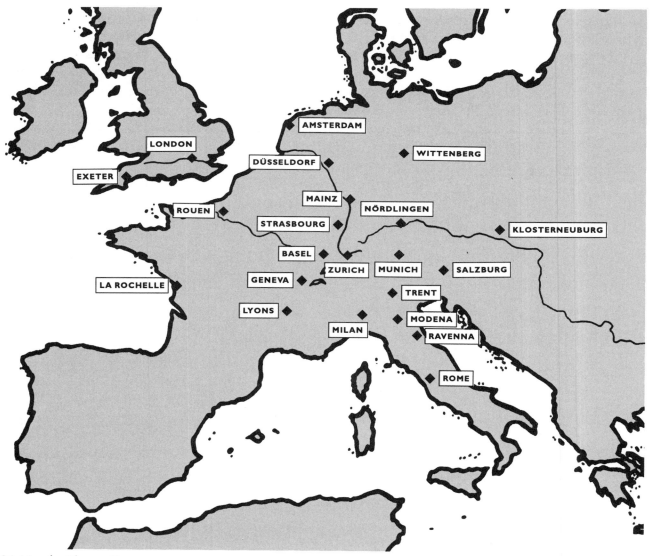

86. Map for Chapter Six.

CHAPTER SIX

Revolt,

Reform and Rigidity:

1517 to 1903

The liturgical disintegration of the late Middle Ages was symbolic of a church in serious political and moral decline. The fourteenth and fifteenth centuries in particular were a time of greed and corruption in the church. Lust for personal gain was a contributing factor in the Great Western Schism (1378–1417 CE), which resulted in the simultaneous existence of three rival popes.

The papacy had been acquired by several unsavory individuals through financial intrigue and deceit. Alexander VI (d. 1503) virtually bought the papacy in 1492 by promising lucrative appointments to those cardinals who would vote for him. As pontiff, Alexander had affairs with prominent noblewomen and fathered many children.

Because the Vatican as a sovereign state played a critical role in international politics, popes often were mired in secular schemes to protect or expand their territories and influence. Popes such as Julius II (d. 1513) were more warriors than ecclesiastics.

It was only in 1517, when the Augustinian monk Martin Luther (d. 1546) challenged the prevailing theology of his day by nailing his 95 theses to a church door in Wittenberg, that the church awakened to the nightmare of its laxity and corruption. Reform ensued, but it was achieved, tragically, at the price of Christian unity.

That the Reformation took place is not surprising. What is surprising is that it took so long to occur. This era certainly had its quota of saints and honorable clerics, who recognized the corruption around them [quotation 140]. But despite innumerable calls for reform, the general malaise of the late medieval church made radical, voluntary renewal an impossibility.

While liturgical matters were not the primary reason for the reform, liturgy's capacity for expressing the lived faith of the church placed it squarely in the midst of the controversy. One great scandal of the period, for example, was the way that bishops and princes treated the church as a private possession. The ability to buy or sell church

Quotation 140. *Depravity has become so taken for granted that those soiled by it no longer notice the stench of sin.* Hadrian VI (d. 1523), as cited in Jedin V:7

87. Bramante's second groundplan for St. Peter's (After Norberg-Schulz, p. 245.)

Quotation 141. *It is also considered an abuse that a priest would accept gifts from several people for the celebration of Mass and then seek to satisfy these requests with only a single Mass. This admitted abuse leaves a lasting impression, because the title of Mass is actually applied to simple monetary gains. Herein are innumerable scandals, and no little harm thus befalls Christ the Lord and the church. . . . The abuse also is noted that while the conventual Mass is being celebrated, cadavers are carried into church, which completely disrupts the sacred rites. . . . Still more serious is the oft-noted scandalous act of very many priests who balance the chalice on their head with both hands after the consecration, so that sometimes . . . there is the greatest danger of spilling the chalice. Abuses relating to the sacrifice of the Mass, reported by a specially appointed commission of the Council of Trent (8 August 1562)*

property or hierarchical offices contributed to the widespread belief that God's favor likewise could be bought and sold. The marketing of indulgences and Mass intentions confirmed this as a commonly accepted tenet of the medieval church. In reaction, Luther emphasized that the laity—not the hierarchy or nobility—comprised the church. Furthermore, he stressed that God's favor could not be earned or purchased, but was a free gift in Jesus Christ. This translated into simplified liturgical forms, frequent communion, the return of the cup to the people, emphasis on community singing and the preaching of scripture. It also resulted in the elimination of sacrificial language from this new genre of worship.

For reasons yet to be completely understood, Luther's personal revolt was the key that unlocked a tidal wave of dissent within the Roman church. Although various reform movements had arisen during the fourteenth and fifteenth centuries, none of these had challenged the church at its core. A host of political, social and theological factors made Luther's challenge different.

In opposition to the reformers, Rome eventually convened a reforming council at Trent (1545–1563). While condemning the teachings of the reformers, the church implicitly acknowledged many of the abuses that had sparked the revolt [quotation 141]. The Council of Trent achieved important reforms within the church. As a result of this council, for example, the training of the clergy was greatly improved, regular preaching was returned to Sunday worship, and the people received better preparation for receiving the sacraments.

To some extent, however, the reforms achieved by Trent were more matters of discipline than of doctrine. The Roman church held fast to most of the teachings and practices attacked by the reformers. The result was a kind of theological entrenchment that lasted until the twentieth century. A similar stance emerged within many strands of Protestantism during these centuries. The enormous diversity among the various Protestant churches, however, prevented any one set of teachings and practices from becoming a predominant characteristic of the reform.

ARCHITECTURE

Ecclesiastical architecture of the sixteenth century was, largely, either a celebration of or a reaction to the church of Rome. Confronted with the challenge of the Reformation, the Roman Catholic Church responded by announcing its own orthodoxy in an unabashed display of triumphalism. This triumphalism translated into an exuberant and monumental architectural style that came to be known as baroque.

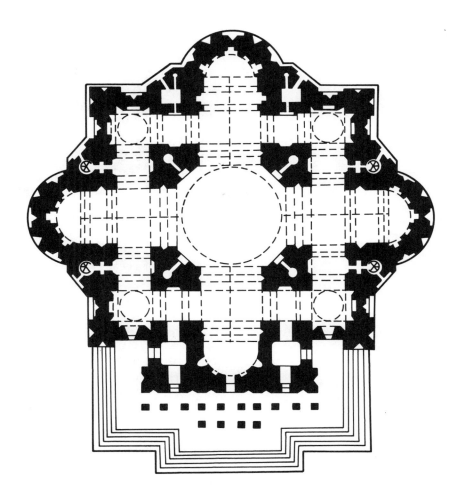

88. Michelangelo's plan for St. Peter's. (After Gardner, p. 552.)

Although various other architectural styles such as rococo and neo-classicism ensued, they never displaced baroque as the symbol of the Tridentine church.

In reaction, many Protestant communities initially sought to create simpler worship settings that were more concerned with enabling the community to hear and respond to the word than with creating a visual impression. Eventually, both sides of the Reformation influenced each other architecturally. Catholic buildings became more suited to preaching and many Protestants adopted the exuberance and dynamism of the baroque.

St. Peter's in Rome

More than any other building project of the sixteenth century, the reconstruction of St. Peter's in Rome chronicled the transition from Renaissance to baroque architecture. The fourth-century basilica built

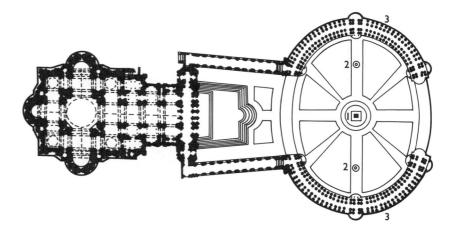

1. Obelisk
2. Fountain
3. Colonnade

89. Groundplan of St. Peter's with Bernini's piazza (After Gardner, p. 635.)

Quotation 142. *Since the church of St. Peter's is the mother of nearly all the others, it had to have colonnades, which would show it as if stretching out its arms maternally to receive Catholics, so as to confirm them in their faith, heretics, to reunite them to the Church, and infidels, to enlighten them in the true faith.* Bernini, translated by Norberg-Schulz

by Constantine had been in disrepair for some time when Julius II laid the cornerstone for the new church in 1506. The sixteenth-century church was first conceived in grand Renaissance style. Donato Bramante (d. 1514) designed a central-plan space consisting of a series of small Greek crosses surrounding one large Greek cross [illustration 87]. This plan would express symbolically this church's position at the center of the Western church, Christianity and the world. After Bramante's death, work slowed until Michelangelo (d. 1564) took over as architect in 1546. By simplifying Bramante's design and enclosing the space in a transverse square, Michelangelo converted St. Peter's from a Renaissance work of static symmetry to one of massive but dynamic unity, announcing the onset of baroque [illustration 88].

After Michelangelo's death, the plan of St. Peter's was altered by the addition of a nave, transforming it from a Greek cross to a Latin cross [illustration 89]. This addition better accommodated the Roman liturgy and the processions that were so integral to that liturgy. Unfortunately, the addition obscured Michelangelo's great dome, which now can be appreciated only from the back of the building. The final step in St. Peter's transition from a Renaissance building to a baroque one was the addition of a piazza designed by Gianlorenzo Bernini (d. 1680). This 645-foot piazza is surrounded by a two-armed, elliptical colonnade that consists of 284 travertine columns surmounted by 162 12-foot-high statues of saints [illustration 89]. Dedicated in 1666, Bernini's piazza is one of the most dramatic public spaces ever created. True to the artist's intentions [quotation 142], the piazza beckons all into the embrace of the mother church of Rome.

Baroque

Among the first of the true baroque churches stands Il Gesù (The Church of Jesus), the mother church of the Jesuits. Il Gesù embodied the vitality and ingenuity of this new community and its founder, Ignatius Loyola (d. 1556). The Jesuits were a novel form of religious life in the sixteenth century: highly centralized, well organized, mobile and free from the demands of a common liturgical life. Designed and built between 1568 and 1584, Il Gesù became one of the most copied designs in ecclesiastical history [illustration 90]. Its popularity was the result of a number of important innovations including the shortening of the apse, the removal of the choir from its place between the altar and the congregation, and the elimination of side aisles. The result was a large open space with its central area emphasized by a dome. Like the hall churches of thirteenth-century Germany, which were popular with medieval preaching orders, these churches gave new attention to the pulpit and the function of preaching. With no choir of monks to obstruct the view and no elongated apse to distance the people from the sacred action, Il Gesù drew the laity into closer proximity to the liturgical action. The people's direct participation, however, remained extraneous to the church's official liturgy. Although fanciful variations on the central plan would be built in the following centuries, these did little to mute the impact of Il Gesù on church architecture of this period.

Reformation Churches

Reform communities initially took over existing churches and adapted them to their own needs, sometimes removing statuary and iconography. In England, the rood screens that divided the church into a nave and a choir area [illustration 91] often were maintained: The nave was

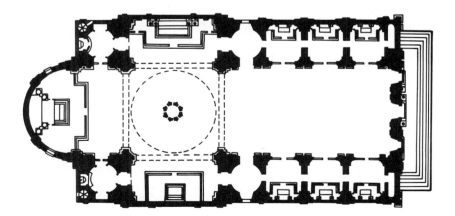

90. Groundplan, Il Gesù (After Norberg-Schulz, p. 277.)

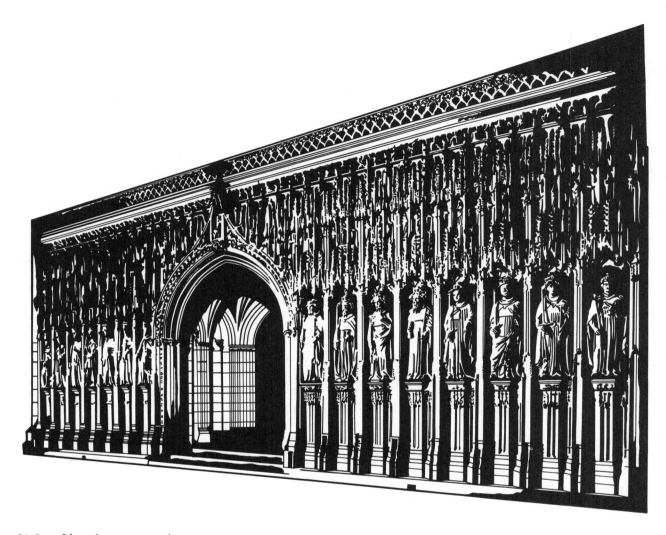

91. Late fifteenth-century rood screen from York Cathedral in England.

used by the assembly for Matins and Evensong, and the choir area was employed for communion services. On the continent, rood screens usually were removed, along with the elaborate reredos and tabernacles. In Calvinist churches, the pulpit was commonly placed in the center. Dissatisfaction with such renovations as well as the need for additional churches led to the creation of new buildings for Protestant worship. One principle common to all these new churches was the centrality of the pulpit [illustration 92], which underscored the centrality of preaching in Protestant worship. As preaching increased in importance, the communion service diminished in many traditions. Consequently, a fixed altar often was eliminated.

As Spiro Kostof has noted, this emerging Protestant architecture meant "a shift from a processional to an auditorium space, from a

92. St. George's United Methodist
Church in Philadelphia, built in 1769.

Quotation 143. *The Romanists, indeed,*
may build larger churches, it is enough
if they hear the murmur of the Mass and
see the elevation of the host, but ours are
to be fitted for auditories. Christopher
Wren (d. 1723) as cited in Addleshaw
and Etchells

Quotation 144. *At Saint Alphege . . . in*
1620, Mr. Loveday was reported for sitting
in the same pew with his wife "which
being held to be highly indecent" he was
ordered to appear; failing to do so,
"Mr. Chancellor was made acquainted"
with his obstinacy. The matter was finally
compromised by the rector giving him
a seat in his pew. John Neal, *History*
of Pues, p. 35

longitudinal to a centralizing plan." Thus the growing emphasis on the visual elements of worship, which especially marked the medieval period, was rejected by major segments of the Reformation. The emphasis on preaching compelled Reformation architects to construct buildings more suitable for hearing than for seeing [quotation 143]. Although benches and stools were in use before the Reformation, the new concern for the hearing of the word contributed to the increased popularity of seating in both Protestant and Catholic churches especially in northern Europe and North America [illustration 92]. In some cases, the introduction of pews coincided with a renewed separation of women and men during worship [quotation 144].

Summary

The changes in worship caused by the Reformation and the Counter-Reformation produced several contradictory architectural trends during the sixteenth century and beyond. Both the Protestant and Catholic reforms renewed the emphasis on preaching, which resulted in churches being designed with shorter apses and other concessions to acoustical concerns. While Protestants generally preferred few embellishments for their churches and often favored central-plan spaces, Roman Catholics embraced the triumphalism and visual display of the baroque.

93. La Scala theatre in Milan (1776–1778). (After Kostof, p. 522.)

Heroic longitudinal designs similar to Il Gesù were the fullest realization of this preference.

It is not a coincidence that this theatrical style of church architecture developed at the same time that opera was emerging as a popular secular art form. To house these often extravagant productions, magnificent new theaters appeared throughout Europe. These theaters consisted of an auditorium with seats for the spectators and a clearly demarcated stage area for the drama [illustration 93]. Similarly, the baroque Roman Catholic Church could be considered an immense ecclesiastical theater divided into an auditorium for the spectators and a holy stage where the drama of redemption was enacted. This style eventually spread beyond denominational borders, and in the following centuries, many Protestant and even Jewish worship spaces were constructed in the baroque style.

As the theological creativity of the Reformation and the Counter-Reformation waned, the church authorities occupied themselves with apologetics rather than speculative theology. They were more concerned with defending previously defined positions than in exploring new doctrinal territory. Despite the advent of the Enlightenment and the intellectual vigor of the eighteenth and nineteenth centuries, the churches entered a period of doctrinal and liturgical stagnation. Popular devotion, in turn, reached new levels of romanticism and sentimentality. Doctrinal stagnation and devotional romanticism found their architectural parallel in the devolution of the baroque—epitomized by the furiously designed St. John Nepomuk in Munich (1733–1746)—and the numerous architectural revivals that marked these centuries. Noteworthy among the revivals were those of the classical, Gothic and Romanesque architecture during the eighteenth and nineteenth centuries. Few fresh ideas emerged in church life or architecture until the twentieth century.

MUSIC

While architectural innovation during the reform might have radiated from Rome, innovations in liturgical music—especially in congregational song—belonged to the reformers. The reasons for this included the musical skill of early reformers such as Martin Luther, the Reformation's focus on the word coupled with music's ability to serve the word, and the strong tradition of vernacular song in the German-speaking countries where the reform began. While reformers emphasized congregational song, the Roman Catholic Church sought a more restrained style of Latin polyphony. The influence of Reformation hymnody, however, could not be avoided completely. As Protestant composers continued to explore hymnody and its many derivatives, Roman Catholic music—like the surrounding architecture—drifted toward the theatrical. In both traditions, the influence of opera and orchestral music was unmistakable.

Reformation Song

In some ways, Martin Luther was a better pastoral musician than he was a systematic theologian. Convinced of the primacy of the word of God, Luther also was convinced that music was a most important way to communicate that word [quotation 145]. Dedicated to the idea of the priesthood of all believers, Luther shifted the emphasis from the music of professional musicians to that of the congregation. With simple musical and textual building blocks—many of them

Quotation 145. *Next to the word of God, music deserves the highest praise. . . . The Holy Ghost himself honors her as an instrument for his proper work when in his Holy Scriptures he asserts that through her his gifts were instilled in the prophets. . . . Thus it was not without reason that the fathers and prophets wanted nothing else to be associated as closely with the word of God as music.* Martin Luther, "Preface to Georg Rhau's *Symphoniae iucundae*" (1538), translated by Ulrich Leupold

94. "A Mighty Fortress" by Martin
Luther. (Leupold, p. 284.)

95. Psalm 136 from the 1562 *Geneva
Psalter.* (Grout, p. 317.)

borrowed—Luther constructed scripturally based music that was
both singable and enduring. His melodies usually were written in
stepwise motion, within the range of a ninth, in syllabic settings, often
employing a self-rehearsing musical form [illustration 94]. His ability
to construct such accessible music contributed mightily to the effectiveness of his reform. Better than anyone else, Luther was able to
transform nonliturgical, religious song into liturgical music. By doing
so, he further integrated the community and vernacular hymnody into
the worship.

Although Luther's influence was widespread, his views were not
shared by every reformer. Ulrich Zwingli (d. 1531), for example,
considered music to be an essentially secular element that had no place
in worship. The most musically gifted of the reformers, Zwingli
eliminated all music from the churches in Zurich during his lifetime.
John Calvin (d. 1564) held the middle ground between Luther and

Zwingli. He banned polyphony from worship because it obscured the word; he also thought that instrumental music distracted one from God. Calvin did allow, however, monophonic singing, especially of the psalms [illustration 95].

The Catholic Response

Aware of the many musical and liturgical abuses that helped bring about the Reformation, the Council of Trent emphasized intelligibility and restraint in church music [quotation 146]. In language reminiscent of John XXII [quotation 131], the 22nd session of the Council (17 September 1562) issued a supplemental decree that banished from the church all music that contained things "lascivious or impure." While Trent sought to restrain composers and performers from indulging in the theatrics of secular music, it never challenged the domination of liturgical singing by professional musicians. Insistence on the intelligibility of texts, for example, referred only to the intelligibility of Latin texts, which generally were not understood by the laity. Although some Roman Catholic leaders favored a vernacular liturgy, this proposal was rejected by Trent. The suggestion that polyphony should be banned from the eucharist also was dismissed.

Quotation 146. Whenever there is singing with the organ in the context of the divine services . . . the texts are to be recited in a clear and simple voice beforehand so that the eternal recitation of the sacred texts may not elude anyone. The whole reason for singing in musical modes is not to give empty pleasure to the ear but so that the words may be understood by all. Discussion at the Council of Trent (10 September 1562)

96. "Kyrie" from Palestrina's *Missa Papae Marcelli* composed c. 1561. (Eulenburg edition.)

97. Top half of page one of Orazio Benevoli's *Missa salisburgansis*, Kyrie. (*Denkmaler der Tonkunst in Oster-reich*, 20:1.)

The reaffirmation of Latin and polyphony, plus the paradoxical emphasis on intelligibility, meant Trent's implicit affirmation of the work of Giovanni da Palestrina (d. 1594). More than any other composer of the Counter-Reformation, Palestrina achieved a clarity and restraint that respected both the dictates of the Council as well as the church's polyphonic tradition. Although Palestrina was a polyphonic composer, his works had a certain affinity with the hymnody of Martin Luther. Like Luther, Palestrina often wrote parts in stepwise motion, frequently within the range of a ninth, relying on consonant harmonies, avoiding chromaticisms, while demonstrating great respect for the text [illustration 96]. In June of 1563, Palestrina performed one of his Masses in the Sistine Chapel, after which the pope affirmed Palestrina's music. Throughout the following centuries, his music was celebrated as the liturgical ideal of the Roman Catholic Church, to be treasured and emulated.

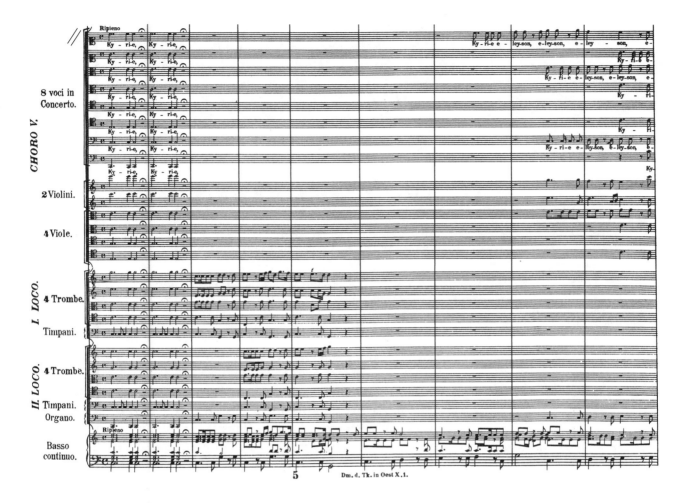

Bottom half of *Missa Salisburgansis,*
Kyrie.

Although Trent did not support vernacular singing, the tradition of popular hymnody fueled by the Reformation spurred the growth of such music within the Roman Catholic Church. The first vernacular Catholic hymnal was Michael Vehe's *A New Little Songbook of Spiritual Hymns* (1537). Many others appeared throughout Germany during the sixteenth century. Although these contained mostly devotional or catechetical hymns, some were used in worship, for example, after the sermon. The *Cantual of Mainz* (1605) borrowed an idea from Luther and allowed the substitution of German hymns for the proper of the Mass. By the eighteenth century, hymns were permitted in some places as substitutes for the ordinary of the Mass. This *Singmesse* gave the people a new sense of participation. In the New World, too, vernacular hymnody was taking root. By 1787, for example, American Catholics had their first collection of vernacular hymns in John Aitken's *A Compilation of the Litanies and Vesper Hymns and Anthems*

Quotation 147. *[On Sundays and feast-days] Mass is to be solemnly celebrated with song. . . . It is hoped that during the various services some hymns or prayers in the vernacular would be sung.* First National Synod in Baltimore (1791), 17

Quotation 148. *The victorious temper of the post-Tridentine age, which once more felt the courage to absorb the entire wealth of the contemporary culture into the Catholic cosmos . . . found its triumphal voice in this music. . . . It sometimes happened that this church music, which had fallen more and more into the hands of laymen, forgot that it was meant to serve the liturgical action. As a result of this, the music often fitted very poorly into the liturgical setting. And since this latter was but little understood, and because esthetic consideration began to hold sway, the liturgy was not only submerged under this ever-growing art but actually suppressed, so that even at this time there were festival occasions which might best be described as "church concerts with liturgical accompaniment."* Jungmann I:148–149

Quotation 149. *I have found to my astonishment that the Catholics, who have had music in their churches for several centuries, and sing a musical Mass every Sunday if possible, in their principal churches, do not to this day possess one which can be considered even tolerably good, or in fact, which is not actually distasteful and operatic. This is the case from Pergolese and Durante, who introduced the most laughable little trills into their Gloria, down to the opera finales of the present day. Were I a Catholic, I would set to work at a Mass this very evening; and whatever it might turn out, it would at all events be the only Mass written with a constant remembrance of its sacred purpose.* Felix Mendelssohn, Letter to Pastor Bauer, Dusseldorf (January 12, 1835) as cited in Wienandt.

as They Are Sung in the Catholic Church (Philadelphia, 1787). Although vernacular hymnody was recommended by the First National Synod in Baltimore in 1791 [quotation 147], it remained an isolated trend in the church. Congregational participation never became central to Catholic worship and thus any congregational song was more music *in* worship than music *of* worship. The assembly still was musically dispensable.

Elaboration, Reform and Sentimentality

Although it took longer to develop, the characteristics that marked baroque architecture during the sixteenth and seventeenth centuries also came to mark baroque music during the seventeenth and eighteenth centuries. Especially under the influence of opera, sacred music in almost every denomination underwent a process of elaboration [quotation 148]. Contrary to the will of Calvin, who sanctioned only single-line melodies, Calvinists turned to multiple-part settings for the psalter. Composers of the English reform wrote polyphonic anthems and settings of the Service, which included music for Morning Prayer, Evening Prayer and Holy Communion. Lutherans composed Masses, chorale motets, chorale concerti and chorale or church cantatas. In the Catholic Church, the compositional restraint of Palestrina was abandoned. Massive choral works such as the 53-part *Missa salisburgensis* by Orazio Benevoli (d. 1672) [illustration 97], instrumental church music such as the *sonata da chiesa* of Arcangelo Corelli (d. 1713) and operatic vocal compositions such as the *Stabat Mater* by Giovanni Pergolesi (d. 1736) overwhelmed the worship [quotation 149].

While opera influenced the composition of larger ecclesiastical works, a new spirit of pietism influenced the smaller congregational works of the era. Inspired by English Puritanism and the Swiss reform, pietism emerged in seventeenth-century Lutheranism. Its emphasis on the personal piety and morality of believers eventually influenced the congregational song of all denominations. One result of this movement was a rich and beautiful body of hymnody [illustration 98]. These hymns consisted of simple texts written in the first person singular and wedded to attractive and accessible melodies. In the hands of less-talented composers and poets, however, another result was sentimental, formulaic and unimaginative music.

Important moderating voices did exist in the midst of the theatrical and pietistic tendencies of the seventeenth and eighteenth centuries. Because the organ and other instruments were forbidden in the papal chapel, the *a cappella* style of Palestrina found a permanent home and sponsor in Rome. In Germany, the Lutheran master Johann Sebastian Bach (d. 1750) was a thoroughly liturgical baroque composer who

98. Example of a pietist hymn with tune by Johann Cruger (d. 1662) and text by Johann Franck (d. 1677). "Jesus, priceless treasure," translation by Catherine Winkworth (d. 1878). *(The Catholic Hymnal and Service Book,* Benziger, 125)

could illuminate a text while achieving new heights of musical expression. By the end of the eighteenth century, however, liturgical music was in a general state of decline as the churches were displaced as patrons of the arts by secular princes. Although a few great religious works were written for the church (such as the Masses of Mozart, d. 1791), most, like Beethoven's (d. 1827) *Missa Solemnis* or Brahms' (d. 1897) *Ein deutsches Requiem,* were written for the concert hall. The predominance of the low Mass in Roman Catholicism resulted in a great decline in the number of Mass compositions. Instead, incidental motets and organ interludes occupied church composers.

The emergence of sacred art-music for the concert hall was met by a new reform in Catholic church music. This Catholic restoration movement sought a return to Gregorian chant and polyphony in the style of Palestrina. One of the most celebrated proponents of this reform was the Society of St. Cecilia, whose work was sanctioned by Pius IX in 1870. Although it was effective in rejecting the elaborations characteristic of the baroque and romantic periods, this reform virtually eliminated all vernacular music from Roman Catholic worship. While vernacular hymnody flourished in the various reform traditions, it could not escape the effects of pietism and personalism that marked the eighteenth and nineteenth centuries. Consequently, much of the hymnody of this period is marked by romanticism and sentimentality.

Summary

Although the various reforms that erupted during the sixteenth century were not musical at their root, the music of the period reflected the positions of the Reformation and the Counter-Reformation. In the ensuing centuries, music continued to symbolize the basic tendencies of Protestant and Catholic theology and worship. In general, the Protestant churches rejected the emphasis on the visual that was increasingly characteristic of Roman Catholic worship and turned instead to the auditory. Luther's belief in the word, and in music's ability to serve the word, was critical to this development. The Roman Catholic Church corrected many musical and liturgical abuses but ultimately maintained its affirmation of the primacy of the visual elements of worship. Celebrated for its architectural developments during this period, the Roman Catholic Church made few musical concessions to the members of the assembly in its reform. Consequently, they were reduced to silent spectators.

BOOKS

The impact of the printing press on the Reformation and Counter-Reformation cannot be overstated. Johann Gutenberg (d. 1468) is credited with inventing movable type toward the end of the 1440s. The early alliance between this new technology and religion is symbolized by Gutenberg's first printed book: the 42-line Bible (1453–1455). Almost 100 printings of the Vulgate appeared by the year 1500. In addition to being used to reproduce the Bible or classical texts, this new

99. Woodcut portrait of Martin Luther on the title page of his pamphlet, *The Babylonian Captivity of the Church,* printed in Strasbourg by Johann Pruess in 1520.

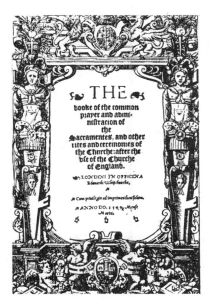

100. Title Page of the first edition of the *Book of Common Prayer or the First Prayer Book of King Edward VI*, published in London in 1549.

Quotation 150. *With Gutenberg, Europe enters the technological phase of progress, when change itself becomes the archetypal norm of social life.* McLuhan, p. 155

Quotation 151. *I would gladly have a German Mass today. I am also occupied with it. But I would very much like it to have a true German character. For to translate the Latin text and retain the Latin tone or notes has my sanction, though it doesn't sound polished or well done. Both the text and notes, accent, melody, and manner of rendering ought to grow out of the true mother tongue and its inflection, otherwise all of it becomes an imitation in the manner of the apes.* Martin Luther, *Against the Heavenly Prophets* (1524), translated by Leupold

invention also could be employed to disseminate new ideas through books, pamphlets and even single pages. Given the debate that would arise over the selling of indulgences in Luther's time, it is ironic that the earliest datable example of printing from movable type is a letter of indulgence issued by Pope Nicholas V in 1451 and printed by Gutenberg in 1454.

Printing enabled the rapid exchange of ideas and served as a catalyst for change [quotation 150]. Paradoxically, it also served to stem the tide of change by creating new standards of uniformity. Previous to the printing press, manuscripts had to be copied by hand. Sometimes errors were made, changes introduced or glosses added to these texts. No matter how conscientious the scribe, no two medieval manuscripts were exactly alike. Even changes in the Roman Canon— whose very title means unchanging—were commonplace. The printing press, however, made it possible to produce identical copies of the same book. A new age of uniformity had begun.

Protestant Books

In the early stage of the reform, printed liturgical books seldom were meant to be comprehensive. Often a combination of instruction, rite and commentary, these books frequently had more affinity with the primitive church orders than with the liturgical books of the Middle Ages.

EARLY EFFORTS   In 1520, Luther issued a formal attack on the church's sacramental system in his pamphlet *The Babylonian Captivity of the Church* [illustration 99]. Although this document severely criticized the Roman liturgy, Luther did not publish a revision of the eucharist. On Christmas of 1521, he did celebrate in Wittenberg a modified Mass that eliminated the canon and set the words of institution in German. The first published reformed Mass was probably the 1522 *Evangelical Mass* of the Carmelite brothers in Nördlingen. In 1523, another Mass was authored by the Anabaptist Thomas Müntzer, who also published a German setting of the Divine Office. In December of 1523, Luther finally published *The Rite for Mass and Communion for the Church of Wittenberg*. This Latin revision satisfied few reformers—including its author [quotation 151]—who continued to produce vernacular liturgies. Zwingli's pamphlet *An Attack upon the Canon of the Mass* (1523) included a proposal for the reform of the Eucharist. His *Action or Use of the Lord's Supper* (1525) offered an even more radical revision. In 1524, Diebold Schwartz published a vernacular rite in Strasbourg. About the same time, William Farel prepared the first reformed liturgy in French and John Oecolampadius

101. Tabernacle built into high altar in Modena, Italy. (After Anson, p. 88.)

102. Baroque chalice from the seventeenth century.

published *Form and Manner of the Lord's Supper in Basel.* This avalanche of vernacular liturgies pressured Luther into publishing the *German Mass and Order of Worship* in October of 1525.

THE MATURING OF THE REFORMED RITES   The second decade of the reform witnessed the slow emergence of more comprehensive publications. In addition to the innumerable hymnals that appeared during this period, followers of Luther—such as the popular Wittenberg pastor Johann Bugenhagen—produced *Kirkenordnungen,* or "church orders," for almost every city and principality in Germany. These contained instructions for reformed church life and worship. Martin Bucer (d. 1551), who exerted significant influence on Calvin's thought, revised the Strasbourg liturgy in his *Psalter, with Complete Church Practice* (1539). John Calvin published a now lost rite for Strasbourg in 1540, although both a 1542 edition and a 1545 edition of his *The Form of Church Prayers and Hymns* still exist. In England, Henry VIII's death in 1547 paved the way for new liturgical publications that were largely the work of Thomas Cranmer. The first *Book of Common Prayer* or *Prayer Book of King Edward VI* appeared in 1549 [illustration 100]. Discontent with this volume led to *The Second Prayer Book of King Edward VI* (1552). Under the influence of Calvin and Cranmer, John Knox published *The Form of Prayers and Ministration of the Sacrament* (1556) for the English Protestant congregations in Geneva. This work was adopted by the Scottish Church in 1562. Puritans adapted Knox's work in *The Book of the Forme of Common Prayers* (1586).

THE SEVENTEENTH AND EIGHTEENTH CENTURIES   Although the directions of reformed liturgies were set during the sixteenth century, significant liturgical publications continued to appear during the seventeenth and eighteenth centuries. For example, in the midst of its war against Charles I (d. 1649), the English Parliament accepted a new *Directory for the Public Worship of God,* or the *Westminster Directory for Worship* (1644). For a brief period, this ordo displaced the *Book of Common Prayer.* After the restoration of the English monarchy in 1660, a new edition of the *Book of Common Prayer* was issued in 1662. The first service intended for use solely in North America was John Wesley's *The Sunday Service of the Methodists in North America* (1784).

Roman Books

The call to reform Rome's liturgical books was sounded long before the Reformation. As early as the fifteenth century, the bishop of Brixen, Nicholas of Cusa, ordered that all diocesan missals be brought into conformity with one approved model. During the early sixteenth century, similar demands for reforms emanated from various quarters. Soon, these were calls not only for the realignment of books within a single diocese but for uniform books throughout the Latin church. The 14th session of the Council of Trent anticipated the work on liturgical books in its decree on scripture (8 April 1546). In this decree, the council fathers ordered that books of scripture and commentaries could not be printed without ecclesiastical approval [quotation 152]. On 20 July 1562, Pius IV (d. 1565) appointed a commission to compile a list of abuses in the Mass. The first list, circulated on 8 August 1562, was long and implied enormous work for a council that was drawing to a close [quotation 141]. While condemning some of the most blatant abuses in the 22nd session (17 September 1562), the council left the reform of the liturgy and its books to the pope [quotation 153].

Initially, only the missal and breviary were to be reformed. Their appearance in 1568 and 1570 led to the adoption of the Roman breviary, missal and rubrics by the whole Latin church. Considered more a purification of the existing rites than original works, this Roman missal and breviary were imposed on all dioceses and religious communities whose own liturgical traditions were less than 200 years old. The hoped-for uniformity eventually achieved with these books was hailed in the Bull of Pius V, printed in every Roman Missal from 1570 until 1965 [quotation 154]. Such uniformity could not have been achieved without Gutenberg's invention. The success of the new breviary and missal encouraged further reform. The Roman martyrology was promulgated in 1584, the bishop's ceremonial in 1600 and the Roman ritual in 1614. Though minor revisions of these rites occurred in succeeding centuries, the liturgical books published in the 50 years after Trent remained in force until the second half of the twentieth century.

Summary

Like the different ways that Catholics and Protestants developed music and architecture during the sixteenth century, the different ways that Protestants and Roman Catholics used Gutenberg's invention are notable. For Protestant reformers, the printing press was an instrument of change. Innumerable orders of worship rolled off primitive presses into the hands of ministers and laity alike. These vernacular rites, economically and linguistically accessible to all believers, did much to support the belief in the priesthood of the laity, a primary tenet of the reform. In contrast, the Roman Catholic Church used the printing press to achieve uniformity and obedience. Texts and rubrics approved by Rome were reproduced for the entire church. These Latin texts, however, were produced only for the clergy. Continued prohibitions against the translation of official prayers—especially the canon

Quotation 152. And wishing . . . to impose a restraint in this matter on printers also who, now without restraint, thinking what pleases them is permitted them, print without permission of ecclesiastical superiors the books of the Holy Scriptures and the notes and commentaries thereon of all persons indiscriminately, often with the name of the press omitted, often also under a fictitious press-name, and what is worse, without the name of the author, and also indiscreetly have for sale such books printed elsewhere, [this council] decrees and ordains that in the future the Holy Scriptures, especially the old Vulgate Edition, but printed in the most correct manner possible, and that it shall not be lawful for anyone to print or to have printed any books whatsoever dealing with sacred doctrinal matters without the name of the author, or in the future to sell them, or even to have them in possession, unless they have first been examined and approved by the ordinary, under penalty of anathema and fine prescribed by the last Council of the Lateran. Council of Trent, fourth session (8 April 1546), translated by Schroeder

Quotation 153. The holy council . . . commissioned some Fathers to consider what ought to be done concerning various censures and books either suspected or pernicious and to report to this holy council. Hearing now that they have put the finishing hand to this work, which, however, by reason of the variety and multitude of books the holy council cannot distinctly and easily estimate, it commands that whatever has been done by them be given over to the most holy Roman pontiff, that it may by his judgment and authority be completed and made public. Council of Trent, 25th session, (3–4 December 1563), translated by Schroeder

Quotation 154. It is most fitting that there be one way of singing the psalms in the church of God and one rite of celebrating Mass. . . . and henceforth nothing is to be added, eliminated or changed. Pius V (14 July 1570)

Quotation 155. *In France certain sons of perdition . . . have translated the Roman Missal—written in ecclesiastical Latin and long approved for use in the church these many centuries—into common French. . . . We damn, condemn and interdict this publication, its reading and preservation by any and all of the faithful whatever their sex, regardless of their clerical state, order, condition, dignity, honor or prominence.* Alexander VII (12 January 1661)

103. Baroque monstrance from Klosterneuburg (1712–1714) in Germany.

Quotation 156. *We decree that the eucharist, viaticum or the body of Christ as well as chrism, holy oil and the oil of the sick— in order that they may be cared for with appropriate devotion in a distinct and secure place—may be stored in churches or in sacristies in places designated and prepared for this.* Synod of Ravenna (1311)

Quotation 157. *The bishop should take the utmost care so that in cathedral churches, collegiate churches, parishes church and any other church where the sacred eucharist is customarily reserved, it should be located on the main altar, except in case of necessity or for what seems to be another valid reason for it.* Council of Milan (1565)

of the Mass [quotation 155]—perpetuated the gap between lay and clerical prayer. Contrary to these directives, many prayer books for the laity did appear, such as America's first vernacular missal, *The Roman Missal, Translated into the English Language for the Use of the Laity* (1822), by Bishop John England of Charleston. Such translations, however, did little to draw people into the liturgy. Rather, they tended to encourage private prayer in the midst of public worship. Such books confirm Marshall McLuhan's insight that print is the technology of individualism.

VESSELS

As already noted, the size and shape of eucharistic vessels often is related to the size and shape of the worship spaces in which they are used. Domestic spaces were complemented by domestic vessels, imperial buildings required impressive cups and plates forged of precious materials, and ornate Gothic churches were the setting for chalices and monstrances adorned with bells and tiny Gothic arches. After the sixteenth century, an explicit relationship between architecture and eucharistic vessels still was apparent in the Roman Catholic Church. Within the Protestant churches, the reform emphasis on communion for everyone from the cup and the decline in the frequency of eucharist led to divergent developments in eucharistic vessels.

Roman Catholic Vessels

After the Council of Trent, no new types of vessels developed within the Roman Catholic Church. The major structural change was the wedding of the tabernacle to the high altar. The baroque and rococo styles especially were influential in the design of chalices and monstrances.

TABERNACLE   Before the sixteenth century, the eucharist often was reserved in a pyx suspended over the altar, in a sacristy cupboard or in a sacrament house. Although there are instances of the eucharist being reserved on the altar as early as the ninth century, this was only one of many options for reservation [quotation 156]. During the sixteenth century, reservation on the altar became the preferred option in Italy [illustration 101], as noted in various diocesan and provincial synods [quotation 157]. The 1584 ritual for the diocese of Rome contained the first explicit Roman directive for placing the tabernacle on the altar. A similar directive was included in the Roman Ritual of 1614 [quotation 158] although, unlike other Tridentine directives, this ritual was only proposed for—not imposed on—the universal church. While this proposal was widely accepted, wall tabernacles in France and sacrament houses in Germany continued to be commonplace. Only during the nineteenth century did the Sacred Congregation of Rites forbid churches to reintroduce the practices of reserving the sacrament in sacrament houses, suspended pyxes or other ancient methods of reservation. This decision underscored the custom of the era not only to place tabernacles on the altar, but also to build them into the church's high altar. This transformed the tabernacle from an independent eucharistic vessel to a part of the architecture.

CHALICES AND MONSTRANCES   Much of the artistic development in Roman Catholic vessels during the post-Tridentine era concerned vessels that had nothing to do with the communion of the faithful. The removal of the cup from the laity in the previous era contributed to the standardization of the chalice's shape and size: Chalices held only a few drops of wine and water for the priest. Further artistic elaborations had no ritual function. In addition, the medieval preference for watching, rather than receiving, the host encouraged the elaboration of vessels for display of the bread. Frequently, chalices and monstrances in the post-Tridentine era assumed forms related to the baroque architecture of this period. The conical cup, so popular in the Gothic era, often was abandoned for a rounded bell- or tulip-shaped cup. Angular stems with single nodes and geometric bases were replaced by rounded stems with softly defined nodes that often melded into two or three smaller nodes and terminating in a moundlike base [illustration 102]. Monstrances also reflected the architecture of post-Tridentine churches. Rather than the static and symmetrical monstrances of the Gothic or Renaissance periods, baroque monstrances often were exuberant vessels adorned with rays of precious metals emanating from the host [illustration 103].

104. Chalice created for Evangelical community at Oberwinter, Germany, 1659, approximately seven inches high, of silver.

Protestant Vessels

The various Protestant groups held divergent views on the role and frequency of the eucharist. Luther, for example, considered weekly eucharist normative. Zwingli preferred a weekly preaching service, with eucharist celebrated only four times a year. Emphasis on the word in virtually every segment of Protestantism, coupled with the influences of pietism and rationalism during the eighteenth century, contributed to a decline in the frequency of eucharist, even in the most sacramental traditions. Thus, in a sacramental revival such as Methodism, the ideal of weekly eucharist in practice became three communion services a year.

105. Pyx or host container from reformation church in Essen, in the Rheinland of West Germany, made in 1685.

Quotation 159. *The pixe deface and sold to Thomas Clepole in presence of parishioners, 1564.* Report of the church in Edenham as cited in Peacock

These divergent theological views and pastoral practices produced a similar divergence in eucharistic vessels. In some places, beautiful eucharistic vessels were created, while in other places, these vessels were virtually eliminated. When new vessels were required after a purge of the old chalices and patens, domestic pieces often were used. At times, new types of vessels developed. The various developments fall into four categories: elaboration, elimination, substitution and invention.

ELABORATION   Luther and Cranmer were two of the reformers who held the eucharist in high esteem. Not surprisingly, their traditions and those influenced by them produced communion vessels that were great works of art. In Germany and other places, this meant that the kind of beautiful vessels once produced for the Roman Catholic Church were later made for the evangelical churches. These vessels included chalices [illustration 104], patens and pyxes [illustration 105]. Besides using vessels specifically designed for worship, the evangelical churches sometimes incorporated vessels designed for secular use into their worship. These vessels originally had graced the tables of the wealthy, who later presented them to their churches.

ELIMINATION AND SUBSTITUTION   Many Reformation churches during the sixteenth century experienced purges, including the destruction of images, the elimination of architectural barriers, the removal of tabernacles and even the burning of pipe organs. The need of some reformers to establish a definitive break with the traditional Roman Mass contributed to the elimination of many eucharistic vessels. In England, for example, all but one cup and plate were removed from every church during the reign of Edward VI (d. 1553). Monstrances and pyxes frequently were destroyed, sold or given away [quotation 159]. On the continent, a simplified eucharist celebrated only three or four times a year often resulted in a drastic reduction in the number of sacred vessels retained by a particular congregation. When the need arose for new vessels, it was customary in many places on the continent, in England and in the New World to borrow secular vessels. Tankards, porringers, wine glasses and mugs became communion cups for many congregations. A similar array of trays and plates held the eucharistic bread. This practice was reminiscent of the early church's instinct to use domestic vessels for eucharist.

INVENTION   The restoration of the cup to the laity by the reformers eventually produced two new vessels for wine. Special vessels for carrying wine before its consecration had appeared by the fourth century. Such vessels were emptied into chalices, which then held the wine for

106. Flagon from Cirencester, England (1576), made of silver, and standing 14½ inches high.

107. A contemporary communion tray.

the duration of the service. Evidence indicates that during the Reformation, containers other than the chalice held the wine before and after its consecration. Flagons or tankards [illustration 106] were used to convey the wine to the table, where some was poured into a cup. Because the cups of the period were seldom large enough to hold sufficient wine for all the faithful, a large amount of wine remained in these flagons, which were used to refill the cups during communion. Another vessel that resulted from returning the cup to the community was the communion tray. This American contribution consisted of a tray that held several small cups for individual communion [illustration 107]. James White believes that communion trays were a nineteenth-century invention. Concern for hygiene apparently contributed to this development in the same century that Louis Pasteur (d. 1895) and others established the basic understanding of the nature and spread of bacteria. The use of individual cups placed popularized scientific theory and pastoral convenience above the ancient symbol of one cup for the one community of faith.

Summary

Although some changes in vessels occurred during this period, the time after the Reformation was not primarily an era when emphasis was given to communion or communion vessels. Roman Catholics customarily watched the elements at Mass; the reception of communion remained an infrequent event. Only the priest received the wine and thus his chalice became more elaborate. More significantly, the tabernacle was changed from a vessel into an architectural element. The tabernacle was moved to the center of the worship space at the same time, ironically, that the people were restricted from that space.

Generalizations about Protestant vessels are more difficult. In some places, tabernacles were retained and in other places they were destroyed. Some Protestant communities continued to make and use elaborate vessels, while others borrowed from home traditions, as the early Christians did. It was especially the reintroduction of lay communion from the chalice that led to the appearance of new vessels during this period.

THOMAS

For as long as he could remember, Thomas had wondered what it was like behind the great choir screen. It seemed strange now to be sitting in the choir stalls that before he could only glimpse from a distance. How much things had changed in the cathedral since he was a child!

Thomas remembered the worship in the church when King Henry was still alive. Once the King himself had come to their cathedral for Mass. It was a glorious ceremony! There were banners and officials everywhere, more clergy and soldiers than Thomas had ever seen, and a corps of trumpeters in the gallery.

That day was also Thomas's first memory of the great stone screen. He was only five or six at the time, scarcely ten hands high, and his view of the pageant was blocked by the crowds. He caught only glimpses of the procession of clerics and royalty as it wound its way through the nave. Then it disappeared behind the choir screen. Thomas didn't think that was fair. He stood outside the screen with his Uncle Geoffry for a long time, trying to discover what was going on inside. Young Tom could hear the service, but he didn't understand it. Uncle Geoff told him that it was in Latin. For all young Tom knew, it could have been in Egyptian. It certainly wasn't the King's English. Tom felt cheated that he could not watch the King and the rest of the royal escort during the Mass.

Things certainly changed after the death of old Henry. Almost as soon as the boy Edward took the throne, the innovations began. Thomas doesn't remember much about the early variations in the service, except that the priests looked very confused. The only consolation, to Thomas's thinking, was that the service was in English, so that the priest and people could be confused together.

Just when things seemed to be settling down and the clergy and congregation were getting used to the new liturgy, Bloody Mary ascended the throne. Then, as Uncle Geoff used to say, "all hell broke loose." Within a few years, the Mass was back in Latin. This time Thomas knew it was Latin and he still didn't like it. But there were many, including his mother, who preferred the mysterious language. He never understood why. Happily for Thomas, that situation didn't last very long. Bloody Mary died just three years after restoring the Latin Mass. Then Elizabeth assumed the throne, and the following year the Mass was back to English. What years of turmoil those were!

Thomas liked many things about the new liturgy besides the fact that he could understand it. Ever since he attended the Mass for King Henry, he had been fighting the choir screen in his mind. He wondered what it was like behind the stone wall, and he asked his mother why he couldn't stand inside the screen during the services. He promised that he would be quiet and no one would even know that he was there. His mother just gave him that look reserved for impossible requests and unanswerable questions. A few times after services, young Tom had taken matters into his own hands and stood at the edge of the doorway, looking into the great choir. He never got completely inside. The one time he tried, he was caught by the sacristan and pushed back outside the door.

Recalling that boyhood memory was a special pleasure as Thomas sat in his favorite seat in the choir stalls inside the great screen. Being able to sit there during the communion service was maybe the best part of the new worship. Instead of standing out in the nave with the rest of the people during the Latin Mass, Thomas now sat in the choir stalls where they attended the new "Mass." Others called it the Lord's Supper or Holy Communion, but it would always be the Mass to Thomas. Like the old Latin service, the new service had a lot of prayers and readings and a long sermon. He didn't mind so much, though, because he could sit during the whole first part of the worship, studying all the carvings in the seats or pondering the fancy vault that towered above the choir. When he did have to stand or kneel, he was comforted in his old age by the presence of wooden risers, much preferred to the damp stone pavement of the nave. All in all, Thomas thought that the changes he had experienced over the years were welcome ones, though he still enjoys regaling his own children with stories of the great cathedral from when he was a boy.

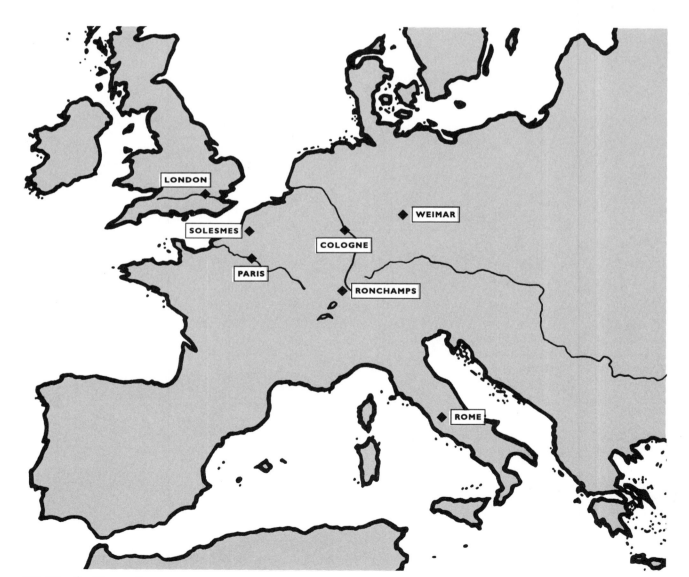

108. Map for Chapter Seven.

The Return
to Change:
1903 and Beyond

It is too early for a definitive introduction to the current period of liturgical change and reform. Although much has happened in this century that indicates a radical break from the previous period, it is difficult to know in what direction the current reform will continue, or how long this era will last. All that is possible at this juncture is to note that the twentieth century has been a period of unusual liturgical ferment.

The heralds of this change were heard before this century. Continuous liturgical reform marked the evolution of various Protestant churches. Some developments—such as Methodism in eighteenth-century America, the Lutheran confessionalism of Wilhelm Löhe in nineteenth-century Bavaria and the Oxford movement in nineteenth-century England—were strongly sacramental. Within the Roman Catholic Church, various attempts at liturgical reform surfaced after the Council of Trent. One of the most notable of these found voice at the Italian Synod of Pistoia in 1786, which called for communion under both forms, active participation of the people, the use of the vernacular and the reform of popular devotions. The recommendations of this synod eventually were condemned by Rome.

A very different Roman Catholic liturgical movement took place in France. During the seventeenth and eighteenth centuries, a group of reformers centered in Paris made significant strides in achieving lay participation within Roman Catholic worship. Known as Jansenists, these reformers shaped what could be considered a French Catholic rite, one in the language of the people that would consciously engage them in the heart of the worship [quotation 160]. Although the Jansenists eventually were condemned by Rome for various teachings, their liturgical reforms continued to influence official worship and popular devotions in France. The French monk Prosper Guéranger—who refounded the Benedictine order in France at the abbey of Solesmes—was a nineteenth-century reformer credited with helping

Quotation 160. *The canon of the Mass [is recited] aloud in a voice intelligible to all the people; [as we are] certain that in [earlier] times what was said aloud and what was said in lowered tones was what was sung, and what was not sung was said intelligibly at the altar. . . . The clergy and the people receive communion at the Mass of their pastor and from his hand, and each responds according to the ancient custom, upon receiving the body of Jesus Christ, immediately after the pastor has pronounced the words:* Corpus Domini nostri Jesu Christi. *The people say Amen. The priest continues:* custodias animam tuam in vitam eternam. Church News *(July 1690), translated by F. Ellen Weaver*

Quotation 161. *Special efforts must be made to restore the use of Gregorian chant by the people, so that the faithful may again assume a more active role in worship, as they did in ancient times.* Pius X, *The Restoration of Church Music* (1903), 3

Quotation 162. *. . . a remarkably wide-spread revival of scholarly interest in the sacred liturgy took place towards the end of the last century and has continued through the early years of this one. . . . The majestic ceremonies of the sacrifice of the altar became better known, understood and appreciated. With more widespread and more frequent reception of the sacraments, the worship of the eucharist came to be regarded for what it really is: the fountain-head of genuine Christian devotion. . . . While we derive no little satisfaction from the wholesome results of the movement just described, duty obliges us to give serious attention to this revival as it is advocated in some quarters, and to take proper steps to preserve it at the outset from excess or outright perversion.* Pius XII, *The Sacred Liturgy* (1947), 4–7

Quotation 163. *The liturgy is the summit toward which the activity of the church is directed; at the same time it is the fount from which all the church's power flows.* *Constitution on the Sacred Liturgy* (1963), 10

to stem the influence of such "Gallicanisms" by reintroducing the Roman liturgy into France. Although sometimes more interested in historical accuracy than in living worship, Guéranger did manage to hold up classic Roman liturgy as the model for public and private prayer. His liturgically centered reform generated great enthusiasm for the Roman liturgy, especially in certain monasteries of France and Germany.

The work of Guéranger and the monks of Solesmes was affirmed by Pius X (d. 1914), who approved their restoration of Gregorian chant for the whole church. Pius X's concern for sacred music surfaced in his 1903 apostolic letter *Tra le Sollicitudini.* Besides instructions about music, this letter also included a call for the active participation of the people [quotation 161]—one of the grand themes of twentieth-century liturgical reforms. Although anticipated in the writings of Pius X, the modern liturgical movement found full expression through the Benedictine Lambert Beauduin (d. 1960). His paper on active participation of the people for the Catholic Congress at Malines, Belgium, in 1909, is traditionally recognized as the birth of this movement.

After this, the twentieth century witnessed an uninterrupted avalanche of liturgical scholarship, pastoral experimentation and ecumenical dialogue directed toward the renewal of Christian liturgy. This was not an exclusively Roman Catholic phenomenon. It did, however, first become systemic within the Roman Catholic Church. The 1947 encyclical of Pius XII (d. 1958), *Mediator Dei*—sometimes called the Magna Charta of the liturgical movement—affirmed the liturgical movement for Catholics [quotation 162]. The liturgical movement within the Roman Catholic community culminated in the first document issued by Vatican II (1962–1965), the *Constitution on the Sacred Liturgy* (1963). While written for Roman Catholics, this document became pivotal in the reform of worship throughout the Christian churches. Probably more than any other treatise or pronouncement, this document articulates the role of worship in the life and mission of the church [quotation 163].

The why of the twentieth-century liturgical movement is yet to be completely understood. Contributing factors include the legacy of the eighteenth-century Enlightenment, which put new emphasis on human reason. From this movement developed the scholarly tools that enabled historians such as Louis Duchesne (d. 1922) and Josef Jungmann (d. 1975) to write great histories of the liturgy and to offer a critical picture of the development of Christian worship. Perhaps more important than the emergence of the scientific method, however, were the many political, social and scientific developments that asserted the value of the individual and of human interaction. Democracy and individual liberty became important political ideas during the late

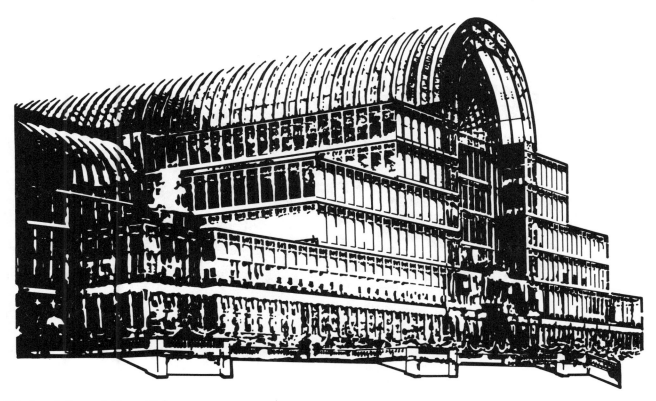

109. Joseph Paxton's Crystal Palace, 1851.

eighteenth and nineteenth centuries. The nineteenth century witnessed the birth of behavioral sciences such as psychology and anthropology, and the affirmation of human development and interaction implicit in them. Social theories arose that stressed the equality of all human beings and the state's responsibility to assure their well-being. These developments are indicative of a larger movement in Western culture that asserted the values of liberty, participation and relationship. In the liturgy, these came to mean a return of the worship to the people. Thus, in the twentieth century, as in ages past, the worship of the church does not exist outside the culture of the people.

ARCHITECTURE

Baroque architecture, a product of Roman Catholicism, was the last Western architectural style with ecclesiastical roots. During the eighteenth century, architecture, like other arts and sciences in the West, became independent of the church. After the Enlightenment and the industrial revolution, the church and the nobility no longer dictated society's building needs. Instead, the industrial and commercial sectors

110. Frank Lloyd Wright's Robie House (Chicago, 1909).

became the driving forces in architecture. These developments must be considered before turning to ecclesiastical architecture in the twentieth century.

Secular Developments

Architecture is an expression of culture. The developments in secular architecture in the modern period were influenced by the philosophical and political movements that changed the face of Western civilization. The rise of systems that upheld the value of the individual and the individual's inalienable right to basic freedoms especially were influential. In architecture, these ideals were expressed by open spaces that related to their environment—a spatial concept very different from that of the previous era [quotation 164].

One early example of this new spatial openness was Joseph Paxton's (d. 1865) Crystal Palace [illustration 109], built for the London Exhibition of 1851. Almost 1,900 feet long, this edifice was built completely of iron and glass framed in wood. Constructed in six months from thousands of prefabricated parts, the Crystal Palace announced a new architectural era through its materials, size, style and even construction technique. This feat was possible because of technological advances from the industrial revolution. One such advance was the use of iron and, after the middle of the century, steel rather than masonry and wood in construction. Economical, fire-resistant and strong, these materials allowed the construction of vast open spaces symbolizing a new freedom and openness. Eventually, buildings began

Quotation 164. *When discussing the architecture of the nineteenth century, we have repeatedly used the term "open space" to indicate the image of a limitless and continuous environment where people may act and freely move about—not for the sake of movement as such, but as an expression of a new freedom of choice, that is, the freedom to search and create one's own place. The new image, then, is the opposite to the Baroque. Whereas Baroque space represented an integrated system, the open space of the nineteenth century expressed a new ideal of human freedom.* Norberg-Schulz, p. 351

expanding vertically rather than horizontally, and the skyscraper emerged, especially in Chicago and New York.

While some architects experimented on this grand scale, Frank Lloyd Wright (d. 1959) focused on the single-family dwelling [illustration 110]. Although concern for domestic architecture might appear to refute the spirit of the Crystal Palace, both were statements about a new openness and freedom, one industrial and the other domestic. Wright considered his work an architecture of democracy. He abandoned the principle of a single room for a single use and, instead, arranged flexible spaces that flowed naturally from the outside, in which people could move freely [quotation 165].

Functionalism

At the turn of the century, a trend against ornamentation in building arose. Adolf Loos (d. 1933) offered a dramatic summation of this trend by suggesting that ornamentation was a crime [quotation 166]. The rejection of ornamentation contributed to a preference for buildings that did not hide their structure behind elaborate masonry, but rather revealed the essential elements of their construction and materials. This move against the artificiality of traditional ornamentation, combined with the emphasis on revealing the interior structure of the building exteriorly, is called "functionalism." A primary maxim of functionalism, articulated by the Chicago architect Louis Sullivan (d. 1924), was "form follows function." In Sullivan's view, the need for continuity between the interior and the exterior design did not eliminate the need for ornamentation. Sullivan, rather, shunned ornamentation that would obscure or hide the function of the building.

Functionalism became a dominant architectural principle during the twentieth century. In Germany, this principle was foundational to the Bauhaus school of design established in Weimar in 1919. A former director of the Bauhaus, Mies van der Rohe (d. 1969), moved to Chicago's Illinois Institute of Technology in 1937, where he gave new expression to functionalism [illustration 111]. The Swiss-born Charles-Edouard Jeanneret-Gris (d. 1966)—more commonly known as Le Corbusier—was a brilliant exponent of functionalism.

A broad acceptance of functionalism contributed to the development of an international style that spread throughout Western Europe and the United States. This style avoided ornamentation. Its preferred construction material was reinforced concrete. Often employing white stuccoed walls, long horizontal bands of windows and flat roofs, buildings in the international style frequently projected a strong sense of volume, rather than simply a sense of mass.

Quotation 165. *What then is the nature of this idea we call organic architecture? We are here calling this architecture "The Architecture of Democracy." Why? Because it is intrinsically based on nature-law: law for [people], not law over [people]. . . . It is simply the human spirit given appropriate architectural form. Simply, too, it is the material structure of every [person's] life on earth now seen by him as various forms of structure—in short, organic. Democracy possesses the material means today to be enlarged intelligently and turned about now to employ machine power on super materials for [human] superiority. Therefore, organic architecture is not satisfied to be employed merely to make money—not if that money is to be stacked against [humanity itself]. Our growing dissatisfaction with autocratic power or bureaucracy of any kind requires wisdom. Old wisdom and good sense are modern even now; it is their application that changes. Still more ancient is the wisdom, and it too is modern, that recognizes this new democratic concept of [humans] free in life wherein money and land-laws are established as subordinate to rights of the human being. That means first of all that all good architecture is good democracy.* Frank Lloyd Wright, The Living City, p. 28

Quotation 166. *Cultural evolution means that we have to eliminate any ornament from our artifacts. It shows the greatness of our age that it is unable to produce a new ornament.* Adolf Loos, "Ornamentation and Crime," cited in Norberg-Schulz

111. Mies van der Rohe's Seagram Building in New York (1956–1958).

Quotation 167. The object of the present lecture is to set forth and explain the true principles of Pointed or Christian Architecture, by the knowledge of which you may be enabled to test architectural excellence. . . . Strange as it may appear at first, it is in pointed architecture alone that these great principles have been carried out; and I shall be able to illustrate them from the vast cathedral to the simplest erection. Moreover, the architects of the middle ages were the first who turned the natural properties of the various materials to their full account and made their mechanism a vehicle for their art. Augustus Pugin, The True Principles of Pointed or Christian Architecture (1841)

In recent decades, functionalism and the international style have given way to a more pluralistic approach to building. As Norberg-Schulz explains, this postmodern pluralism does not begin with preconceived styles or basic principles. Rather, a pluralistic approach attempts first to understand the nature of each task and then to generate a series of compatible solutions. Thus, pluralism is more a method than a specific style and can allow for regional and stylistic variations.

Ecclesiastical Architecture

Although the nineteenth century was a revolutionary time for Western architecture, this was not true for church architecture. The most notable development in church architecture during this period was the Gothic Revival. Augustus Pugin (d. 1852) was the revival's most outspoken proponent [quotation 167]. Pugin's argument that Gothic was the only appropriate ecclesiastical style was accepted not only by the Catholic church, but also by other religious traditions in his native England. This revival, however, had little impact outside of England, the United States and, to a lesser degree, France.

Some innovations did occur in church buildings in the early twentieth century, but these essentially were structural. St. Eugene (1854–1855) in Paris, designed by Louis-Auguste Boileau (d. 1896), for example, was the first ironframed church. Northwest of Paris in Le Raincy, Auguste Perret (d. 1954) constructed the church of Notre-Dame (1922–1923) completely out of reinforced concrete, a design that had much in common with the hall churches of the thirteenth century. A few years later, Otto Bartning (d. 1959) created the steel and copper *Stahlkirche* in Cologne that, again, offered technological innovation within a traditional configuration.

It was not until Le Corbusier designed Notre-Dame-du-Haut in Ronchamps (1950–1955) that a breakthrough occurred in church architecture [illustration 112]. Beyond new technology, this church offers a fresh vision of sacred space [quotation 168], but without a fully renewed vision of the liturgy. For example, although innumerable barriers traditionally found between the assembly and the sanctuary were omitted, the space does not assert the primacy of the assembly [quotation 169]. Rather, the interior of Notre-Dame-du-Haut appears as a collection of devotional spaces under a single roof—a perspective that Le Corbusier's own words seem to confirm [quotation 170]. However, the processional path to the church and the exterior choir, which faces east—calling the eucharistic community to stand in the light of day—are compelling liturgical elements. Overall, Notre-Dame-du-Haut exists more as a triumph of sacred architecture than as a model of liturgical space.

Quotation 168. *Although the plan does not follow the traditional disposition of churches, le Corbusier has succeeded in recovering the basic properties of the Christian sanctuary. His building is receptacle and giver, fortress and poetic vision of otherness. Above all he has managed to re-create the interiority of the early churches with means which are simultaneously new and old, making the interior in Ronchamp a space which simultaneously protects and liberates.* Norberg-Schulz, pp. 408–12

Quotation 169. *Among the symbols with which liturgy deals, none is more important than this assembly of believers.* U.S. Bishops' Committee on the Liturgy, *Environment and Art in Catholic Worship* (1978), 28

Quotation 170. *In building this chapel I wished to create a place of silence, prayer, of peace and spiritual joy. Our efforts were inspired by their sacred aim. . . . The Virgin is extolled by various symbols and some written words. The cross—the real cross of suffering—is erected in this ark; henceforth the Christian drama is in possession of the place. . . . What all of us have recorded here will, I hope, find an echo in you and in those who climb this hill.* Le Corbusier's address to the bishop (June 25, 1955)

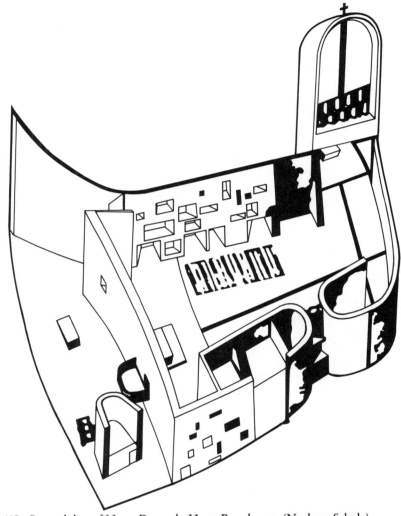

112. Groundplan of Notre Dame du Haut, Ronchamp. (Norberg-Schulz)

Ultimately, it was not the accumulation of technological advances, nor even the new vision of the sacred offered by Le Corbusier, that changed the face of twentieth-century Christian architecture in the West. Rather, it was the success of the liturgical movement, which reasserted the corporate nature of worship and the centrality of the community in that worship. Although this perspective was held by many reformers, who often opted for central-plan churches, many Protestant churches lost this vision. Under the influence of the nineteenth-century Cambridge Movement, many English-speaking churches returned to more traditional forms in the various architectural revivals (Gothic, classical and Romanesque) that marked that century. James White has noted a

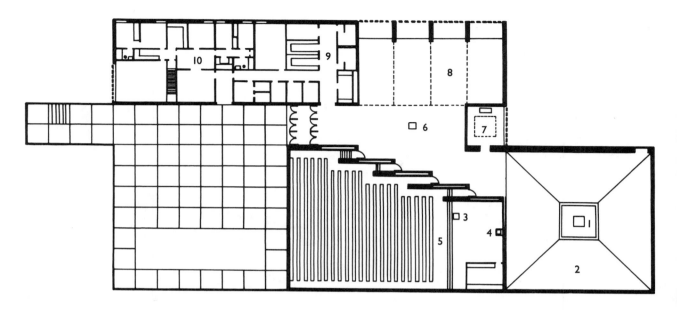

1. Altar
2. Hall of celebration
3. Lectern
4. Chair
5. Place for liturgy of the word
6. Baptistry
7. Chapel
8. Multipurpose space
9. Meeting area
10. Residential area

113. A radical example of the emphasis on the double axis of ambo and altar. Design of St. Rita's Church in Cottage Grove, Minnesota. The plan calls for two separate spaces: an auditorium-style building for the word, and an open "hall of celebration" for the liturgy of the eucharist. (After *Liturgical Arts* 38 [1970], 46.)

Quotation 171. *A space acquires a sacredness from the sacred action of the faith community which uses it.* U.S. Bishops' Committee on the Liturgy, *Environment and Art in Catholic Worship* (1978), 41

similar return to traditional forms resulting from nineteenth-century revivalism, where emphasis on pulpit personalities and massed choirs developed the concert-stage arrangement.

Although a few visionaries, including Otto Bartning, experimented with central-plan spaces as a way to affirm the unity and centrality of the assembly, these remained isolated experiments. Eventually, however, the liturgical movement, reflecting the movement in society toward freedom and equality, brought a greater emphasis to the communal aspect of worship. At first this emphasis took place mainly through scholarship, but it eventually had an impact on the worship space. In some sense, this meant an adoption of "functionalism" in liturgy [quotation 171], more commonly expressed in terms of the "ritual requirements" of the space. Thus, a space must serve not only as a place for individual encounter with the Holy, but also, and primarily, as a place for the enactment of public ritual. Christian liturgical space is rendered sacred first of all by the action of the community.

In many respects, functionalism in the liturgy is grounded in the architectural principles that dominated Europe and the United States earlier in the twentieth century: respect for individuals and their freedom; a preference for open, free-flowing, flexible spaces suited to their environment; the achievement of a sense of volume rather than of

114. Renovation of Madonna della Strada Chapel of Loyola University, Chicago.

mass; a concern for the authenticity of materials; the exposure of the essential elements of the construction and the nature of the materials; and the rejection of ornamentation. Whereas Frank Lloyd Wright shaped his domestic spaces around a huge open hearth, an increasing number of liturgical churches are shaping their space around the ambo and the altar [illustration 113].

This renewed awareness that the liturgy must shape the space has resulted in numerous church renovations reminiscent of those that followed the Reformation. In some churches, the interior has been completely reoriented, giving a building designed as a longitudinal arch the feeling of a central plan [illustration 114]. Newer constructions also reflect a preference for central-plan interiors [illustration 115]. These buildings attempt to place the assembly concretely, and not simply theoretically, at the center of the church's prayer.

Summary

Although twentieth-century architecture in the West was not by nature ecclesial, it did express certain principles that were well accepted in ecclesial circles. Most important were the functionalists' attention to the purpose of the building and the need for integrity in materials, construction and design in fulfilling that purpose. This has resulted in a revolution in ecclesiastical architecture since the 1950s. No longer

115. Sanctuary of St. Peter Lutheran Church in Columbus, Indiana. Architect: Gunnar Kirkerts & Associates 1988.

is the repetition of a particular "sacred" design acceptable merely because it is traditional. Rather, each building's design must respect and support the reformed liturgy and the community responsible for its enactment. Only then will communities again understand that it is not any structure, whatever its style, but the assembly that is the church of living stones.

MUSIC

Just as ecclesiastical influence on Western architecture waned during the eighteenth and nineteenth centuries, so did the churches lose their leadership in the development of music in the West. The resulting division between worship music and nonliturgical, sacred music allowed the latter to flourish in the concert halls, without reference to the liturgy. This division between the concert hall and the church was further marked by radically different musical styles. While composers of secular music explored new dimensions of rhythm, harmony and

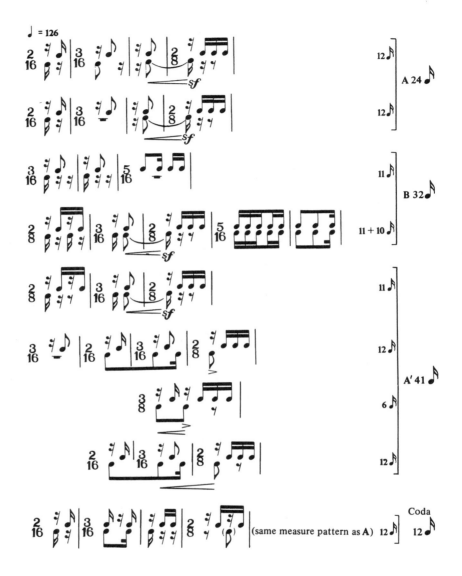

116. Examples of rhythms used by Stravinsky in "The Rite of Spring." (Grout, p. 844–845.)

form, the churches reverted to music from their past. Although artistic advances eventually influenced church music, it was not the composers of liturgical music who transformed twentieth-century worship music. It was, rather, the liturgical movement, which insisted that worship song was the people's song.

Secular Developments

Outside the church, three important musical developments affected twentieth-century liturgical music: changes in the sound of the music itself, the evolution of a new musical philosophy called *Gebrauchsmusik* and the emergence of a new musical science, ethnomusicology.

117. A song for the initiation of a girl in the Venda Society of South Africa.

CHANGING SOUNDS   Early in the twentieth century, the West experienced dramatic musical changes. Harmonic, rhythmic and melodic experiments abounded. Composers such as Arnold Schoenberg (d. 1951) explored atonal music in works such as his "Three Piano Pieces" (1909). Igor Stravinsky (d. 1971) shattered existing concepts of rhythm with "The Rite of Spring" (1913) [illustration 116]. Others, such as Béla Bartók (d. 1945) in "Music for Strings, Percussion and Celesta" (1936), experimented with new musical forms. Later in the century, visionaries such as Karlheinz Stockhausen (b. 1928) turned to the composition of electronic music. Like the nineteenth-century technological advances in architecture, such ground-breaking compositions gave the West not only great works of art, but also new tonal materials and techniques.

Quotation 172. *Characteristic traits of Gebrauchsmusik are: forms of moderate length, simplicity and clarity of style; small ensembles; avoidance of technical difficulties; parts of equal interest and so designed that they can be played on what instruments are available; soberness and moderation of expression; emphasis on 'good workmanship.' Harvard Dictionary of Music, Apel, p. 342*

GEBRAUCHSMUSIK   Besides tonal changes, the early twentieth century witnessed an important philosophical development in music. Carl Orff (d. 1982) was one of the composers and theorists in Germany after World War I who were interested in a socially oriented music. Sometimes called *Gebrauchsmusik* or "utility music" [quotation 172], this style of composition was especially attuned to the amateur musician. In reaction to composers such as Richard Wagner (d. 1883) and Gustav Mahler (d. 1911), the adherents of *Gebrauchsmusik* sought a new musical clarity and accessibility.

Gebrauchsmusik is meant to be socially useful and culturally relevant. Besides music for amateur performance, it included music for radio dramas and films. *Gebrauchsmusik* is something of a musical counterpart to architectural functionalism: It was stripped of ornamentation and employed elementary building blocks and, like many buildings of the era, it was self-consciously purposeful. Both architectural and musical functionalism flourished in Germany after World War I.

ETHNOMUSICOLOGY   Another important trend in twentieth-century music was an increased interest in folk music, in the music of non-Western cultures [illustration 117] and in the role of music in culture. During the nineteenth century, scholarly interest in the music of exotic cultures generated a new science called comparative musicology. This discipline, which acquired the name ethnomusicology in the 1950s, is concerned with every kind of music a culture produces [quotation 173]. Combining the tools of anthropology and musicology, ethnomusicologists want to know what music exists and how it functions in a given society. Because music is integral to the rituals of many peoples, ethnomusicologists often study the ritual music of traditional societies. In contrast to proponents of *Gebrauchsmusik*, who wanted to create music with an identifiable use, ethnomusicologists were coming to understand that all music has a function in society.

Quotation 173. *Ethnomusicology is closest of all to ethnology, in spite of its obvious features of musicological specialization. It studies living musics: it envisages musical practices in their widest scope; its first criterion is to address itself to phenomena of oral tradition. It tries to replace the facts of music in their socio-cultural context, to situation them in the thinking, actions and structures of a human group and to determine the reciprocal influences of the one on the other; and it compares these facts with each other across several groups of individuals of analogous or dissimilar cultural level and technical milieu. Marcel-Dubois, cited in Krader.*

Church Music before Vatican II

During the first half of this century, two significant currents in church music were the revival of traditional music and experimentation with twentieth-century sounds.

REVIVALISM   Rather than advocating new sounds or musical forms, many churches during the nineteenth and early twentieth centuries advocated a return to traditional music. This musical revivalism was related to the various architectural revivals of the nineteenth century.

XI. In Dominicis infra annum.
(For Sundays throughout the Year.)
(Orbis factor)

118. Accompanied version of the Kyrie from Mass XI from 1937. (*Kyriale*. Accompaniment by Achille P. Bragers, p. 58.)

Quotation 174. *Sacred music should consequently possess, in the highest degree, the qualities proper to the liturgy and precisely sanctity and goodness of form, from which spontaneously springs its other character, universality. . . . These qualities are possessed in the highest degree by the Gregorian chant which is, consequently, the chant proper to the Roman Church, the only chant it has inherited from the ancient fathers, which it has jealously guided for centuries in its liturgical codices, which it directly proposes to the faithful as its own, which it prescribes exclusively for some parts of the liturgy and which the most recent studies have so happily restored to their integrity and purity. Upon these grounds the Gregorian chant has always been regarded as the supreme model for sacred music, so that the following rule may be safely laid down: The more closely a composition for church approaches in its movement, inspiration and savor the Gregorian form, the more sacred and liturgical it is. . . . The ancient traditional Gregorian chant must, therefore, be largely restored in the functions of public worship. Pius X, The Restoration of Church Music (1903), Introduction, 2–3*

The Roman Catholic Church, for example, sought to restore Gregorian chant in its worship [quotation 174]. This revival engendered new liturgical insights with limited pastoral application. Pius X (d. 1914), for example, mandated chant for the universal church while simultaneously calling for the active participation of the assembly [quotation 161]. His attempt to reintegrate the song of the assembly into the liturgy while prohibiting the use of the vernacular meant that congregations were expected to sing music written for specialists. In most places, this was possible only by accompanying chant on the organ, which drastically changed the nature of the music [illustration 118].

In the Church of England, adherents of the Oxford Movement sought to restore traditional carols, plainsong hymns and German chorales to their worship. Of lasting significance were the translations of ancient texts by masters such as John Mason Neal (d. 1866) [illustration 119]. Lutherans also experienced a musical revival during

Veni veni Emmanuel;	O come, O come, Immanuel (Isaiah. 7:14)
captivum solve Israel,	and ransom captive Israel
qui gemit in exilio,	that mourns in lonely exile here
privatus Dei Filio.	until the Son of God appear.
Gaude, gaude, Emmanuel	Rejoice! Rejoice! Immanuel
nascetur pro te, Israel.	shall come to thee, O Israel.
Veni, o Jesse virgula;	O come, thou Rod of Jesse, free (Isaiah 11:1)
ex hostis tuos ungula	thine own from Satan's tyranny;
de specu tuos tartari	from depths of hell thy people save
educ et antro barathri.	and give them victory o'er the grave.
Gaude, gaude, Emmanuel	Rejoice! Rejoice! Immanuel
nascetur pro te, Israel.	shall come to thee, O Israel.
Veni, veni, o Oriens;	O come, thou Dayspring come and cheer (Luke 1:78)
solare nos adveniens;	our spirits by thine advent here;
noctis depelle nebulas	disperse the gloomy clouds of night
dirasque noctis tenebras.	and death's dark shadows put to flight.
Gaude, gaude, Emmanuel	Rejoice! Rejoice! Immanuel
nascetur pro te, Israel.	shall come to thee, O Israel.
Veni, Clavis Davidica;	O come, thou Key of David, come, (Isaiah 22:22)
regna reclude caelica;	and open wide our heavenly home; (Revelation 3:7)
fac iter tutum superum,	make safe the way that leads on high,
at claude vias inferum.	and close the path to misery.
Gaude, gaude, Emmanuel	Rejoice! Rejoice! Immanuel
nascetur pro te, Israel.	shall come to thee, O Israel.
Veni, veni Adonaï	O come, O come, thou Lord of might (Exodus 20)
quo populo in Sinaï	who to thy tribes on Sinai's height
legem dedisti vertice	in ancient times didst give the law
in maiestate gloriae.	in cloud and majesty and awe.
Gaude, gaude, Emmanuel	Rejoice! Rejoice! Immanuel
nascetur pro te, Israel.	shall come to thee, O Israel.

119. John Mason Neal's translation of "Veni veni Emmanuel." (Routley, *A Panorama of Christian Hymnody,* p. 76.)

this time. After the death of Bach (d. 1750), the quality of Lutheran church music in Europe declined. The interest of King Friedrich Wilhelm IV (d. 1861) in traditional music, as well as the tendency of the age to value things from the past, contributed to a revival of older musical forms in nineteenth-century Lutheran Prussia. Interest in their musical heritage spread throughout Lutheranism.

These revivals were aided by advances in historical and musicological studies during the nineteenth century. Such advances, coupled with a renewed reverence for traditional music, helped to generate a series of important denominational hymnals. Often produced by committees of experts, these hymnals raised the standards of church music by recovering quality composition from the past and encouraging contemporary composition of equal artistry.

NEW SOUNDS   Another development in twentieth-century music was the return of outstanding Western composers to liturgical composition. Ralph Vaughan Williams (d. 1958) wrote a "Mass in G Minor";

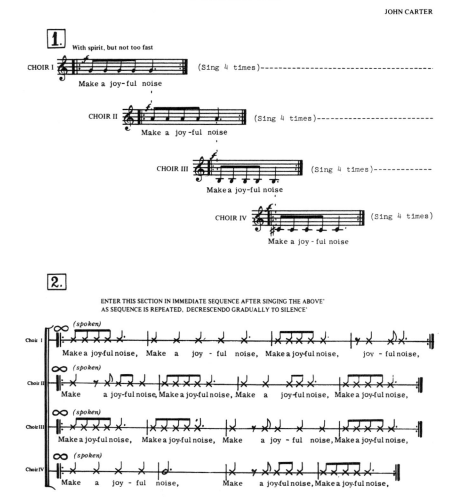

120. Contemporary setting of Psalm 100 by John Carter. (Walton Music Corp., 1974.)

Igor Stravinsky contributed his "Mass for Mixed Voices and Wind Instruments"; Zoltán Kodály (d. 1967) and Benjamin Britten (d. 1976) each composed a "Missa Brevis." In the spirit of *Gebrauchsmusik*, such compositions were written for a specific liturgical use within a given tradition. They also served to introduce many of the musical advances of the century into church music. Like the church at Ronchamps, however, they provided a renewed artistic perspective, but without a renewed liturgical perspective that placed the assembly at the center of the prayer.

The Liturgical Movement and Vatican II

Concurrent with these various musical currents was the growing influence of the liturgical movement. Because of its Roman Catholic

℗ The Lord be with you.

℃ And al-so with you.

℗ Lift up your hearts.

℃ We lift them to the Lord.

℗ Let us give thanks to the Lord our God.

℃ It is right to give him thanks and praise.

29. The preface appropriate to the day or season is sung or said.

℗ It is indeed right and salutary . . . we praise your name and join their unending hymn:

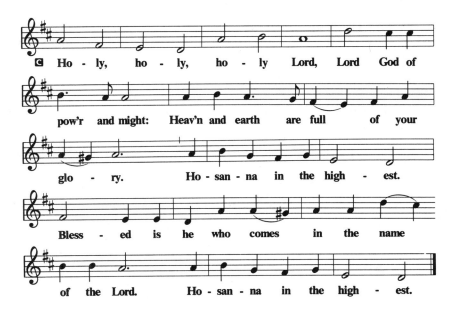

℃ Ho - ly, ho - ly, ho - ly Lord, Lord God of pow'r and might: Heav'n and earth are full of your glo - ry. Ho - san - na in the high - est. Bless - ed is he who comes in the name of the Lord. Ho - san - na in the high - est.

121. Holy Communion, Setting Two.
(*Lutheran Book of Worship* [1978],
pp. 88–89.)

Text: Afro-American Spiritual
Tune: Afro-American Spiritual; Harm. by J. Jefferson Cleveland, b.1937, and Verolga Nix, b.1933, © 1981, Abingdon

122. Traditional African American text and tune made available for Roman Catholic worship in the African American Catholic hymnal *Lead Me, Guide Me* (Chicago: GIA, 1987).

Quotation 175. *The musical tradition of the universal church is a treasure of inestimable value, greater even than that of any other art. The main reason for this pre-eminence is that, as sacred song closely bound to the text, it forms a necessary or integral part of the solemn liturgy. Holy scripture itself has bestowed praise upon sacred song and the same may be said of the Fathers of the church and of the Roman pontiffs, who in recent times, led by St. Pius X, have explained more precisely the ministerial function supplied by sacred music in the service of the Lord. Therefore sacred music will be the more holy the more closely it is joined to the liturgical rite, whether by adding delight to prayer, fostering oneness of spirit, or investing the rites with greater solemnity.* Constitution on the Sacred Liturgy (1963), 112

Quotation 176. *To determine the value of a given musical element in a liturgical celebration, a threefold judgment must be made: musical, liturgical, and pastoral.* U.S. Bishops' Committee on the Liturgy, Music in Catholic Worship (1972), 25

origins, the effects of the movement first surfaced within that tradition. Early in the century, for example, the dialogue Mass emerged among German Catholics. In such Masses, the people recited some of those parts previously taken over by the choir (such as the *Kyrie* and the *Gloria*), first in Latin and eventually in the vernacular. Experimentation with the vernacular, popular hymnody and other forms of congregational participation helped prepare the way for the *Constitution on the Sacred Liturgy* (1963).

This pivotal document reiterated the insights of Pius X and others that music serves the liturgy and forms an integral part of the worship. One reason for music's integral role is its ability to serve liturgical texts. The *Constitution* broke new ground, however, when it asserted that the "holiness of the music" is determined by how closely the music is wedded to the ritual [quotation 175]. This text officially opened the way for what might be considered a functionalist approach to liturgical music.

Like all *Gebrauchsmusik*, worship music no longer could be considered an end in itself. Music must serve a style of liturgy in which the people again assumed a central role. With the ministerial function of music as a first principle, a completely different set of standards for judging the effectiveness of music for worship arose [quotation 176]. Some have argued, however, that the only requirement of music for worship is that it enables the community to pray the liturgy. The result

THE HYMNAL

THE CHRISTIAN YEAR

*At the end of each section are listed additional hymns
also appropriate for the season or the occasion.*

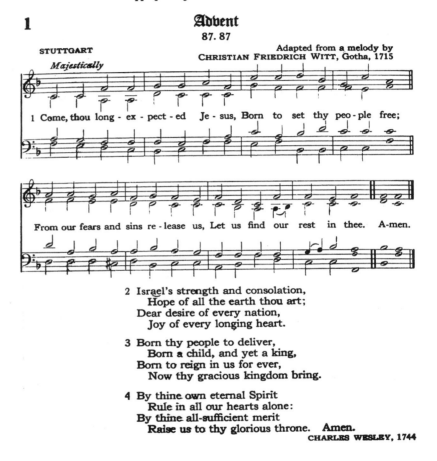

123. Opening hymn from the 1940
Episcopal Hymnal.

has been much new and sometimes controversial worship music
[illustration 120].

While many Protestant churches never displaced the assembly's
song in prayer, their worship music still has undergone a significant
change. As many Protestant churches have come to recover the
sacramental aspects of their traditions, especially the weekly celebration of the eucharist [quotation 177], so have they come to place music
at the very heart of the eucharist. As demonstrated by numerous
hymnal revisions in major Protestant denominations over the past two
decades, song for worship increasingly includes acclamations, responsories and various settings for the eucharistic liturgy [illustration 121],

along with the more traditional psalms and hymns. Although some traditions, such as the Scandinavian Lutherans, never lost this practice, they no longer are the exception.

Summary

Music, perhaps more than any other element in the liturgy, has changed in response to concerns for congregational accessibility, cultural diversity [illustration 122] and liturgical functionalism. This change has come about while attempting to respect the church's rich and varied artistic traditions. It is no wonder that, since Vatican II, music for worship often has been said to be in a state of crisis. While no single direction for liturgical music has yet been agreed on, what is clear is that any resolution must respect the central place that the song of the assembly has in the worship.

BOOKS

A steady stream of new liturgical books emanated from the Christian churches of the West during the twentieth century. The increase in the number of books from many denominations after Vatican II is especially noteworthy. To highlight this increase this section will first consider the books that appeared before this pivotal council and then those that appeared after it. Although a vast number of rituals and hymnals have been published throughout the world in this century, this discussion will focus on books published in the United States.

Liturgical Books before Vatican II

Few significant changes occurred in Roman Catholic liturgical books between the Council of Trent and Vatican II. One exception was the reform of the breviary by Pius X in 1911. The heart of this reform was a reduction in the number of psalms—from twelve to nine—prayed at Matins and the redistribution of the psalms throughout the offices. In theory, this was a startling innovation [quotation 178]. In practice, however, it went unnoticed by the faithful who had been excluded from this prayer for centuries. The restoration of the Easter Vigil (1951), which ended the practice of celebrating the Easter Vigil on Saturday morning, and the *Renewed Order of Holy Week* (1955) were much more significant for ordinary believers.

As James White has documented, the early twentieth century was a time when the Protestant churches of this country produced an unusual number of liturgical books. The Episcopal Church's *Book of*

Quotation 178. *For the first time in the history of Christian morning praise in East or West, the psalms of lauds, Psalms 148–150, were not said daily, but one psalm of praise was assigned to each day of the week, beginning with Saturday: Psalms 148, 116, 134, 145, 146, 147, 150. Furthermore, Psalms 50 and 62 were abandoned as fixed psalms at lauds, as were the traditional canticles except for Lent and vigils. For anyone with a sense of the history of the office, this was a shocking departure from almost universal Christian tradition.* Taft, The Liturgy of the Hours in East and West, *p. 312.*

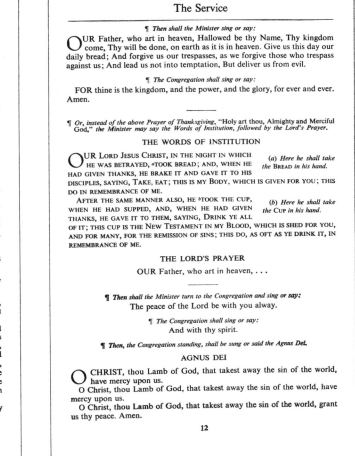

The Communion

¶ *After the Preface shall follow immediately:*

THEREFORE with Angels and Archangels, and with all the company of heaven, we laud and magnify thy glorious Name; evermore praising thee, and saying:

¶ *Then shall be sung or said the Sanctus.*

THE SANCTUS

HOLY, holy, holy, Lord God of Sabaoth; Heaven and earth are full of thy glory; Hosanna in the highest.
Blessed is he that cometh in the Name of the Lord; Hosanna in the highest.

¶ *Then may the Congregation kneel.*

¶ *The Minister standing before the Altar, and facing it, shall say the Prayer of Thanksgiving.*

THE PRAYER OF THANKSGIVING

HOLY art thou, Almighty and Merciful God. Holy art thou, and great is the Majesty of thy glory.
Thou didst so love the world as to give thine only-begotten Son, that whosoever believeth in him might not perish, but have everlasting life; Who, having come into the world to fulfill for us thy holy will and to accomplish all things for our salvation, IN THE NIGHT IN WHICH HE WAS BETRAYED, ᵃTOOK BREAD; AND, WHEN HE HAD *(a) Here he shall take the* BREAD *in his hand.* GIVEN THANKS, HE BRAKE IT AND GAVE IT TO HIS DISCIPLES, SAYING, TAKE, EAT; THIS IS MY BODY, WHICH IS GIVEN FOR YOU; THIS DO IN REMEMBRANCE OF ME.
AFTER THE SAME MANNER ALSO, HE ᵇTOOK THE CUP, WHEN HE HAD SUPPED, AND, WHEN HE HAD GIVEN *(b) Here he shall take the* CUP *in his hand.* THANKS, HE GAVE IT TO THEM, SAYING, DRINK YE ALL OF IT; THIS CUP IS THE NEW TESTAMENT IN MY BLOOD, WHICH IS SHED FOR YOU, AND FOR MANY, FOR THE REMISSION OF SINS; THIS DO, AS OFT AS YE DRINK IT, IN REMEMBRANCE OF ME.
Remembering, therefore, his salutary precept, his life-giving Passion and Death, his glorious Resurrection and Ascension and the promise of his coming again, we give thanks to thee, O Lord God Almighty, not as we ought, but as we are able; and we beseech thee mercifully to accept our praise and thanksgiving, and with thy Word and Holy Spirit to bless us, thy servants, and these thine own gifts of bread and wine, so that we and all who partake thereof may be filled with heavenly benediction and grace, and, receiving the remission of sins, be sanctified in soul and body, and have our portion with all thy saints.
And unto thee, O God, Father, Son, and Holy Spirit, be all honor and glory in thy holy Church, world without end. Amen.

11

The Service

¶ *Then shall the Minister sing or say:*

OUR Father, who art in heaven, Hallowed be thy Name, Thy kingdom come, Thy will be done, on earth as it is in heaven. Give us this day our daily bread; And forgive us our trespasses, as we forgive those who trespass against us; And lead us not into temptation, But deliver us from evil.

¶ *The Congregation shall sing or say:*

FOR thine is the kingdom, and the power, and the glory, for ever and ever. Amen.

¶ *Or, instead of the above Prayer of Thanksgiving, "Holy art thou, Almighty and Merciful God," the Minister may say the Words of Institution, followed by the Lord's Prayer.*

THE WORDS OF INSTITUTION

OUR LORD JESUS CHRIST, IN THE NIGHT IN WHICH HE WAS BETRAYED, ᵃTOOK BREAD; AND, WHEN HE *(a) Here he shall take the* BREAD *in his hand.* HAD GIVEN THANKS, HE BRAKE IT AND GAVE IT TO HIS DISCIPLES, SAYING, TAKE, EAT; THIS IS MY BODY, WHICH IS GIVEN FOR YOU; THIS DO IN REMEMBRANCE OF ME.
AFTER THE SAME MANNER ALSO, HE ᵇTOOK THE CUP, WHEN HE HAD SUPPED, AND, WHEN HE HAD GIVEN *(b) Here he shall take the* CUP *in his hand.* THANKS, HE GAVE IT TO THEM, SAYING, DRINK YE ALL OF IT; THIS CUP IS THE NEW TESTAMENT IN MY BLOOD, WHICH IS SHED FOR YOU, AND FOR MANY, FOR THE REMISSION OF SINS; THIS DO, AS OFT AS YE DRINK IT, IN REMEMBRANCE OF ME.

THE LORD'S PRAYER

OUR Father, who art in heaven, . . .

¶ *Then shall the Minister turn to the Congregation and sing or say:*
The peace of the Lord be with you alway.

¶ *The Congregation shall sing or say:*
And with thy spirit.

¶ *Then, the Congregation standing, shall be sung or said the Agnus Dei.*

AGNUS DEI

O CHRIST, thou Lamb of God, that takest away the sin of the world, have mercy upon us.
O Christ, thou Lamb of God, that takest away the sin of the world, have mercy upon us.
O Christ, thou Lamb of God, that takest away the sin of the world, grant us thy peace. Amen.

12

124. One significant change in the 1958 *Service Book and Hymnal* was the introduction of a complete eucharistic prayer which could be used instead of the words of institution alone. (*Service Book and Hymnal*, [1958] pp. 11–12.)

Common Prayer, first approved for use in the United States in 1789, was revised in 1892 and again in 1928. The Episcopal Church also revised its hymnal twice during the first half of this century: *The New Hymnal* (1916–1918) and the *Hymnal* (1940) [illustration 123]. *The New Hymnal* was the first musical edition of an Episcopal hymnal authorized by a general convention. The 1940 *Hymnal* became one of the most celebrated hymnals of the century.

The various Lutheran churches in the United States often produced a combined hymnal and prayer book. The first of these produced in English was John Christopher Kunze's (d. 1807) *A Hymnal and Prayer-Book* (1795). Throughout the eighteenth and nineteenth centuries,

ORDO MISSÆ

THE ORDINARY
OF THE MASS

1. *After the celebrant has made the required reverence to the altar, he signs himself with the sign of the cross, saying in an appropriate tone of voice:*

In the name of the Father, and of the Son, and of the Holy Spirit. Amen.

Then, with his hands joined, he adds:

℣. I will go to the altar of God.
℟. To God who gives joy to my youth.

2. *And he continues immediately:*

℣. Our help is in the name of the Lord.
℟. Who made heaven and earth.

Next, bowing deeply, he makes the following confession:

I confess to almighty God, to blessed Mary ever Virgin, to blessed Michael the Archangel, to blessed John the Baptist, to the holy apostles Peter and Paul, to all the saints, and to you, brethren, that I have sinned exceedingly in thought, word and deed; (*he strikes his breast three times, saying:*) through my fault, through my fault, through my most grievous fault. Therefore I beseech blessed Mary ever Virgin, blessed Michael the Archangel, blessed John the Baptist, the holy apoltles Peter and Paul, all-the saints, and you, brethren, to pray to the Lord our God for me.

The ministers or those present respond:

May almighty God have mercy on you, forgive you your sins, and bring you to life everlasting.

The celebrant says: Amen, and stands erect. Next the ministers or those present make the confession. Where the celebrant has said to you, brethren, *and* you, brethren, *they* say to you, father *and* you, father.

1. *Celebrans, facta altari debita reverentia, signans se signo crucis, congrua voce dicit:*

In nómine Patris, et Fílii, et Spíritus Sancti. Amen.

Deinde, iunctis manibus, subiungit:

℣. Introíbo ad altáre Dei.
℟. Ad Deum qui lætíficat iuventútem meam.

2. *Et statim addit:*

℣. Adiutórium nostrum in nómine Dómini.
℟. Qui fecit cælum et terram.

Deinde, profunde inclinatus, facit confessionem:

Confíteor Deo omnipoténti, beátæ Maríæ semper Vírgini, beáto Michaéli Archángelo, beáto Ioánni Baptístæ, sanctis Apóstolis Petro et Paulo, ómnibus Sanctis, et vobis, fratres: quia peccávi nimis cogitatióne, verbo et ópere: (*percutit sibi pectus ter, dicens:*) mea culpa, mea culpa, mea máxima culpa. Ideo precor beátam Maríam semper Vírginem, beátum Michaélem Archángelum, beátum Ioánnem Baptístam, sanctos Apóstolos Petrum et Paulum, omnes Sanctos, et vos, fratres, oráre pro me ad Dóminum Deum nostrum.

Ministri vel circumstantes respondent:

Misereátur tui omnípotens Deus, et, dimíssis peccátis tuis, perdúcat te ad vitam ætérnam.

Sacerdos dicit: Amen et erigit se. Deinde ministri vel circumstantes faciunt confessionem: et ubi a celebrante dicebatur vobis, fratres, *et* vos fratres, *ab eis dicitur tibi, pater, et te, pater.*

563

125. The English-Latin Sacramentary for the United States of America (1966), showing the hybrid state of the eucharistic liturgy immediately after the Second Vatican Council with a partially revised ritual in English and Latin. (Benziger Edition, 1966.)

Quotation 179. *When the music edition of the* Common Service Book *came from the press in 1917, it was hailed as one of the most significant events of the quadricentennial observance of the Protestant Reformation. But it also had far-reaching practical results. The spirit of fellowship engendered by 33 years of joint liturgical and hymnological studies on the part of the three general bodies was undoubtedly one of the most potent factors which led to their organic union in 1918 a the United Lutheran Church in America.* Ernest Ryden, cited in Stulken, p. 100

many others were published, such as the *Church Book*, which was prepared for the 1868 convention of the General Council and subsequently went through many editions. In 1917, three groups—the General Council, the General Synod and the United Synod South— produced a single worship book and hymnal. This publication, the *Common Service Book*, played an important role in the merger of these three synods into the United Lutheran Church in America in 1918 [quotation 179]. Another notable joint venture was the *Service Book and Hymnal* (1958) [illustration 124]. Produced by eight different church bodies, this hymnal also contributed to the merger of various groups. Four of these groups—the American Lutheran Church, the Evangelical Lutheran Church in America, the United Evangelical

126. Opening of the Order of Mass from a twentieth-century edition of the Dominican Rite, eliminated by Vatican II. (*Missale Ordinis Praedicatorum,* Rome, 1939.)

Lutheran Church and the Lutheran Free Church—joined to form the American Lutheran Church in 1961. The remaining four—the Augustana Lutheran Church, the American Evangelical Lutheran Church, the Finnish Evangelical Lutheran Church and the United Lutheran Church in America—formed the Lutheran Church in America in 1962.

Other significant collaborative efforts in this century include the work of three Methodist churches. In anticipation of their union in 1939, the Methodist Episcopal Church, the Methodist Episcopal Church-South and the Methodist Protestant Church jointly published *The Methodist Hymnal.* After their union, the new Methodist Church published a *Book of Worship* (1944). A second *Hymnal* and *Book of Worship* were approved in 1964.

Although not a joint venture, the 1906, 1932 and 1946 editions of the *Book of Common Worship,* which were published by the Presbyterian Church in the U.S.A. (North), eventually were approved by the Presbyterian Church in the U.S. (South). This certainly contributed to their joint publication of *The Hymnbook* (1955), foreshadowing the 1983 reunion of these two churches.

Twentieth-century American Protestantism again demonstrates that liturgical books are not simply neutral ritual objects. They embody belief and thus, in some situations, serve as instruments of unity. Ordinary worshipers participated in this experience because the changes occurred in the books they used week after week. Although approved by recognized ecclesiastical bodies, these books were not simply books of the liturgical specialists; they were the people's books, especially the hymnals.

Liturgical Books after Vatican II

In a series of deceptively simple statements, Vatican II decreed the reform of virtually every liturgical book in the Roman Catholic Church [quotation 180]. Like those at the Council of Trent, the bishops at Vatican II did not attempt the work of revision themselves. This was given to a series of commissions, special committees and Roman congregations that continue the work today.

New liturgical books for the Roman Catholic Church appeared very quickly because of the technologies available. The books published in the years immediately following the council were hybrid books, often in both Latin and the vernacular, reflecting a preliminary stage of the reform [illustration 125].

Eventually, a series of standard editions for the universal church (each called an *editio typica*) was promulgated by Rome. These, in turn, were published in vernacular translations approved by the national conferences of bishops and Rome. Thus, for example, the standard edition of the *Roman Sacramentary* was issued in 1969 and an approved English translation appeared in 1973.

A third step is the adaptation of the books to various cultures, as presumed by the council [quotation 181]. For example, after the standard edition of the *Order of Funerals* was issued in Latin (1969), an approved English translation appeared (1970). A revised version, prepared by the International Commission on English in the Liturgy (ICEL), approved by the Catholic Bishops of the United States and confirmed by Rome, then appeared (1989).

With the promulgation of the various standard editions of the rites, Vatican II created a liturgical uniformity never before known to the Roman Catholic Church. Even the Council of Trent had allowed all

Quotation 180. *Quotations from the Constitution on the Sacred Liturgy:*

The Order of Mass is to be revised. (50)

Both of the rites for the baptism of adults are to be revised. (66)

The rite for the baptism of infants is to be revised. (67)

The rite of confirmation is also to be revised. (71)

The rite and formularies for the sacrament of penance are to be revised. (72)

In addition to the separate rites for anointing of the sick and for viaticum, a continuous rite shall be drawn up. (74)

Both the ceremonies and texts of the ordination rites are to be revised. (76)

The marriage rite . . . is to be revised. (77)

The sacramentals are to be reviewed. (79)

The rite for the consecration to a life of virginity . . . is to be revised. (80)

The rite of funerals should express more clearly the paschal character of Christian death. (81)

When the office is revised . . . (89)

Quotation 181. *Provisions shall also be made, even in the revision of liturgical books, for legitimate variations and adaptations to different groups, regions and peoples, especially in mission lands, provided the substantial unity of the Roman Rite is preserved; this should be borne in mind when rites are drawn up and rubrics devised. Constitution on the Sacred Liturgy, 38*

liturgical traditions over 200 years old to continue. Vatican II elimi-nated all such rites [illustration 126]. That council did, however, allow the use of the vernacular and it presumed the adaptation of the rites. Having passed through the translation stage, the Roman Catholic Church is currently in the process of adapting the standard rites to the needs of various cultures and peoples. This again could allow for enormous diversity in the Roman Catholic Church's liturgy. Whatever the outcome, this church understands again that liturgical books are always in need of revision, if for no other reason than the fact that living languages change. Contemporary questions on the role of inclusive language, for example, make that eminently clear.

The explosion of liturgical books after Vatican II in the Roman Catholic Church was matched by similar activity in the Protestant churches. The Episcopal Church, for example, revised virtually all of

III

P You are indeed holy,
  almighty and merciful God;
  you are most holy,
  and great is the majesty
  of your glory.

You so loved the world
  that you gave your only Son,
  that whoever believes in him
  may not perish
  but have eternal life.

Having come into the world,
  he fulfilled for us your holy will
  and accomplished our salvation.

In the night
  in which he was betrayed,
  our Lord Jesus took bread,
  and gave thanks; broke it,
  and gave it to his disciples,
  saying: Take and eat;
  this is my body, given for you.

Do this for the remembrance of me.

Again, after supper,
  he took the cup, gave thanks,
  and gave it for all to drink,
  saying: This cup is
  the new covenant in my blood,
  shed for you and for all people
  for the forgiveness of sin.

Do this for the remembrance of me.

Remembering, therefore,
  his salutary command,

his life-giving Passion and death,
his glorious resurrection
and ascension,
and his promise to come again,
we give thanks to you,
Lord God Almighty,
not as we ought,
but as we are able;
and we implore you
mercifully to accept
our praise and thanksgiving,
and, with your Word
and Holy Spirit,
to bless us, your servants,
and these your own gifts
of bread and wine;
that we and all who share
in the body and blood
of your Son
may be filled
with heavenly peace and joy,
and, receiving the forgiveness
of sin,
may be sanctified
in soul and body,
and have our portion
with all your saints.
All honor and glory are yours,
  O God, Father, Son,
  and Holy Spirit,
  in your holy Church,
  now and forever.

C Amen

127. Eucharistic Prayer 3 from *The Lutheran Book of Worship: Minister's Desk Edition* (p. 297)

Quotation 182. *Baptism, confirmation, marriage and burial all appeared, not as they had been in the context of choir offices, but in specialized forms of the pro-anaphora. The rest of the eucharist can, and usually does, follow. So, too, is the case with special rites for Ash Wednesday and Palm Sunday. Although extensive space is devoted to the daily offices, the new American Prayer Book is eucharistically centered.* Porter, in *New Eucharistic Prayers*, edited by Frank Senn, p. 64

its rites and the psalter. The result of this process was *The Book of Common Prayer and Administration of the Sacraments and Other Rites and Ceremonies of the Church together with the Psalter or Psalms of David* (1979). This volume includes newly revised rites, a lectionary based on the Roman lectionary, an expanded liturgical calendar and four new eucharistic prayers. Furthermore, the new configuration of the rites—placing baptism, confirmation, marriage and burial rites in the context of eucharist—downplays the traditionally more important rites of Morning and Evening Prayer. The eucharist is central in this revision [quotation 182]. The Episcopal Church also issued a new hymnal in 1982.

During the year after the end of Vatican II, an Inter-Lutheran Commission on Worship began a 12-year project that culminated in the publication of *The Lutheran Book of Worship* (LBW). Proposed as a joint publication of the Lutheran Church in America, the American Lutheran Church, the Evangelical Lutheran Church of Canada and the Lutheran Church-Missouri Synod, this volume led to further unions. Although the Lutheran Church-Missouri Synod withdrew from the project and produced its own volume, *Lutheran Worship* (1982), the LBW nonetheless became one more vehicle to unity in the American Lutheran community. The Lutheran Church in America, the American Lutheran Church and the Association of Evangelical Lutheran Churches together formed the Evangelical Lutheran Church in America in 1988. The LBW is its official worship book. It contains the richest liturgical calendar in a Lutheran publication since the reformation. It also adopts the Roman lectionary with its three-year cycle of readings and includes four musical settings of the eucharistic rite together with three forms of the eucharistic prayer. The *Lutheran Book of Worship: Minister's Desk Edition* (1978) contains three more eucharistic prayers. This builds on the tradition of the 1958 *Service Book,* which introduced a full eucharistic prayer as an alternative to the preface, *Sanctus* and words of institution traditionally used in Lutheran churches [illustration 127].

In 1970, the newly formed United Methodist Church—created through a merger of the Methodist Church with the Evangelical United Brethren Church in 1968—established a commission to revise its worship and books. As was also true of the Episcopalians and Lutherans, the work of this body first resulted in a series of individual rites published in the *Supplemental Worship Resources* series. These revisions culminated in *The United Methodist Hymnal* (1989), which is a single volume of worship and song. Most significant in these revisions was the use of a three-year lectionary—called the common lectionary, it is widely shared with other Protestant churches today—and a greatly expanded calendar. The large number of eucharistic prayers—

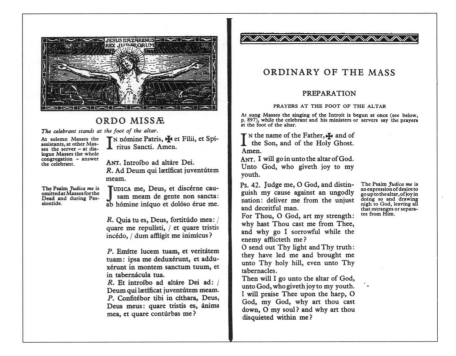

128. Opening rites of the Mass (*The Saint Andrew Daily Missal* [1952], pp. 890–91.)

24 in the 1987 publication *Holy Communion,* for example—also is notable.

Summary

In the various traditions surveyed here, the revised books, especially those revised after Vatican II, are the result of deliberate and sometimes long processes. The Roman Catholics published standard editions after years of consultations. These currently are being adapted around the world. Various Protestant denominations in the United States prepared for the publication of major liturgical books through a series of preliminary publications. The Episcopal Church published 28 volumes of *Prayer Book Studies* from 1950 to 1976. The United Methodists published 17 volumes of *Supplemental Worship Resources* between 1972 and 1988. Since 1984, the Presbyterian Church U.S.A. has been publishing *Supplemental Liturgical Resources,* which are preparing the way for a combined hymnal and service book projected for publication during the 1990s.

In this process of revision, there has been considerable cross-fertilization. For example, Protestant churches often have adopted the Roman lectionary, and Roman Catholics are learning about vernacular liturgy, even to the point of borrowing texts from other vernacular liturgies [quotation 183].

Quotation 183. *In sure and certain hope of the resurrection to eternal life through our Lord Jesus Christ, we commend to almighty God our brother/sister N., and we commit his/her body to the ground; earth to earth, ashes to ashes, dust to dust. The Lord bless him/her and keep him/her, the Lord make his face to shine upon him/her and be gracious to him/her, the Lord lift up his countenance upon him/her and give him/her peace.* Prayer of Committal from *The Book of Common Prayer* (1979) employed in the Roman Catholic *Order of Christian Funerals* (1989)

One great difference is that in most Protestant churches, the revised book is the people's book. This is true especially when churches publish a combined service book and hymnal. Such books belong to the assembly and it is not unusual for members of the congregation to have their own books. Roman Catholics, however, have revised books only for the liturgical specialists. There is no official book for the congregation. For decades, the unofficial liturgical book for the laity was a hand missal, which guided people through the Latin liturgy [illustration 128]. With the return to the vernacular, these missals have become obsolete. Their replacements range from newsprint missalettes and paperback songbooks to finely crafted hymnals. In view of the expensive sanctuary books used by the priest and other ministers, the range of these replacements continues to communicate a mixed message about the role of the assembly in worship.

129. Monstrance of stainless steel, with 24-karat gold pyx by Alexander Schaffner. (*Liturgical Arts,* 39 [1971], 77)

Quotation 184. Zwingli believed that "it is clear and indisputable that no external element or action can purify the soul" and was completely consistent to discount the use of physical objects and actions in worship. A sense of the sign value of things in conveying God's grace is altogether lacking. This disjuncture between the physical and spiritual sets Zwingli apart from Luther and Calvin. Essentially it is a matter of piety. If the physical cannot lead one to God, one has to draw a circle around much of the traditional Christian cultus and mark it for destruction. White, Protestant Worship, 61

VESSELS

Changes in twentieth-century worship vessels have been less dramatic than those that occurred, for example, in the worship spaces. Unlike the evolution of liturgical music in this era, there was no organization comparable to the Society of St. Cecilia to champion a restoration of cups or plates parallel to the restoration of Gregorian chant. Furthermore, unlike the revision of liturgical books in the same period, changes in the materials, styles and shapes of liturgical vessels seldom were achieved at the request of some church board or Roman congregation. Nonetheless, the metamorphosis of worship vessels—perhaps more than that of spaces, music or books—symbolizes the desire to rediscover the power of blessing God through sharing simple gifts of bread and wine in the spirit of early Christian worship. This especially was true of the Roman Catholic community, whose eucharist after Trent had so little in common with that of the domestic church.

Stylistic Changes

As already noted, some Protestant churches introduced domestic vessels into their worship early in the reform. For those who rejected a place for artistry in the liturgy, such as the followers of Zwingli [quotation 184], simple domestic ware was most appropriate for celebrating the Lord's Supper. Similar styles continue to be used in these traditions. For others, however, domestic wineglasses and serving trays were only an interim solution after the purge of "popish" vessels. The sacramental revivals of the nineteenth century prompted the displacement of domestic ware by more specialized vessels in some

128   ESTABLISHED 1872 · JOHN P. DALEIDEN CO. 1530-32 SEDGWICK ST. CHICAGO. INCORPORATED 1902

CHALICES
(ORNAMENTAL YET INEXPENSIVE)

No. A296/30
A nice low priced style 8⅝ inches high.
              Free Import
Cup and Paten silver, all gold plated........$22.50
Solid silver, all gold plated.................$30.00
Ciborium to Match.
Diameter of cup, 4 inches.
Silver Cup, all gold-plated...................$22.50
Solid silver, all gold-plated.................$30.00

No. 274/30.
            Free Import
Three mat silver medallions on base, 9½ inch, silver
   cup and paten, all gold plated.............$47.50
All silver, gold plated $62.50

No. A290/30
Three medallions in silver on base. Crucifixion,
Blessed Virgin and St. Joseph, 9 inches high.
             Free Import
Cup and paten silver, all gold-plated........$ 75.00
Solid silver, all gold plated................$ 95.00
Ciborium to Match.
Diameter of cup, 4¼ inches.
Silver cup, all gold-plated..................$ 75.00
Solid silver, gold-plated $100.00

No. A293/30
Three silver medallions on base, the Crucifixion,
Annunciation and Nativity; six medallions on cup,
three of the Doctors of the Church and Sacred Heart
of Jesus, Mater Dolorosa and St. Joseph. The knob
has the name of Jesus.
9¼ inches high.   **Free Import**
Cup and paten, silver, all gold-plated.......$120.00
Solid silver, all gold-plated................$145.00
   Ciborium to Match.
Cup 4⅞ in. diameter.   **Free import**
Cup, silver, all gold-plated.................$120.00
Solid silver, gold-plated....................$155.00

No. A294/30
Grape design, chased, column in enamel, knob
open work.
9 inches high.   **Free Import**
Cup and paten, silver, all gold-plated.......$110.00
All silver, gold-plated $140.00

No. A298/30
Six apostles on base and six on cup in enamel
9¾ inches high.   **Free Import**
Cup and paten, silver, all gold-plated.......$260.00
Solid silver, all gold-plated................$300.00
Ciborium to Match
Cup 4¾ inches diameter
Silver cup, all gold-plated..................$260.00
Solid silver, all gold-plated................$330.00

130. Page from the 1930 catalogue of the John P. Daleiden Company, Chicago.

131. Eucharistic bread and appropriately enlarged paten for the reformed liturgy. (*Liturgical Arts*, 1971.)

132. Bronze and gold chalice by William Frederick.

Protestant churches. Forged from precious metals by professional artisans, the vessels of many Protestant churches during the nineteenth and twentieth centuries often had little in common with those used in the home. For these Protestant churches, as well as for the Roman Catholic Church, the early twentieth century was a time of essentially stylistic changes in worship vessels. These changes were brought about by two influences: the acceptance of the principles of functionalism and the tendency to mass-produce such vessels.

Functionalism

A strong correlation between the architecture of a space and the style or shape of the vessels used in that space has been pointed out many times in this book. Thus, it is not surprising that the early twentieth-century tendency to reject ornamentation and artificiality in architecture affected the design of eucharistic vessels as well. Although this approach affected vessels much later than it did church architecture, the mid-twentieth century eventually saw the emergence of eucharistic vessels with little or no ornamentation. The results often were sleek, contemporary works of art. Sometimes this was achieved with traditional materials of silver and gold. Other times, however, new alloys such as stainless steel were the preferred materials [illustration 129].

Mass Production

The principles of functionalism contributed to the creation of some truly artistic vessels. The twentieth-century propensity for mass production, however, had the opposite affect. Although liturgical books had been mass-produced since the advent of the printing press in the fifteenth century, vessels were not manufactured in this way until the invention of the assembly line at the turn of the twentieth century. Originally conceived for the production of heavy equipment—the automobile, for example—assembly-line techniques eventually were adapted to a variety of products. By the 1930s, this included the mass production of eucharistic vessels. The result of this technological advance, apparent especially in the United States, was an approach to the production, marketing and acquisition of eucharistic vessels similar to that used for other mass-produced commodities. Catalogues of vessels and other church goods emerged [illustration 130]. Although available in various styles and materials, these vessels had to appeal to a broad market. Consequently, they often were manufactured according to mediocre standards of design and artistry. Through these catalogues, the revivalist tendencies apparent in nineteenth- and early twentieth-century architecture and music persisted in liturgical vessels.

Quotation 185. *Theologians began to turn their thoughts in quite a different direction after the Second World War. . . . [Between 1949 and 1960] a different question was already preoccupying most theologians—that of the relationship between the metaphysical approach and the sacramentality of the eucharist. The tendency to approach the eucharist, not ontologically and via the philosophy of nature, but anthropologically, became increasingly prevalent at this time. . . . Emphasis could again be given in post-war theology to the fact that sacraments are first and foremost symbolic acts or activity as signs—"sacramentum est in genere signi."* Schillebeeckx, The Eucharist, 96–97

Quotation 186. *Quotations from the Constitution on the Sacred Liturgy:*

In this reform both texts and rites should be so drawn up that they express more clearly the holy things they signify. (21)

It is from the scriptures that actions and signs derive their meaning. (24)

The visible signs used by the liturgy to signify invisible divine realities have been chosen by Christ or the church. (33)

Quotation 187. *The term "sign," once suspect, is again recognized as a positive term for speaking of Christ's presence in the sacrament. For, though symbols and symbolic actions are used, the Lord's supper is an effective sign: It communicates what it promises" . . . the action of the church becomes the effective means whereby God in Christ acts and Christ is present with his people."* The Eucharist: A Lutheran-Roman Catholic Statement, 2.1

Quotation 188. *The bread for the celebration of the eucharist . . . must be made solely of wheat and, in accordance with the tradition proper to the Latin Church, it must be unleavened. By reason of the sign, the matter of the eucharistic celebration "should appear as actual food." This is to be understood as linked to the consistency of the bread and not to its form, which remains the traditional one. No other ingredients are to be added to the wheaten flour and water.* John Paul II, On Certain Norms Concerning Worship of the Eucharistic Mystery, 1980

Pseudo-Gothic and pseudo-baroque chalices were produced by the thousands. Reproductions of classic designs from the past became available to the consumer. Such mass-produced vessels continue to proliferate in the twentieth-century church.

THE SYMBOLIC REVOLUTION   Like the parallel changes in music and architecture during the early part of this century, the changes in eucharistic vessels brought about by the principles of functionalism and mass production essentially were stylistic. A more profound change would not occur until the middle of the century, when the shift in liturgical and sacramental thought would place renewed stress on the symbolic nature of the liturgy [quotation 185].

During the nineteenth century, a symbolists' movement in the visual arts and literature—epitomized in the writing of Paul Verlaine (d. 1896)—swept across Europe. During the twentieth century, philosophers such as Ernst Cassirer (d. 1945), Susanne Langer (d. 1985) and Paul Ricoeur (b. 1913) advanced symbolic theory, while anthropologists such as Victor Turner (b. 1920) explored the ritual symbolism of traditional societies. Their work provided a framework for theologians searching for more satisfying explanations of sacraments than those afforded by medieval theologies, which emphasized intention and abstraction rather than perception or experience. Thus, theologians such as Edward Schillebeeckx (b. 1914) reasserted the primary place of symbols in understanding and celebrating Christian liturgy. Vatican II affirmed such thinking in the *Constitution on the Sacred Liturgy* [quotation 186]. It also has become part of the ecumenical consensus on worship since the council [quotation 187].

Bread and Its Vessels

The reassertion of the primacy of symbols heralded a return to full, rich symbols in worship, such as bread that could be perceived as bread. This, in turn, resulted in vessels shaped to hold more natural forms of bread [illustration 131]. Many Protestant churches that had continued the Western practice of employing unleavened wafer-bread have returned to the ancient practice of a single loaf of leavened bread.

In the Roman Catholic community, the *General Instruction of the Roman Missal* decreed in 1970 that bread had to appear as real food. This contributed to changes in the size and shape of bread vessels. Ironically, Pope John Paul II decreed in 1980 that although the bread was to appear as real food, it could not contain anything other than flour and water [quotation 188].

Wine and Its Vessels

The sharing of the cup within this richer symbolic framework meant that wine should be drunk by all from a common vessel. The Protestant churches had returned the chalice to the laity at the Reformation, but some abandoned the common cup, which so clearly symbolizes the unity of the community [illustration 107]. The *Constitution on the Sacred Liturgy* approved in principle the return of the cup to the laity within the Roman tradition [quotation 189]. Since 1970, Roman Catholics in the United States have been allowed to receive communion from the cup on weekdays; in 1978, this permission was extended to all eucharistic celebrations. The return of the cup to the community meant a change in the design of the chalice. It no longer could hold only a sip of wine for the priest but rather was to be large enough to be used for the communion of the assembly [illustration 132].

Another consequence of returning the cup to the laity was the introduction of the flagon into the Roman Catholic eucharist. Because the symbolism of a single cup does not allow more than one chalice on the table, the rest of the wine should be held in another vessel, such as the flagon, until it is poured into other cups during the fraction rite before communion [illustration 133].

Materials

The move toward more authentic symbols also effected a change in the materials for the eucharistic vessels. Although gold and silver continue to be employed, precious metals often are replaced by glass, pottery and wood. Even wicker baskets, reminiscent of primitive Christian worship, are used again in some places to hold the eucharistic bread. For the Roman Catholic Church, this required a change in laws prescribing that patens and chalices would be made of gold or silver. In 1962, for example, permission was given to modify only slightly the design of a chalice [quotation 190]. Only seven years later, the new *General Instruction of the Roman Missal* virtually removed every specific requirement for the fabrication of eucharistic vessels [quotation 191].

Summary

A hallmark of the twentieth-century liturgical movement has been a renewed belief in the centrality of the assembly in public worship. This belief has manifested itself in various ways. One manifestation is the acknowledgment that the intention of the presider or even the assembly at eucharist is insufficient for the fullness of the sacramental act.

Quotation 189. *The dogmatic principles laid down by the Council of Trent [regarding communion under both species] remain intact. In instances to be specified by the Apostolic See, however, communion under both kinds may be granted both to clerics and religious and to the laity at the discretion of the bishops.* Constitution on the Sacred Liturgy, 55

Quotation 190. *The Reverend Romuald Bissonnette, Rector of the Pontifical Canadian College, in the name of his eminence, the ordinary of Montreal, asked this Sacred Congregation whether chalices without a node below the cup may be consecrated. Reply: The Sacred Congregation of Rites, after mature consideration of everything, replied: "It suffices that the priest can satisfactorily hold the chalice with his thumb and index finger joined."* Private Response of the Sacred Congregation of Rites (1962), cited in Seasoltz

Quotation 191. *Vessels should be made from materials that are solid and that in the particular region are regarded as noble. . . . Chalices and other vessels that serve as receptacles for the blood of the Lord are to have a cup of nonabsorbent material. The base may be of any other solid and worthy material. . . . The artist may fashion the sacred vessels in a shape that is in keeping with the culture of each region, provided each type of vessel is suited to the intended liturgical use.* The General Instruction of the Roman Missal, 290, 291, 295

133. Participation cups on tray and flagon with wine.

Liturgy is an action that requires the use of perceivable symbols to bring about its hoped-for meaning. The evolution of eucharistic vessels and of the material gifts of bread and wine that they hold attests to the churches' growing awareness of the importance of symbols. Vessels are not sacred because of the beauty of their design or the preciousness of their materials. Rather, they are sacred because they mediate presence to the assembly. And it is in the hands of the assembly that they belong. Thus, it is primarily the hand of the assembly, rather than the hand of the artist or the theologian, that once again has come to craft these vessels of hope.

HATTIE JOHNSON

"Blessed assurance, Jesus is mine! O what a foretaste of glory divine!" As the entrance procession moved down the center aisle, the choir and congregation sang with gusto, urged on by an insistent pianist with a heavy left hand. Jessica Brown carried the cross high, followed by her brother Freddie and Adrian Washington carrying tall white candles. The choir, red robes accentuating rich brown skin, marched after them in hesitation step to the music, singing at full volume, "This is my story, this is my song." Then came old Mrs. Williams, leaning on her cane but walking proud with the lectionary tucked under her arm. Deacon Tim and Father Charles, dressed in matching vestments of red, black and green, brought up the rear of the procession.

Hattie Johnson was not the strongest voice in the assembly, but she certainly was one of the most earnest. "Perfect submission, perfect delight, visions of rapture now burst on my sight." Who would have guessed that she would be singing the songs of her grandmother in the Catholic church? Grandma had belonged to Christ First Pentecostal Church in the old neighborhood. Hattie's mother never let her go to the tiny church with Grandma. Instead, she took Hattie to Mass at the Catholic Church — what Grandma used to call the "white man's church." Sunday afternoons after services, though, Grandma would hold Hattie in her lap and tell her all about the worship at First Pentecostal: the preaching, the gifts of the Spirit manifest that morning, and especially the music. Oh, how Hattie loved the songs that Grandma sang to her! And no one is more astounded than she that 50 years later they would be singing some of those same songs in a Catholic church.

Here at St. Michael's a lot of things have changed besides the music. One of the best changes, from Hattie's point of view, is that, while there are white faces and yellow faces in the pews, every face in the sanctuary is like her own. St. Michael's is certainly no white man's church, she thought to herself. Hattie knew it wasn't like this everywhere in Chicago, and there still were many churches where all the faces in the sanctuary and in the pews were white. Those will change in time, she thought. And besides, I don't need those places. St. Michael's is my church and it suits me just fine. The idea brought a smile to her lips as she and the rest of the congregation sat down for the readings.

Old Mrs. Williams sure knew how to read the prophets. The years of raising a family in the projects and fighting for a decent wage must have accounted for some of the conviction in her voice. The prophet's call for justice was just a little more believable, coming from the lips of someone like Clarice Williams. Father Charles's preaching also was more convincing than most of the preaching Hattie had heard over the years. And she didn't think it was just because he was an African American. She had heard other African American preachers, but they didn't have the power of Father Charles. Maybe it was the fact that here at St. Michael's, African Americans felt at home and it was Father Charles who, more than anyone else, helped make this their home. When he preached or talked to the congregation, people talked right on back — and not just "Amen" or "Preach it, pastor." Sometimes people disagreed with him or added another example or gave their own witness. And he just let them do it. Hattie was convinced that Grandma would have liked Father Charles.

A lot of other people also made St. Michael's

feel like home to Hattie: Clara and Bobby Turner, who baked the bread for Mass; Rodney Harris and his son, Jimmy, who took the collection; Adele Thompson, who got the congregation singing and clapping; and whoever was standing close enough to take Hattie's hand while they sang the Our Father. Hattie especially liked that part. She remembered when she was a little girl, how she had to kneel or stand or sit real quiet and not talk or even look at the other people during Mass. From what she remembered, it was a pretty barren experience. How shocked that old congregation would be if they could see the people at St. Michael's today during the sign of peace. As little Michelle Eugene once said during the peace, "There's some serious huggin' going on here."

The communion song today was one of Hattie's favorites, "Thank you, Lord." Darrel the pianist played it very slowly and rhythmically as members of the congregation stepped forward to receive the bread from the big wicker baskets and drink from one of the pottery cups offered to them by the ministers of communion. Hattie found herself keeping step with the music as she walked back to her place. Sitting down, she let the sounds of the baby grand and the gospel choir wash over her. After communion there always were a lot of announcements. Luckily, most of the important ones were also in the bulletin. Otherwise, Hattie surely would have forgotten them all.

After the last announcement, the congregation stood for the closing prayer and Father Charles's blessing. Then Darrel dug his left hand into the keyboard as the choir began to sing "Go ye therefore and teach all nations, go, go, go." The congregation joined in on the second phrase as Jessica raised the cross and led the ministers down the center aisle. "Baptizing them in the name of the Father and Son and Holy Ghost. Go, go, go." As Hattie joined the informal procession, making its way toward the coffee and rolls in the back of church, she thought again of Grandma and the Christ First Pentecostal Church in the old neighborhood. Maybe if Grandma were alive today she might feel at home at St. Michael's, too.

Glossary

A cappella. Italian for "as in the chapel"; refers to choral music sung without instrumental accompaniment.

Ambo. A raised platform or lectern for the proclamation of the word of God.

Ambulatory. A semicircular or polygonal passageway designed for walking around the outer perimeter of the sanctuary.

Amidah. Hebrew for "standing"; originally the 18, now 19, benedictions that are central to Jewish synagogue services.

Anastasis. Greek for "resurrection"; the central plan structure in Jerusalem that is thought to house the tomb of Christ, originally connected with and now incorporated into the Church of the Holy Sepulchre.

Anglican Church. *See* Church of England.

Apologetics. A branch of theology that deals with the defense and proof of Christianity.

Atonal music. Twentieth-century Western music not written in a specific key.

Atrium. Originally the open-air courtyard in the center of an ancient Roman house, often in the shape of a square, which usually contained a pool. The term later was used for the courtyard in front of a church.

Babylonian Talmud. *See* Talmud.

Basilica. Greek for "hall of the king." The term originally referred to a large public Roman building, usually rectangular in shape; it eventually referred to the Christian church buildings that developed from this form.

BCE. Abbreviation for "before the common era" or the time before the birth of Christ.

Buttress. An exterior mass of masonry or brickwork built against a wall to give it additional strength and support.

Byzantium. *See* Constantinople.

Canon (of the Mass). The one eucharistic prayer used by the Roman church from about the fifth century to the twentieth century; also called the "Roman canon."

Canon (ecclesiastical title). Secular clergy belonging to a large church or cathedral, who share a common life and derive an income from the church or cathedral by singing the offices and providing other pastoral services.

Cantatory. The medieval Roman name for the book that contained chant texts sung by a soloist. The Frankish name for this book was the gradual *(graduale),* referring to the step *(gradus)* from which these chants were sung.

Carolingian dynasty. Dynasty of Frankish kings that ruled over Gaul from 751 to 982 CE. The name is probably a combination of the Latin word for Charles *(Carolus),* after Charles Martel (d. 741), the founder of the dynasty, and Merowig, the legendary founder of the Merovingian dynasty.

CE. Abbreviation for "common era" or the time after the birth of Christ.

Central plan. A round or polygonal structure.

Chalice. The traditional term for the cup filled with wine and water at Mass.

Church of England. The national church of England, which separated from the Roman Catholic Church under Henry VIII (d. 1547).

Church orders. Generic term for various pastoral handbooks from the early church that contain instructions about various aspects of the community's life and prayer. The term reemerged during the Reformation to designate similar books *(Kirchenordungen)* for the developing Protestant churches.

Ciborium (plural ciboria). Vessel that developed from the pyx for holding the consecrated bread.

Colonnade. A number of columns arranged in order.

Common lectionary. Lectionary proposed by the Consultation on Common Texts in 1983. It is based on the three-year Roman lectionary (1969) and harmonized with the major variants of this lectionary in use at the time in the United States.

Concomitance. The doctrine that in the eucharist, Christ's body and blood are present in both the bread and the wine.

Confessionalism. The principle that a church should have a confession of faith.

Constantinople. City in northwest Turkey on the Strait of Bosporus whose ancient name was "Byzantium." Constantine renamed it after himself and moved the capital of the empire there; its modern name is "Istanbul."

Divine Office. *See* "office."

Editio typica. Standard edition of a Roman Catholic liturgical book issued for the universal church.

Enlightenment. A philosophical movement of the eighteenth century, concerned with the critical examination of previously accepted doctrines and institutions from the viewpoint of human reason.

Episcopal Church. American church that developed from the Church of England.

Epistolary. Liturgical book that contained the readings for Mass other than the gospel.

Ethnomusicology. A twentieth-century branch of musical science that studies the anthropology of music.

Evangeliary. Liturgical book that contained the gospel readings for Mass.

Franks (adjective Frankish). Generic term for the Germanic tribes that conquered Gaul about 500 CE and established an extensive kingdom there.

Gallican. *See* Gaul.

Gaul (adjective Gallican). Ancient name for the region roughly equivalent to modern France and Belgium.

Gebrauchsmusik. German for "music for use"; a style of musical composition that flourished in Germany after World War I that was meant to be socially useful and culturally relevant. In reaction to extravagant nineteenth-century composition for the concert hall or opera, it was conceived as a simpler style of music, and designed for children or amateur musicians, although it also included music for radio dramas and films.

General convention. The legislative body of the Episcopal church.

General Council. A nineteenth-century union of Lutheran synods in the United States, committed to the historic principles of confessional Lutheranism.

General Synod. An early nineteenth-century union of four Lutheran synods (Pennsylvania, New York, North Carolina and Maryland-Virginia).

Geonim (singular gaon). Talmudic scholars who were active in Babylonia from the sixth to the tenth centuries.

Gnosticism (adjective gnostic). General name for a movement within Christianity, identifiable from the second century, that emphasized the acquisition of a special knowledge (Greek, *gnosis*) beyond faith, through which salvation was attainable.

Gradual. *See* cantatory.

Great Western Schism. The period between 1378 and 1417, when Western Christendom was divided by the simultaneous reign of two, sometimes three, popes in Rome, Avignon and Pisa.

Greek cross. A cross with four equal arms.

Hall church. A church in which the nave and the aisles are approximately the same height.

Hellenistic. Greek; from the Greek word *Hellas,* meaning "Greece."

Impluvium. A small pool, constructed in the atrium of ancient Roman houses, for catching and storing rainwater from the roof.

International Commission on English in the Liturgy (ICEL). A joint commission of 26 English-speaking conferences of Roman Catholic bishops that is responsible for preparing English texts for use in the liturgy.

Introit. The entrance chant, originally consisting of an entire psalm sung by a small choir *(schola)* while the assembly responded with a short refrain (antiphon), concluded by a doxology. By the eleventh century, all but the antiphon, one verse from the psalm and the doxology remained, sung only by the choir.

Latin cross. A cross with three short arms and one long arm.

Lectionary. Liturgical book containing the readings for eucharist.

Libelli Missarum. Literally "little books of Masses"; small booklets for the priest containing various prayers for use at Mass existing by the end of the fourth century. These were the forerunners of the sacramentaries.

Martyrium (plural martyria). A church, often central plan, built over the tomb of a martyr.

Martyrology. A list of martyrs that expanded into a liturgical book listing martyrs and other saints and feasts for every day of the year.

Merovingian dynasty. The first dynasty of Frankish kings that ruled over Gaul from about 500 CE until 751 CE; the name is derived from Merowig (d. 458), the grandfather of Clovis (d. 511) and legendary founder of this dynasty.

Middle Ages. A generic term for the period in European history between antiquity and the Renaissance, often dated from the deposition of the last Roman emperor in the West (475 CE) to the fall of Constantinople to the Turks (1453 CE).

Minor orders. The lower ranking degrees of ministry, below the major orders of bishop, priest, deacon and formerly subdeacon (suppressed in 1972): porter, lector, exorcist and acolyte. In 1972, porter and exorcist were suppressed while lector and acolyte were transformed into ministries that could be conferred on laity.

Mishnah. Hebrew for "instruction, repetition"; a collection of legal interpretations and instructions, originating as oral tradition and codified around 200 CE.

Monophony (adjective monophonic). Music consisting of a single musical line for voice or instrument, such as Gregorian chant.

Narthex. The enclosed vestibule at the entrance of a church.

Nave. The main body of a church, especially in a basilica-style church, extending from the narthex to the sanctuary, flanked by the side aisles.

Neumes. The signs used for musical notation in Europe from about the eighth to the fourteenth centuries.

Node. A knob inserted along the stem of a chalice or other drinking goblet, between the base and the bowl.

Office, Divine. The daily prayer of the church, which in the West developed into eight separate "hours" or independent prayer rituals: matins, lauds, prime, terce, sext, none, vespers and compline. The Divine Office or Liturgy of the Hours was reformed by the Roman Catholic Church in 1971.

Oration. A brief prayer, offered by the presider in the name of the assembly, concluded with their "Amen." It often consists of an opening invocation to God, a recalling of God's wondrous deeds in the past, a petition for the future and a doxology. The opening prayer, prayer over the gifts, and prayer after communion are the three orations in the eucharistic liturgy.

Ordinary of the Mass. Collective name for the *Kyrie* (Lord, have mercy), *Gloria* (Glory to God), *Sanctus* and *Benedictus* (Holy) and *Agnus Dei* (Lamb of God).

Ordo. Liturgical book containing the directions for worship. Originally these were single pages or small booklets that were compiled into collections, the earliest known of which appeared at Rome in the seventh century.

Ottonian architecture. Pre-Romanesque architecture from Germany during the rule of the Ottonian emperors in the second half of the tenth century.

Oxford Movement. Movement within the Church of England originating at Oxford University in 1833 that sought to link that church more closely to the Roman Catholic Church.

Palestinian Talmud. *See* Talmud.

Pericope. A passage from the scriptures, particularly one designated to be read during the liturgy.

Piazza. A public open space, often oblong, surrounded by buildings.

Pier. A vertical column designed for support.

Pilgrim festivals. Three Jewish festivals: the combined Feast of Passover and Unleavened Bread, the Feast of Weeks or Pentecost and the Feast of Booths or *Sukkoth*. Each adult male was required to journey to Jerusalem each year for at least one of these festivals, thus the name "pilgrim" festivals.

Polyphony (adjective polyphonic). Music consisting of several independent parts that sound simultaneously.

Porringer. A shallow cup or bowl with a handle

Proper of the Mass. Collective name for the chants formerly sung at the entrance, between the readings, during the offertory and during communion.

Pyx. Small vessel for holding consecrated bread outside of eucharist.

Reredos. An ornamental screen or wall at the back of an altar.

Rib. A protruding band on the ceiling or vault, often providing support, although sometimes only decorative.

Ribbed vault. A vault in which the diagonal arched ribs support, or seem to support, the web of the vault.

Roman Canon. *See* canon.

Rood. Anglo-Saxon word for cross.

Roman Canon. *See* canon.

Rood. Anglo-Saxon word for cross.

Sacramentary. A liturgical book containing the prayers for the priest at Mass. The first authentic sacramentary was compiled in Rome sometime during the seventh or early eighth century.

Sacrament house. A type of tabernacle common in medieval Germany that resembled a small tower or cathedral spire, often located within the sanctuary.

Shema. Jewish profession of faith, composed of three passages from the Bible: Deuteronomy 6:4–9, Deuteronomy 11:13–21, Numbers 15:37–41. It takes its name from the first Hebrew word, "hear."

Showbreads. A special form of meal offering, placed in the temple sanctuary and eaten by the priests according to the directives found in Exodus 25.30 and Leviticus 24:5–8.

Siddur. Hebrew for "order, arrangement"; commonly refers to the Jewish prayer book containing prayers for the various daily, weekly and festival services of the year.

Stational liturgy. Public worship celebrated by the bishop of Rome in alternating churches on designated days throughout the city, in evidence by at least the fifth century. Some other cities throughout the empire eventually adopted similar practices based on the Roman model.

Synagogue. Place of assembly for nonsacrificial Jewish worship.

Talmud. Hebrew for "instruction, learning"; contains the Mishnah and commentary known as the Gemara. Two versions, representing different Gemara, exist: The Palestinian version was completed in the fifth century, the Babylonian version in the sixth century. The Gemara in the latter is almost three times as long as the former.

Torah. Hebrew for "instruction, teaching"; refers to first five books of the Bible, often called "the Law."

Tract. The chant between the readings that formerly took the place of the "alleluia" on certain penitential days or in penintential seasons.

Transept. The side arms of a cross-shaped church.

Tridentine. Adjective referring to the Council of Trent (1545–1563).

Tunnel vaulting. The simplest kind of vaulting, with an unbroken, semi-cylindrical roof; also called barrel vaulting.

Vault. An arched structure, usually of stone, brick or concrete, forming a roof or ceiling.

Vulgate. The Latin translation of the Bible made by St. Jerome (d. 420).

Westwork. The west end of a Carolingian or Romanesque church.

Bibliography

General Bibliography

[All scripture quotes are taken from the New Revised Standard Bible.]

Peter F. Anson. *Churches: Their Plan and Furnishing.* Ed. and rev. by Thomas F. Croft-Fraser and H. A. Reinhold. Milwaukee: Bruce Publishing Company, 1948.

Willi Apel. *Harvard Dictionary of Music.* 2nd rev. ed. Cambridge: Belknap Press, 1969.

Denis Arnold, ed. *New Oxford Companion to Music.* 2 vols. New York: Oxford University Press, 1983.

Karl Atz. *Die Christliche Kunst in Wort und Bild.* Regensburg: Nationale Verlagsanstalt, 1899.

André Biéler. *Architecture in Worship: The Christian Place of Worship.* Edinburgh–London: Oliver & Boyd, 1965.

Joseph Braun. *Der Christliche Altar in seiner geschichtlichen Entwicklung.* Munich: Guenther Koch & Co., 1924.

_____. *Das Christliche Altargerät in seinem Sein und in seiner Entwicklung.* Munich: Max Hueber, 1932.

Lukas Brinkhoff, et al. *Liturgisch Woordenboek.* 9 vols. Roermond: J. J. Romen and Sons, 1958–1962.

Robert Cabié. *L'Eucharistie.* Vol. II of *L' Église in Prière.* Ed. by A. G. Martimort. Paris: Desclée, 1983.

C. Callewaert. *Liturgicae Institutiones. Vol. 3: De Missalis Romani Liturgia.* Brugge: Car. Beyaert, 1937.

William Thomas Cavanaugh. *The Reservation of the Blessed Sacrament.* The Catholic University of America Canon Law Studies 40. Washington, DC: The Catholic University of America, 1927.

Kenneth John Conant. *Carolingian and Romanesque Architecture, 800–1200.* 2nd ed. The Pelican History of Art. Harmondsworth and New York: Penguin, 1966.

Solange Corbin. *L'Èglise à la Conquête de sa Musique.* Pour la Musique. Ed. by Roland-Manuel. Paris: Gallimard, 1960.

Archibald Davidson and Willi Apel. *Historical Anthology of Music.* 2 vols. Rev. ed. Cambridge: Harvard University Press, 1949.

Charles Dufresne Du Cange. *Glossarium ad Scriptores Mediae et Infirmae Latinitatis.* Ed. by L. Favre. 10 vols. Niort, 1883–1887.

Margaret English Frazer. *Medieval Church Treasures.* New York: Metropolitan Museum of Art, 1986.

Helen Gardner. *Art Through the Ages.* 8th ed. rev. by Horst de la Croix and Richard Tansey. San Diego: Harcourt, Brace, Jovanovich, 1986.

Alfred Heales. *History and Law of Church Seats or Pews.* 2 vols. London: Butterworths, 1872.

The Holy Bible, New Revised Standard Version. New York: Oxford University Press, 1989.

H. E. Jacob. *Six Thousand Years of Bread.* Trans. by Richard and Clara Winston. Westport, Connecticut: Greenwood Press, 1944.

R. C. D. Jasper and G. J. Cuming. *Prayers of the Eucharist, Early and Reformed.* 2nd ed. New York: Oxford University Press, 1980.

Hubert Jedin and John Dolan, eds. *History of the Church.* 10 vols. New York: Crossroad, 1980–1981.

Cheslyn Jones, et al. *The Study of Liturgy.* New York: Oxford University Press, 1978.

Pierre Jounel. "Places of Christian Assembly: the First Millenium." *The Environment for Worship.* Washington, DC: United States Catholic Conference, 1980. 15–27.

Josef Jungmann. *The Early Liturgy to the Time of Gregory the Great.* Trans. by Francis Brunner. Notre Dame: University of Notre Dame Press, 1959.

_____. *The Mass of the Roman Rite: Its Origins and Development.* Trans. by Francis Brunner. 2 vols. New York: Benziger Brothers, Inc., 1950.

Theodor Klauser. *A Short History of the Western Liturgy.* Trans. by John Halliburton. London: Oxford University Press, 1979.

Spiro Kostof. *A History of Architecture: Settings and Rituals.* New York: Oxford University Press, 1985.

Franz Xaver Kraus. *Geschichte der Christlichen Kunst.* 2 vols. Freiburg: Herder, 1896.

Richard Krautheimer. *Early Christian and Byzantine Architecture.* 4th ed. Pelikan History of Art 24. Harmondsworth: Penguin Books, 1986.

J. D. Mansi, ed. *Sacrorum Conciliorum Nova et Amplissima Collectio.* 31 vols. Florence-Venice: 1757–1798. Reprinted and expanded to 53 vols. by L. Petit and J. B. Martin. Paris: 1889–1927.

Thomas Mathews. *Early Churches of Constantinople, Architecture and Liturgy.* University Park: Pennsylvania State University Press, 1971.

A. G. McKay. *Houses, Villas, and Palaces in the Roman World.* Ithaca, NY: Cornell University Press, 1975.

James McKinnon, ed. *Music in Early Christian Literature.* Cambridge Studies in Music. Cambridge: University Press, 1987.

Jacques Paul Migne, ed. *Patrologia Graeca.* 162 vols. Paris, 1857–1866.

————. *Patrologia Latina.* 221 vols. Paris, 1844–1864.

Nathan Mitchell. *Cult and Controversy: The Worship of the Eucharist Outside Mass.* New York: Pueblo Publishing, 1982.

John Mason Neale. *History of Pues.* Cambridge: The Camden Society, 1841.

Christian Norberg-Schulz. *Meaning in Western Architecture.* New York: Praeger Publishers, 1975.

J. B. O'Connell. *Church Building and Furnishing: A Study in Liturgical Law.* Liturgical Studies. Notre Dame: University of Notre Dame Press, 1955.

Adolf K. Placzek, ed. *MacMillan Encyclopedia of Architects.* 4 vols. New York: The Free Press, 1982.

Mario Righetti. *Manuale di Storia Liturgica.* 4 vols. Milan: Ancora, 1945–1953.

Stanley Sadie, ed. *New Grove Dictionary of Music and Musicians.* New York: W. W. Norton, 1988.

A. J. Schulte. "Host." *Catholic Encyclopedia* (1910) 7: 489–497.

Marilyn Kay Stulken. *Hymnal Companion to the Lutheran Book of Worship.* Philadelphia: Fortress Press, 1981.

Robert Taft. *The Liturgy of the Hours in East and West.* Collegeville: The Liturgical Press, 1986.

F. van der Meer and Christine Mohrmann. *Atlas of the Early Christian World.* Trans. and ed. by Mary F. Hedlund and H. H. Rowley. London: Thomas Nelson and Sons Ltd., 1958.

Cyrille Vogel. *Medieval Liturgy: An Introduction to the Sources.* Trans. and rev. by William Storey and Niels Rasmussen. Washington, DC: Pastoral Press, 1986.

Elwyn A. Wienandt, ed. *Opinions on Church Music.* Waco, Texas: Baylor University Press, 1974.

Robert Wilken. *The Myth of Christian Beginnings.* Notre Dame: University of Notre Dame Press, 1981.

Bibliography for Chapter One

Raymond Brown, Joseph Fitzmyer, Roland Murphy, eds. *The New Jerome Biblical Commentary.* Englewood Cliffs, New Jersey: Prentice-Hall, Inc., 1990.

R. H. Charles, ed. *The Book of Jubilees or The Little Genesis.* London, 1902.

Frederick E. Crowe. *Theology of the Christian Word: A Study in History.* New York: Paulist Press, 1978.

Reinhard Deichgräber. *Gotteshymnus und Christushymnus in der frühen Christenheit.* Göttingen: Vandenhoeck and Ruprecht, 1967.

Edward Foley. "The Cantor in Historical Perspective." *Worship* 56 (1982) 194–213.

————. "The Question of Cultic Singing in the Christian Community of the First Century." Unpublished thesis, University of Notre Dame, 1980.

Joseph Gelineau. "Music and Singing in the Liturgy." *The Study of Liturgy.* 440–49.

Robert Grant. "Roman Empire." *Interpreter's Dictionary of the Bible.* IV:103–9.

Joseph Heinemann. *Prayer in the Talmud: Forms and Patterns.* Studia Judaica 9. Berlin–New York: Walter de Gruyter, 1977.

Lawrence Hoffman. *The Canonization of the Synagogue Service*. Notre Dame–London: University of Notre Dame Press, 1979.

A. Z. Idelsohn. *Jewish Music in its Historical Development*. New York: Schocken Books, 1967 [1929].

Joachim Jeremias. *The Eucharistic Words of Jesus*. Trans. by Norman Perrin. Philadelphia: Fortress Press, 1977.

Ralph Martin. *Worship in the Early Church*. Rev. ed. Grand Rapids: Wm. B. Eerdmans, 1975.

Wayne A. Meeks. *The First Urban Christians: The Social World of the Apostle Paul*. New Haven–London: Yale University Press, 1983.

The Mishnah. Ed. and trans. by Jacob Neusner. New Haven-London: Yale University Press, 1988.

Jerome Murphy-O'Connor. "The Corinth that Saint Paul Saw." *Biblical Archaeologist* 47/3 (1984) 147–59.

Jacob Neusner. *The Way of Torah*. 3rd ed. North Scituate, Massachusetts: Duxbury Press, 1979.

Past Worlds. The Times Atlas of Archaeology. London: Times Books Ltd., 1988.

Norman Perrin and Dennis C. Duling. *The New Testament: An Introduction*. 2nd ed. New York: Harcourt, Brace, Jovanovich, 1982.

Jakob J. Petuchowski and Michael Brocke, eds. *The Lord's Prayer and Jewish Liturgy*. New York: Seabury Press, 1978.

H. H. Rowley. *Worship in Ancient Israel: Its Forms and Meaning*. London: SPCK, 1967.

Carroll Stuhlmueller. *Psalms 1 & 2*. 2 vols. Old Testament Message 21 & 22. Wilmington: Michael Glazier, 1983.

Roland de Vaux. *Ancient Israel*. 2 vols. New York–Toronto: McGraw-Hill, 1965.

Eric Werner. *The Sacred Bridge*. Vol. 1. New York: Columbia University Press, 1959.

_____. *The Sacred Bridge*. Vol. 2. New York: Ktav Publishing House, 1984.

Geoffrey Wigoder. *The Story of the Synagogue*. San Francisco: Harper & Row, 1986.

Bibliography for Chapter Two

Jean-Paul Audet. *La Didachè, Instructions des Apôtres*. Etude Bibliques. Paris: J. Gabalda, 1958.

Henry Chadwick. *The Early Church*. Pelican History of the Church 1. Harmondsworth: Penguin Books, 1967.

James Charlesworth, ed. and trans. *The Odes of Solomon: The Syriac Texts*. Texts and Translations 13, Pseudepigrapha Series 7. Missoula, Montana: Scholars Press, 1977.

Clement of Alexandria. Ed. by Alexander Roberts and James Donaldson. Hymns trans. by W. L. Alexander in *Ante-Nicene Fathers*. New York: Charles Scribner's Sons, 1926. II:296.

R. H. Connolly, ed. and trans. *Didascalia Apostolorum*. Oxford: Oxford University Press, 1929.

Louis Duchesne. *Le Liber Pontificalis*. Bibliotheque des Ecoles Francaises d'Athenes et de Rome. 3 vols. Paris: E. de Boccard, 1981.

Eusebius. *The History of the Church*. Trans. by G. A. Williamson. Harmondsworth: Penguin Books, 1965.

F. X. Funk, ed. *Didascalia et Constitutiones Apostolorum*. 2 vols. Paderborn: F. Schoeningh, 1905.

Gesta apud Zenophilum. Ed. by Carolus Ziwsa. Corpus Scriptorum Ecclesiasticorum Latinorum 26. Vienna: F. Tempsky, 1893. 185–197.

Edgar Hennecke. *New Testament Apocrypha*. 2 vols. Ed. by Wilhelm Schneemelcher. English trans. by R. Mcl. Wilson. Philadelphia: Westminster Press, 1963–1965.

Ignatius of Antioch. "Letter to the Ephesians." *The Apostolic Fathers*. Ed. and trans. by Kirsop Lake. The Loeb Classical Library 24. London: W. Heinemann, 1930.

C. H. Kraeling. *Excavation at Dura Europos. Final Report 8, Part 2: The Christian Building*. New Haven: Yale University Press, 1967.

James McKinnon. "The Meaning of the Patristic Polemic against Musical Instruments." *Current Musicology* 1 (1985) 69–82.

David Magie, ed. and trans. *Scriptores Historiae Augustae*. 3 vols. Loeb Classical Library 139, 140 & 263. Cambridge: Harvard University Press, 1967.

Pliny. "Letter to the Emperor Trajan." *Pliny: Letters and Panegyricus*. Trans. by Betty Radice. Loeb Classical Library 59. Cambridge: Harvard University Press, 1969.

Erik Routley. *The Music of Christian Hymns*. Chicago: GIA Publications Inc., 1981.

Tacitus. *Annals: Books 13–15*. Trans. by John Jackson. Loeb Classical Library 322. London: William Heinemann Ltd., 1937.

Bibliography for Chapter Three
Michel Andrieu. *Les Ordines Romani du Haut Moyen Age*. 5 vols. Spicilegium sacrum Lovaniense 11, 23–24, 28–29. Louvain, 1960.

Willi Apel. *Gregorian Chant*. Bloomington: Indiana University Press, 1958.

John Baldovin. "Kyrie Eleison and the Entrance Rite of the Roman Eucharist." *Worship* 60 (1986) 334–47.

John Chrysostom. "Second Baptismal Instruction." Trans. by Paul Harkins. *Ancient Christian Writers* 31. Westminster, MD: Newman Press, 1963.

Peter Cobb. "The Architectural Setting of the Liturgy." *The Study of Liturgy*. Ed. by Cheslyn Jones et al. New York: Oxford University Press, 1978. 473–87.

Noele M. Denis-Boulet. *The Christian Calendar*. Trans. by P. Hepburne-Scott. The Twentieth Century Encyclopedia of Catholicism 113. New York: Hawthorn Books, 1960.

Louis Duchesne. *Liber Pontificalis*. 3 vols. Bibliothèque des Ecoles Francaises d'Athènes et de Rome. Paris: E. de Boccard, 1981.

Peter Jeffery. "The Introduction of Psalmody into the Roman Mass by Pope Celestine I (422–32)." *Archiv für Liturgiewissenschaft* 26 (1984) 147–165.

Thomas Mathews. "An Early Roman Chancel Arrangement and Its Liturgical Function." *Revista di Archeologia Cristiana* 38 (1962) 73–95.

Kenan Osborne. *Priesthood: A History of the Ordained Ministry in the Roman Catholic Church*. New York: Paulist Press, 1988.

Mario Mirabella Roberti. *Grado*. 3rd ed. Triest, n.d.

Brian Spinks. "The Jewish Sources for the Sanctus." *The Heythrop Journal* 21 (1980) 168–179.

John Wilkinson. *Egeria's Travels to the Holy Land*. Rev. ed. Warminster, England: Aris & Phillips, 1981.

G. G. Willis. "The Consecration of Churches Down to the Ninth Century." *Further Essays in Early Roman Liturgy*. Alcuin Club 50. London: SPCK, 1968. 133–173.

Bibliography for Chapter Four
Michel Andrieu. *Les Ordines Romani du Haut Moyen Age*. 5 vols. Spicilegium Sacrum Lovaniense 11, 23–24, 28–29. Louvain, 1960.

Bede. *A History of the English Church and People*. Trans. by Leo Sherley-Price. Rev. ed. Middlesex: Penguin Books, 1968.

Eucharistic Vessels of the Middle Ages. n. p.: Garland Publishing, 1975.

Angelus Albert Häussling. *Mönchskonvent und Eucharistiefeier*. Liturgiewissenschaftliche Quellen und Forschungen 58. Münster: Aschendorff, 1973.

Helmut Hucke. "Toward a New Historical View of Gregorian Chant." *Journal of the American Musicological Society* 33 (1980) 437–67.

K.-H. Kandler. "Wann werden die Azyma das Brotelement in der Eucharistie im Abendland?" *Zeitschrift für Kirchengeschichte* 75 (1964) 153–55.

Edgar Lehmann. "Die Anordnung der Altäre in der Karolingischen Kosterkirche zu Centula." *Karl Der Grosse: Lebenswerk und Nachleben*. Ed. by Wolfgang Braunsfels and Hermann Schnitzler. Dusseldorf, 1966. 374–83.

Arthur Mirgeler. *Mutations of Western Christianity*. Notre Dame: University of Notre Dame Press, 1968 [1961].

Leo C. Mohlberg, ed. *Liber Sacramentorum Romanae Aeclesiae Ordinis Anni Circuli*. Rerum Ecclesiasticarum Documenta: Series maior, fontes 4. Rome: Herder, 1960.

————. *Missale Francorum*. Rerum Ecclesiasticarum Documenta: Series maior, fontes 2. Rome: Herder, 1957.

————. *Missale Gallicanum Vetus*. Rerum Ecclesiasticarum Documenta: Series maior, fontes 3. Rome: Herder, 1958.

————. *Missale Gothicum*. Rerum Ecclesiasticarum Documenta: Series maior, fontes 2. Rome: Herder, 1961.

Cyrille Vogel. "Orientation dans les Ordines Romani." *La Maison Dieu* 70 (1962) 67–99.

_____. "La Multiplication des Messes Solitaires au Moyen Âge: Essai de Statistique." *Revue des Sciences Religieuse* 55 (1981) 206–13.

G. G. Willis. *Further Essays in Early Roman Liturgy.* Alcuin Club Collections 50. London: SPCK, 1968.

Bibliography for Chapter Five

Peter Browe. *Die Verehrung der Eucharistie im Mittelalter.* Rome: Herder, 1967 [1932].

Ernst Cassirer. *The Philosophy of the Enlightenment.* Boston: Beacon Press, 1955.

S. J. P. van Dijk and J. Hazelden Walker. *The Origins of the Modern Roman Liturgy.* London: Darton, Longman and Todd, 1960.

Edward Foley. *The First Ordinary of the Royal Abbey of St.-Denis in France.* Spicilegium Friburgense 32. Fribourg: The University Press, 1990.

Adrian Fortescue. *The Mass: A Study of the Roman Liturgy.* London: Longmans, Green & Co., 1912.

J. A. Froude. *Life and Letters of Erasmus.* New York: Charles Scribner's Sons, 1895.

Harold Gleason, ed. *Examples of Music before 1400.* New York: Appleton-Century-Crofts, Inc., 1942.

John Harthan. *The Book of Hours.* New York: Park Lane, 1977.

Richard H. Hoppin. *Medieval Music.* New York: W. W. Norton, 1978.

Erwin Panofsky. *Gothic Architecture and Scholasticism.* Cleveland–New York: The World Publishing Company, 1957.

Patrick Quinn. "The Architectural Implications of the Choir in the Worshipping Community." *Liturgical Arts* 34 (1966) 38–46.

Gustave Reese. *Music in the Middle Ages.* New York: W. W. Norton & Company, 1940.

_____. *Music in the Renaissance.* Rev. ed. New York: W. W. Norton & Company, 1959.

Otto Von Simson. *The Gothic Cathedral.* 3rd ed. Bollingen Series 48. Princeton: Princeton University Press, 1988.

Walter Wiora. "The Origins of German Spiritual Folk Song: Comparative Methods in a Historical Study." *Ethnomusicology* 8 (1964) 1–13.

Bibliography for Chapter Six

G. W. O. Addleshaw and F. Etchells. *The Architectural Setting of Anglican Worship.* London: Faber and Faber, 1948.

Henry Bett. *Nicholas of Cusa.* Merrick, NY: Richwood Publishing Co., 1976 [1932].

Boston Museum of Fine Arts. *American Church Silver of the Seventeenth and Eighteenth Centuries.* Boston: 1911.

Yngve Brilioth. *Eucharistic Faith and Practice Evangelical and Catholic.* Trans. by A. G. Herbert. London: SPCK, 1930.

Canons and Decrees of the Council of Trent. Trans. by H. J. Schroeder. St. Louis-London: B. Herder, 1941.

Catalogue of Silver Treasures from English Churches. London: Christies, 1955.

Concilium Tridentinum. Ed. by Societas Goerresiana. Vol. 8. Freiburg–Bresgau: Herder, 1964 [1919].

Raymond Creytens. "L'Ordinaire des Frères Prêcheurs au Moyen Âge." Archivum Fratrum Praedicatorum 24 (1954) 108–88.

John De Visser and Harold Kalman. *Pioneer Churches.* New York: W. W. Norton, 1976.

John Tracy Ellis. *Perspectives in American Catholicism.* Benedictine Studies 5. Baltimore: Helicon, 1963.

Samuel Gardner. *A Guide to English Gothic Architecture.* Cambridge: University Press, 1922.

Martin Luther. *Luther's Works.* Volume 53: *Liturgy and Hymns.* Ed. by Ulrich S. Leupold. Philadelphia: Fortress Press, 1965.

Marshall McLuhan. *The Gutenberg Galaxy: The Making of Typographic Man.* Toronto: University of Toronto Press, 1962.

Irm. Pahl. *Coena Domini.* Vol. 1. Spicilegium Friburgense 29. Freiburg: 1983.

E. Peacock. *English Church Furniture, Ornaments and Decorations at the period of the Reformation as exhibited in a list of the goods destroyed in certain Lincolnshire churches, 1566.* London: 1866.

Jaroslav Pelikan. *Bach among the Theologians.* Philadelphia: Fortress Press, 1985.

Le Psautier de Geneve 1562–1865. Genève: Bibliothèque Publique et Universitaire, 1986.

Gustave Reese. *Music in the Renaissance.* Rev. ed. New York: W. W. Norton & Company, 1959.

Reformatio: 400 Jahre Evangelishces Leben im Rheinland. Cologne: Walter Müller, 1965.

Emil Sehling. *Die evangelischen Kirchenordnungen des 16 Jahrhunderts.* Leipzig: O. R. Reisland, 1902–1913.

Massey Shepherd. *At All Times and in All Places.* Third rev. ed. New York: Seabury Press, 1965.

"Statuta Synodi Baltimorensis Anno 1791 Celebratae." *Concilia Provincialia Baltimori habita ab anno 1829 usque ad annum 1849, Editio altera.* Baltimore: John Murphy and Co., 1851.

Denis Stevens. *Tudor Church Music.* Rev. ed. New York: W. W. Norton and Company, 1966.

Bard Thompson. *Liturgies of the Western Church.* Cleveland–New York: Collins and World Publishing Co., 1962.

W. W. Watts. *Catalogue of Chalices and Other Communion Vessels.* London: Victoria and Albert Museum Department of Metalwork, 1922.

Francis J. Weber. "America's First Vernacular Missal." *America's Catholic Heritage, Some Bicentennial Reflections (1776–1976).* St. Paul Editions, 1976.

James White. *Protestant Worship and Church Architecture.* New York: Oxford University Press, 1964.

Bibliography for Chapter Seven

John Blacking. *How Musical is Man?* Seattle–London: University of Washington Press, 1973.

Bernard Botte. *From Silence to Participation.* Trans. by John Sullivan. Washington DC: The Pastoral Press, 1988.

Common Lectionary. New York: The Church Hymnal Corporation, 1983.

Gilbert Cope, ed. *Making the Building Serve the Liturgy: Studies in the Re-Ordering of Churches.* London: A. R. Mowbray & Co., 1962.

Otto Deri. *Exploring Twentieth-Century Music.* New York: Holt, Rinehart and Winston, Inc., 1968.

Paul Empie and T. Austin Murphy, eds. *Lutherans and Catholics in Dialogue I–III.* Minneapolis: Augsburg Publishing, 1965.

Edward Foley. "When American Roman Catholics Sing." *Worship* 63 (1989) 98–112.

Raymond Glover. *Perspectives on the New Edition.* Hymnal Studies 1. New York: The Church Hymnal Corporation, 1981.

Peter Hammond. *Liturgy and Architecture.* London: Barrie and Rockliff, 1960.

Kyriale. Boston: McLaughlin and Reilly Co., 1937.

Barbara Krader. "Ethnomusicology." *New Groves Dictionary of Music and Musicians.* Ed. by Stanley Sadie. London, 1980, 6:275–282.

Andreas Liess. *Carl Orff: Idee und Werk.* Rev. ed. Zürich–Freiburg im Bresgau: Atlantis, 1977.

Our Lady of the Height Ronchamp. Schnell Art Guide 818. 17th English edition. Munich–Zurich: Verlag Schnell & Steiner, 1986.

Augustus Pugin. *The True Principles of Pointed or Christian Architecture.* New York: St. Martin's Press, 1973 [1841].

Erik Routley. *A Panorama of Christian Hymnody.* Collegeville: The Liturgical Press, 1979.

Thomas Schattauer. "Sunday Worship at Neuendettelsau under Wilhelm Löhe." *Worship* 59 (1985) 370–84.

Edward Schillebeeckx. *The Eucharist.* Trans. by N. D. Smith. New York: Sheed and Ward, 1968.

Frank Senn, ed. *New Eucharistic Prayers.* New York: Paulist Press, 1987.

Lancelot Sheppard, ed. *The People Worship: A History of the Liturgical Movement.* New York: Hawthorn Books, Inc., 1967.

Geoffrey Skelton. *Paul Hindemith: The Man Behind the Music.* London: Victor Gollancz Ltd., 1975.

Norris Kelly Smith. *Frank Lloyd Wright: A Study in Architectural Content.* Englewood Cliffs, NJ: Prentice-Hall, Inc., 1966.

E. A. Sövik. *Architecture for Worship.* Minneapolis: Augsburg Publishing House, 1973.

F. Ellen Weaver. "Liturgy for the Laity: The Jansenist Case for Popular Participation in Worship in the Seventeenth and Eighteenth Centuries." *Studia Liturgica* 19/1 (1989) 47–59.

James White. *Protestant Worship: Traditions in Transition.* Louisville: Westminster/John Knox Press, 1989.

————. "Sources for the Study of Protestant Worship in America." *Worship* 61 (1987) 516–33.

John Willett. *The Theatre of Bertolt Brecht.* New York: New Directions, 1968.

Frank Lloyd Wright. *The Living City.* New York: Horizon Press, 1958.

Index